Oxford Archaeological Guides
General Editor: Barry Cunliffe

Scotland

Anna and **Graham Ritchie** are archaeologists working in Scotland.
Graham is Head of Archaeology in the Royal Commission on the
Ancient and Historical Monuments of Scotland, and Anna is a
Member of the Ancient Monuments Board for Scotland and a Trustee
of the National Museums of Scotland. They are both graduates of the
University of Edinburgh, and have published widely on Scottish
archaeology both jointly and separately. Recent books include
The Ancient Monuments of Orkney, *Viking Scotland*, and *Iona*.

Barry Cunliffe is Professor of European Archaeology at the
University of Oxford. The author of over forty books, including
The Oxford Illustrated Prehistory of Europe and *The Ancient Celts*, he
has served as President of the Council for British Archaeology and
the Society of Antiquaries, and is currently a member of the Ancient
Monuments Board of English Heritage.

'Call it "Travels with my Trowel"—this splendid Oxford
Archaeological Guide to Scotland is an indispensable vade-mecum
for the discriminating traveller.'
MAGNUS MAGNUSSON

'A valuable companion, whether on the desk or in the pocket.'
ANDREW SHERRATT
Author of *Economy and Society in Prehistoric Europe*

'Anna and Graham Ritchie together have an unparalleled knowledge
of the Scottish heritage ... this guide is well laid out, beautifully
illustrated, and with clear instructions regarding access.'
STEVEN MITHEN
Author of *The Prehistory of the Mind*

Oxford Archaeological Guides

Rome	Amanda Claridge
Scotland	Anna and Graham Ritchie
The Holy Land	Jerome Murphy-O'Connor
Spain	Roger Collins

FORTHCOMING:

Egypt	George Hart
Western Turkey	Hazel Dodge
Southern France	Henry Cleere
England	Tim Darvill, Paul Stamper, and Jane Timby
Crete	Colin MacDonald and Sara Paton
Greece	Christopher Mee and Antony Spawforth
Ireland	Conor Newman and Andy Halpin

North Africa

Scotland

An Oxford Archaeological Guide

Anna and Graham Ritchie

Oxford · New York
OXFORD UNIVERSITY PRESS
1998

Oxford University Press, Great Clarendon Street, Oxford OX2 6DP
Oxford New York
Athens Auckland Bangkok Bogota Bombay
Buenos Aires Calcutta Cape Town Dar es Salaam Delhi
Florence Hong Kong Istanbul Karachi
Kuala Lumpur Madras Madrid Melbourne
Mexico City Nairobi Paris Singapore
Taipei Tokyo Toronto Warsaw
and associated companies in
Berlin Ibadan

Oxford is a trade mark of Oxford University Press

First published as an Oxford University Press paperback 1998

British Library Cataloguing in Publication Data
Data available

Library of Congress Cataloging in Publication Data
Ritchie, Anna.
Scotland: an Oxford archaeological guide / Anna and Graham Ritchie.
p. cm.—(Oxford archaeological guides)
Includes bibliographical references and index.
(acid-free paper)
1. Scotland—Antiquities—Guidebooks. 2. Excavations
(Archaeology)—Scotland—Guidebooks. I. Ritchie, J. N. G. (James
Neil Graham) II. Title. III. Series.
DA770.R48 1998 914.1104'859—dc21 97-10485
ISBN 0-19-288002-0

1 3 5 7 9 10 8 6 4 2

Designed by Richard Marston, London
Typeset by Best-set Typesetter Ltd., Hong Kong
Printed in BOOK PRINT, S.L.
Barcelona - Spain

Series Editor's Foreword

Travelling for pleasure, whether for curiosity, nostalgia, religious conviction, or simply to satisfy an inherent need to learn, has been an essential part of the human condition for centuries. Chaucer's 'Wife of Bath' ranged wide, visiting Jerusalem three times as well as Santiago de Compostela, Rome, Cologne, and Boulogne. Her motivation, like that of so many medieval travellers, was primarily to visit holy places. Later, as the Grand Tour took a hold in the eighteenth century, piety was replaced by the need felt by the élite to educate its young, to compensate for the disgracefully inadequate training offered at that time by Oxford and Cambridge. The levelling effect of the Napoleonic Wars changed all that and in the age of the steamship and the railway mass tourism was born when Mr Thomas Cook first offered 'A Great Circular Tour of the Continent'.

There have been guidebooks as long as there have been travellers. Though not intended as such, the *Histories* of Herodotus would have been an indispensable companion to a wandering Greek. Centuries later Pausanias' guide to the monuments of Greece was widely used by travelling Romans intent on discovering the roots of their civilization. In the eighteenth century travel books took on a more practical form offering a torrent of useful advice, from dealing with recalcitrant foreign innkeepers to taking a plentiful supply of oil of lavender to ward off bedbugs. But it was the incomparable 'Baedekers' that gave enlightenment and reassurance to the increasing tide of enquiring tourists who flooded the Continent in the latter part of the nineteenth century. The battered but much-treasured red volumes may still sometimes be seen in use today, pored over on sites by those nostalgic for the gentle art of travel.

The needs and expectations of the enquiring traveller change rapidly and it would be impossible to meet them all within the compass of single volumes. With this in mind, the Oxford Archaeological Guides have been created to satisfy a particular and growing interest. Each volume provides lively and informed descriptions of a wide selection of archaeological sites chosen to display the cultural heritage of the country in question. Plans, designed to match the text, make it easy to grasp the full extent of the site while focusing on its essential aspects. The emphasis is, necessarily, on seeing, understanding, and above all enjoying the particular place. But archaeological sites are the creation of history and can only be fully appreciated against the *longue durée* of human achievement. To provide this, each book begins with a wide-ranging historical overview introducing the changing cultures of the country and the landscapes which formed them. Thus, while the Guides are primarily intended for the traveller they can be read with equal value at home.

Barry Cunliffe

Acknowledgements

We are very grateful both to the Royal Commission on the Ancient and Historical Monuments of Scotland and to Historic Scotland for permission to use plans and photographs from their collections (crown copyright), and to K. H. J. Macleod for his skill in producing the computer-generated maps. In the National Monuments Record of Scotland we have benefited in finding suitable illustrations from the help and advice of Lesley M. Ferguson and Kevin Maclaren. Several friends and colleagues have allowed Oxford University Press to base illustrations on their plans, and we are grateful in particular to David J. Breeze, Audrey S. Henshall, Ian A. G. Shepherd, Alexandra N. Shepherd, and Val Turner.

Contents

How to use this Guide

In the following guide, individual monuments are arranged broadly in geographical areas, from the border with England northwards and westwards. These areas correspond with those of the administrative Local Authorities, in order to make travel arrangements easier, particularly when dealing with local Tourist Boards:

Dumfries and Galloway   Argyll and Bute
Borders   Aberdeenshire and Moray
Lothians and Edinburgh   Highland South
From the Clyde to the Forth   Highland North
Fife, Angus, Stirling,   The Northern Isles
    and Perthshire   The Western Isles

Within these broad geographical areas, monuments are mostly arranged in alphabetical order. As well as road directions, the National Grid Reference is provided for each site to enable it to be located on the relevant sheet of the Ordnance Survey Landranger series of 1 : 50,000 maps. Many monuments are in the care of Historic Scotland, the National Trust for Scotland, or local authorities, but others are in private ownership and visitors are responsible for seeking permission to view them.

Sixty monuments have been given a rating of two stars or a single star. The choice was very difficult to make, and it is based on the state of preservation, interest, and accessibility of each site. Two stars indicate a monument that you really must visit, and one star designates sites not to be missed if you are in the area. But all the sites in this guide will reward a visit.

List of Maps

Scotland

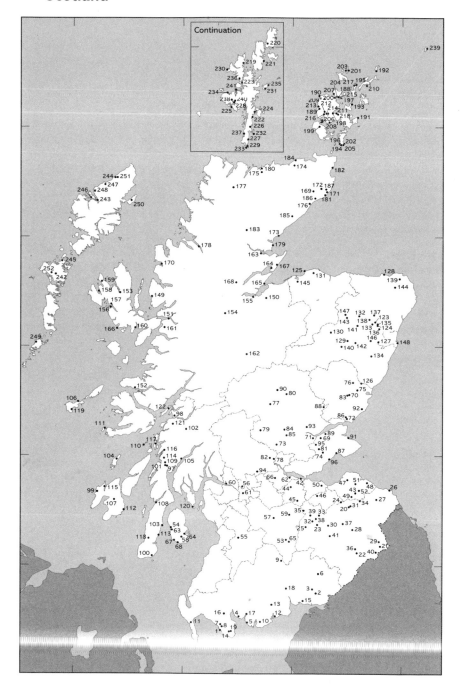

Dumfrics and Galloway

1 Barsaloch Point
2 Birrens
3 Burnswark★★
4 Cairnholy★
5 Castle Haven
6 Castle O'er
7 Druchtag
8 Drumtroddan
9 Durisdeer
10 High Banks
11 Kirkmadrine
12 Mote of Mark
13 Motte of Urr★
14 Rispain Camp
15 Ruthwell Cross★★
16 Torhousekie
17 Trusty's Hill
18 Twelve Apostles
19 Whithorn★★

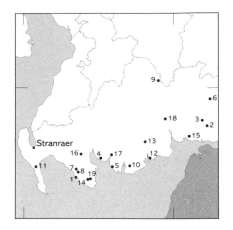

Borders

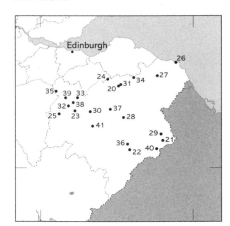

20 Addinston★
21 Blackbrough
22 Bonchester Hill
23 Cademuir Hill
24 Dere Street
25 Dreva★
26 Earns' Heugh
27 Edin's Hall★★
28 Eildon Hill North
29 Hownam Law
30 Innerleithen
31 Longcroft
32 Lyne
33 Milkieston Rings
34 Mutiny Stones
35 North Muir
36 Rubers Law
37 Torwoodlee
38 White Meldon
39 Whiteside Hill
40 Woden Law★
41 Yarrow

★★ Outstanding sites (see p. xi)
★ Highly recommended sites

Lothians & Edinburgh

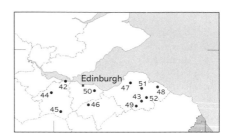

From the Clyde to the Forth

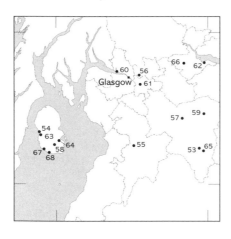

Fife, Angus, Stirling, and Perthshire

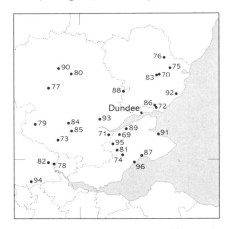

Argyll and Bute

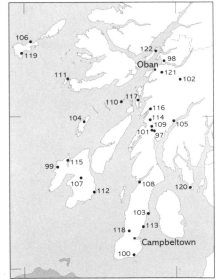

Aberdeenshire and Moray

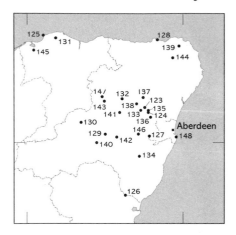

123 Brandsbutt
124 Broomend of Crichie
125 Burghead
126 Capo
127 Cullerlie *
128 Cullykhan
129 Culsh
130 Doune of Invernochty
131 Duffus Castle
132 Dunnideer *
133 Easter Auquorthies
134 Garrol Wood
135 Inverurie

136 Kintore
137 Loanhead of Daviot **
138 Maiden Stone
139 Memsie
140 New and Old Kinord *
141 Old Keig
142 Peel of Lumphanan
143 Rhynie
144 Strichen
145 Sueno's Stone *
146 Sunhoney *
147 Tap o' Noth
148 Tullos Hill

Highland South

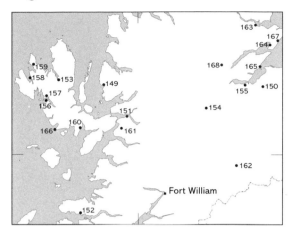

156 Dun Ardtreck
157 Dun Beag★
158 Dun Fiadhairt
159 Dun Hallin
160 Dun Ringill
161 Dun Telve
   and Dun
   Troddan★★
162 Dun-da-Lamh
163 Edderton
164 Nigg★
165 Rosemarkie★
166 Rubh' an
   Dunain★
167 Shanwick
168 Strathpeffer

149 Applecross
150 Balnuaran of
   Clava★★
151 Caisteal Grugaig

152 Camus nan Geall
153 Clach Ard
154 Corrimony
155 Craig Phadrig

Highland North

169 Achavanich
170 An Dun
171 Cairn o' Get
172 Camster★★
173 Carn Liath
174 Cnoc
   Freiceadain
175 Coille na
   Borgie
176 Dunbeath
177 Dun Dornaigil
178 Dun Lagaidh
179 Embo
180 Farr
181 Hill o' Many
   Stanes★

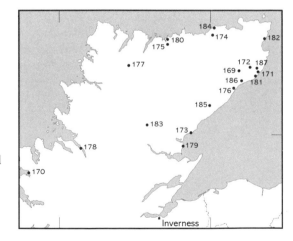

182 Nybster
183 Ord
184 St Mary's
   Chapel

185 Strath of Kildonan
186 Wag of Forse
187 Yarrows

The Northern Isles: Orkney

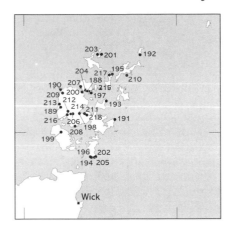

The Northern Isles: Shetland

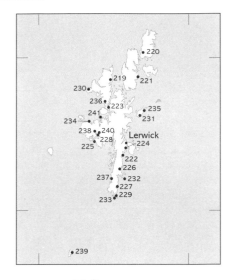

The Western Isles

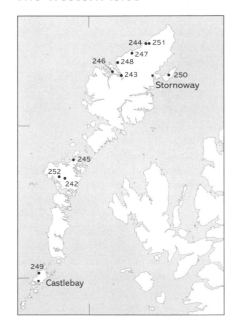

Sites listed by archaeological period

Neolithic

Achnacree
Balbirnie
Balfarg
Balnuaran of Clava★★
Barnhouse
Barpa Langass
Beorgs of Housetter
Blackhammer
Blasthill
Cairn o' Get
Cairnholy★
Cairnpapple Hill★
Calf of Eday
Callanish★★
Camster★★
Camus nan Geall
Capo
Carn Ban
Cnoc Freiceadain
Coille na Borgie
Corrimony
Crarae
Cuween Hill
Dalsetter
Dwarfie Stane
Embo
Garrabost
Gruting School
Holm of Papa Westray
Isbister★
Jarlshof★★
Kilmartin★★
Knap of Howar★
Knowe of Yarso
Machrie Moor★★
Macs Howe★★
Midhowe★
Monamore
Mutiny Stones

Normangill
North Muir
Ord
Pettigarth's Field
Punds Water
Quoyness★
Ring of Brodgar★
Rubh' an Dunain★
Scord of Brouster★
Skara Brae★★
Stanydale★
Stones of Stenness★
Taversoe Tuick
Torrylin
Unival
Unstan
Vementry
Vinquoy
Wideford
Yarrows

Neolithic/ Bronze Age

Achavanich
Achnabreck★
Auchagallon
Balbirnie
Balfarg
Ballinaby
Ballochmyle★
Bordastubble
Broomend of Crichie
Busta
Cairnbaan
Cairnpapple Hill★
Callanish★★
Clach an Trushal
Croft Moraig
Cullerlie★

Dervaig
Drumtroddan
Easter Auquorthies
Fairy Knowe
Garrol Wood
High Banks
Hill o' Many Stanes★
Jarlshof★★
Kilmartin★★
Kintraw
Liddle
Loanhead of Daviot★★
Lundin Links★
Memsie
Old Keig
Quoybune
Sandy Road
Scord of Brouster★
Steinacleit
Strichen
Strontoiller
Sunhoney★
Torhousekie
Tullos Hill
Twelve Apostles

Iron Age

Abernethy
Addinston★
An Dun
Arbory Hill
Ardestie
Barsaloch Point
Black Castle
Black Hill
Blackbrough
Bonchester Hill
Borwick
Brough of Stoal

Brown and White
Caterthuns
Burland
Burnswark★★
Burrian
Burroughston
Cademuir Hill
Caisteal Grugaig
Caisteal Suidhe
Ceannaidh
Carn Liath
Carradale
Castle Law
Castle O'er
Castle of Burwick
Castle Haven
Chesters
Clickhimin★
Craig Phadrig
Cullykhan
Culsh
Culswick★
Dalsetter
Dreva★
Dumyat
Dun an Sticir
Dun Ardtreck
Dun Beag★
Dun Bharabhat
Dun Bragar
Dun Carloway★
Dun Cuier
Dun Dornaigill
Dun Fiadhairt
Dun Hallin
Dun Lagaidh
Dun Mor
Dun Nosebridge★
Dun Ringill
Dun Skeig
Dun Telve★★
Dun Troddan★★
Dun-da-Lamh
Dunbeath
Dunnideer★
Earns' Heugh
East Lomond
Edin's Hall★★

Eildon Hill North
Finavon
Gurness★★
Hare Law
Holyrood Park
Hownam Law
Jarlshof★★
Kildonan
Kinord★
Knockfarril
Laws of Monifieth
Leccamore
Loch of Houlland
Loch of Huxter
Longcroft
Midhowe★
Milkiestone Rings
Mousa★★
Ness of Burgi
Ness of Garth
Norman's Law
Nybster
Queen's View
Ranachan Hill
Rennibister
Rhiroy
Rispain Camp
Rubers Law
South Haven
Strath of Kildonan
Tap o' Noth
Tirefour
Torr a' Chaisteil
Torwoodlee
Traprain Law
Wag of Forse
White Hill
White Meldon
Whiteside Hill
Woden Law
Yarrows

Roman

Antonine Wall
Ardoch★
Bearsden★
Birrens

Burnswark★★
Castle Greg
Dere Street
Durisdeer
Gask Ridge
Kinneil
Lyne
Rough Castle★

5th-9th centuries AD

Abdie Churchyard
Abercorn
Aberlemno★★
Abernethy
Applecross
Brandsbutt
Brechin
Broomend of Crichie
Brough of Birsay★
Brough of Deerness
Burghead
Burwick, St Mary's Church
Clach Ard
Clickhimin★
Colonsay House
Craig Phadrig
Doon Hill
Dumbarton Rock
Dunadd★
Dundurn
Dunfallandy
Edderton
Eileach an Naoimh
Farr
Fowlis Wester
Govan★
Gurness★★
Innerleithen
Iona★★
Jarshof★★
Kildalton Cross★
Kilnave Cross
Kintore
Kirkmadrine
Maiden Stone

Meigle*
Mote of Mark
Nigg*
Rosemarkie*
Ruthwell Cross**
Rhynie
St Andrews*
St Blane's Church
St Ninian's Isle
St Vigeans
Shandwick
Strathmiglo
Strathpeffer
Sueno's Stone*
Trusty's Hill
Wag of Forse
Wemyss Caves
Whithorn**
Yarrow

Viking

Brough of Birsay*
Cunningsburgh
Jarlshof**
Orphir

10th-12th centuries AD

Abercorn
Abernethy
Brechin
Carnwath
Cubbie Roo's Castle
and St Mary's Church
Cunninghsburgh
Doune of Invernochty

Druchtag
Duffus Castle
Govan*
Inverurie
Jarlshof**
Kirkwall
Meigle*
Motte of Urr*
Orphir
Peel of Lumphanan
St Mary's Chapel
St Ninian's Isle
St Vigeans
Sir John de Graham's
Castle
Whithorn**

Introduction

Scotland is relatively small in area but remarkably diverse in the character of its landscape. It has a coastline out of all proportion in length to the enclosed land-mass, because of its long sea-lochs and many islands, and its topography displays equal extremes from grassy sand-dunes to moorland, low rounded hills to dramatic mountains, small swift-flowing burns to grand salmon-rivers and trout-filled lochs. Scottish archaeology is equally diverse, from humble burial-mounds to the awesome splendour of rings of tall standing stones, and the monuments are often exceptionally well preserved. In the past, particularly in times of relatively greater warmth, people have lived at higher altitudes than today, with the result that intact archaeological landscapes can be found, with visible remains of houses, fields, and burial-mounds spanning several millennia.

The monuments highlighted in the gazetteer have been chosen for their interest, good condition, and accessibility, and they are but a sample of what is there to be explored. Space has dictated a limit on time-span, from earliest times to the C12 AD, but the use of a good map will allow

▼ The cairns and standing stone at Kintraw (p. 129) (RCAHMS)

later monuments such as abbeys, castles, and distilleries to be added along the way.

The Physical Environment after the Last Ice Age

Scotland's most dramatic scenery is a legacy from the thousands of years that it lay beneath a deep but far from static blanket of ice. The Highland glens and the long sea-lochs of the west coast were sculpted by moving glaciers, from which Scotland was not finally free until some 10,000 years ago. The ice left a bare scoured landscape, which, as the climate warmed, was gradually colonized by vegetation from unglaciated land to the south. Juniper heaths were followed by birch and hazel, and later by elm, oak, and pine. The establishment of these forests provided habitats for the animals essential to human colonization, from the small mammals such as otters, foxes, and voles to huge wild oxen, moose, and reindeer. In the mean time, the warmer seas, rivers, and lochs acquired a population of fish and molluscs, whales and seals, again vital for human consumption.

The forests also provided timber for building houses and logboats, but in some areas of Scotland tree-cover was minimal from the start and stone was the logical building material. People in Caithness and Orkney, for example, were compensated for their lack of trees by the quality of their flagstones, and here stone-built houses, tombs, and forts have survived the centuries in often remarkably good condition. The most famous site is Skara Brae in Orkney (p. 184), where houses almost 5,000 years old stand to roof level, thanks both to their excellent walling and to the wind-blown sand that finally enveloped and protected them.

Climatic Change

Air temperatures rose rapidly after the end of the last Ice Age, creating a relatively mild climate across Scotland. It has been estimated, on the basis of the spread of certain plants and fish beyond the limit of their modern habitat, that the climate was an average of two degrees centigrade warmer than today. Excavations in Orkney have yielded evidence for the cultivation of wheat in the fourth millennium BC, a crop that no farmer would attempt there now, and for the presence in Orcadian waters of the corkwing wrasse, a fish that could not survive the sea temperatures of today.

The milder climate also made sea-travel easier, for there would have been fewer storms. But there is evidence for the formation of sand-dunes before 3000 BC, suggesting an increase in offshore wind-speeds, which would have had an adverse effect on sea-travel and, particularly in island contexts, on the growth of trees.

Peat had been growing in boggy hollows since post-glacial times, but it was the onset of colder and wetter conditions around 2000 BC that generated the gradual formation of blanket peat. This enveloped upland areas that had once been cultivated, but it also brought a long-term benefit in providing a much-needed source of fuel for treeless areas. Before peat was available, fuel was a real problem. Driftwood not needed for other purposes could be used, otherwise people resorted to drying and burning turf, animal dung, heather, and seaweed. Peat even became a commodity that could be exchanged between communities. It was recorded in the C18 that the inhabitants of Sandness parish in western Shetland grew enough grain to supply the needs of the neighbouring parish and in return obtained peat, of which their parish had little.

This worsening climate in the second millennium was hastened in 1159 BC (a rare precise date!) by a massive and far-reaching eruption of the Hekla volcano in Iceland. This ejected thick dust high into the atmosphere, which spread over a wide area and blocked out the sun, causing very poor growth seasons which can be seen in contemporary tree-rings in Ireland. In Scotland, a number of sites show a fine layer of black volcanic dust (the study of Scottish tree-ring sequences is less advanced than in Ireland). Throughout Britain at this time, there was a marked decline in the manufacture of bronze axes and a corresponding increase in weapon production, which is thought to relate to the competition for land and resources that was the inevitable result of the climatic disaster.

It was a patch of rather better weather that helped to create the Viking Age. Around the middle of the first millennium AD, the climate in NW Europe began to improve, resulting in calmer seas and the incentive for Norwegian boat-builders to develop ships capable not only of crossing the North Sea but ultimately of crossing the Atlantic. There were other factors involved as well, both political and economic, but climate provided the physical context in which the Viking adventure was possible. By the last decade of the C8, Viking longships were harrying the coasts of Scotland, taking advantage of the prevailing winds that blew westwards in the spring, and in the autumn blew eastwards, conveniently aiding the homeward voyage to Norway.

Scottish Archaeology

The tendency now is to avoid using chronological labels, such as Bronze Age, in favour of absolute dating brackets, such as second millennium BC or 2500–1500 BC. This has been made possible by scientific methods of dating, particularly radiocarbon analysis and tree-ring chronologies, and it has the advantage of avoiding too neat a progression through the ages, as if bronze-working were somehow automatically replaced by iron-working at the same time everywhere. But these labels can still be useful as shorthand descriptive terms and are sometimes so used in this volume.

For much of Britain, prehistory begins with a long period known as the palaeolithic, but for Scotland the story begins around 10,000 years ago, after the end of the last Ice Age, with the mesolithic period. While it is theoretically possible that there was a human presence in Scotland in inter-glacial periods before the end of the last Ice Age, evidence is so far lacking. These earliest settlers have left little physical trace compared with later generations, and there are very few sites to which the visitor can be directed. They lived by hunting, fishing, and gathering wild plant-foods, and their existence was semi-nomadic, leaving only minimal traces of their camp-sites. Debris from flint-working is usually the clue to a mesolithic site, sometimes accompanied by traces of hearths, small post-holes, and areas of cobbling, and these, of course, can only be explored through excavation. There is evidence of mesolithic peoples throughout Scotland, as far north as Orkney but not, as yet, Shetland. They favoured good fishing rivers such as the Tweed, river estuaries, sandy shores and islands, and important sites have been excavated at Morton in Fife, and on the inner Hebridean islands of Rum, Jura, Islay, Colonsay, and Oronsay (grass-covered sandy mounds with layers of shell-midden on the latter island are among the few visible mesolithic sites). Inland sites have also been found, and a picture is evolving of a fairly complete mesolithic occupation of Scotland.

Around 4000 BC, the arrival of people with farming skills heralded the beginning of the neolithic period. Doubtless in many areas the two approaches to economic survival co-existed for several centuries, for the advantages of being tied to the land and dependent upon good weather for successful crops may not have been instantly apparent to people accustomed to an abundant natural harvest of fish, deer, berries, and nuts. By 4000 BC, the presence of cereal pollen suggests that agriculture was underway, and the earliest burial monuments can be dated by radio-carbon analysis to the following centuries. The farming life-style was certainly well established by about 3600 BC, to which period can be assigned the oblong stone houses at Knap of Howar in Orkney (p. 195) and a massive timber-built hall beside the River Dee at Balbridie in Aberdeenshire. Neolithic settlement in Scotland was thus as early as anywhere in Britain. Newcomers with their seed corn and young domes-ticated animals were certainly involved in this process, but in time the indigenous mesolithic population appears to have adopted the farming way of life. As well as plant cultivation, stock-rearing, permanent houses and tombs, this life-style was marked by the use of round-based pottery, polished stone axes, and leaf-shaped flint arrowheads—a longbow made of yew wood found in Dumfriesshire has been radiocarbon-dated to this early period.

To the third millennium belong the many stone circles and alignments of Scotland, sometimes grouped in ceremonial centres that reflect a flour-ishing and complex society. In terms of the surviving visible monuments, this was the golden age of Scottish prehistory, but, for reasons as yet little understood, decline set in during the last centuries of the millennium. There is evidence for climatic deterioration and for the arrival of new ideas. Communal burial was replaced by individual burial, new types of pottery were adopted and metalworking was introduced, first in copper and then the stronger copper-alloy known as bronze. Both beaker pottery and metalworking were ideas imported from Europe, and it is likely that there was some settlement in Scotland of new people accustomed to these innovations.

▼ Inside the tomb at Unstan (p. 191) (Historic Scotland)

▲ Aerial view of Longcroft fort (p. 55) (RCAHMS)

The next major development in terms of the surviving monuments took place in the opening centuries of the first millennium BC. This was the appearance of defended settlements, particularly hillforts, which presumably reflect social change with an increased element of aggression and competition for resources. In the north and west of Scotland there was an equivalent change with the adoption of massive stone round-houses, which evolved by about 200 BC into that uniquely Scottish phenomenon, the broch or stone tower. By then, another stage in metal technology had been introduced: iron-working.

Roman Scotland

The Scottish Iron Age was interrupted briefly by the Roman army. The Roman general, Agricola, marched his legions into Scotland in AD 79, reaching almost to the Moray Firth in AD 83, when the famous battle of Mons Graupius was fought and won against the Celtic tribesmen. Agricola's aim to complete the Roman subjugation of the whole of Britain was never achieved, neither by Agricola himself nor by his successors, and the population of Scotland was virtually untouched by the increasingly urban life of the Roman province farther south. There was a military presence in southern Scotland for much of the next three centuries, based on Hadrian's Wall, but the Antonine Wall between the Forth and Clyde estuaries was garrisoned for only about 20 years after its construction began in AD 142 (p. 78). Roman goods reached even the Northern and Western Isles, but the closest that the people in those areas came to the Romans was when Agricola sent his naval fleet round the north of Scotland to check that Britain was indeed an island.

Many of the Roman remains in Scotland are exceptionally well preserved, from the marching camps at Pennymuir in the Borders (p. 63) to the great fortress of Ardoch in Perthshire (p. 89), the watchtowers along the Gask Ridge (p. 99), and the bath house at Bearsden in Glasgow (p. 79).

▼ Aerial view of Ardoch Roman fort (p. 89) (RCAHMS)

One great advantage of the Roman presence was that it brought Scotland into the realm of written history. Calgacus, who led the Celtic force at Mons Graupius, is the first person in Scotland whose name we know, and from the C2 written sources record the names of some of the Celtic tribes, rivers, and places of Scotland. Another important effect of Roman military activity was to stimulate the native tribes into concerted opposition, leading eventually to their political union as the kingdom of the Picts.

Early Historic Scotland

The Roman province was finally abandoned to its own devices in the early C5. Control of southern Scotland reverted to the British tribes, descended from the Celts, who formed the kingdoms of Strathclyde and Rheged in the west and Gododdin in the east. Strathclyde, with its stronghold on Dumbarton Rock in the Clyde (p. 76), survived as one of the four major peoples of early medieval Scotland, but the Gododdin were conquered by invading Angles from Northumbria, and their capital at Edinburgh fell to the Angles in AD 638. Rheged, around the Solway Firth, was also taken over by the Angles.

North of the Forth–Clyde line, the rest of Scotland belonged to the Picts, apart from Argyll which was known as Dalriada and formed the kingdom of the *Dál Riata*. The Picts were the descendants of the earlier Celtic tribes, but the *Dál Riata* were newcomers from Northern Ireland, who gradually took over Argyll in the early centuries AD and finally transferred their ruling dynasty from County Antrim to their new homeland around AD 500. They were Gaelic speakers, a different form of Celtic from that spoken by the Picts and the Britons, and they are sometimes known as Gaels. The more commonly used name is Scots, from the Latin *Scotti*, a general name for the Irish.

Forts have been identified as belonging to this period from the C6 to the C9 both in Pictland (e.g. Burghead, p. 134) and in Dalriada (e.g. Dunadd, p. 128), but domestic settlements are best known from the stone-using north of Scotland. The Picts are celebrated for their stone-carving, especially the symbol-stones which are unique to them (see below, under Art). With the establishment of Christianity from monastic centres in the west such as Iona (p. 113) and Applecross (p. 150), the sculptor's art blossomed into superb cross-slabs, and Pictland could be seen to be participating in the mainstream of early medieval European culture.

Fine metalwork is also a hallmark of this period, for the patrons who could afford carved memorial stones showed their wealth in expensive personal ornaments, weapons, and tableware.

The C9 was a time of intense political change in Scotland. The Viking Age had opened in the last decade of the C8 with a devastating series of raids along the northern and western coasts, and the Northern and Western Isles were lost to Norwegian settlers in the course of the C9. The

Norse earldom of Orkney and Shetland was formally established by the end of the century, and Norse control soon spread into Caithness and Sutherland. The foundations of Viking Age houses can be seen at Brough of Birsay in Orkney (p. 177) and at Jarlshof in Shetland (p. 211).

Meanwhile, control of the kingdom of the Picts was taken over by the royal house of Dalriada around AD 843, and Pictland became Scotland. Pictish sculptors continued to work for new masters, but the hallowed Pictish symbols were dropped from their repertoire.

The monuments featured in this book take the story of Scotland into the C12, with buildings belonging to Norse family estates in Orkney, including chapels and the earliest castle in Scotland (p. 205), and some of the many sites of timber castles (mottes) introduced by new Norman overlords in mainland Scotland south of the Moray Firth.

Sources of Information

Archaeological data are derived from a number of sources, from aerial photography to field survey, but excavation provides the bulk of new information. Excavation is by its nature a destructive process, and it follows that most upstanding monuments have not been excavated or only very partially. Techniques of excavation and recording have improved immeasurably within the last few decades, and thus the information gleaned about the economic and environmental background of

▼ Aerial view of Jarlshof (p. 211) (RCAHMS)

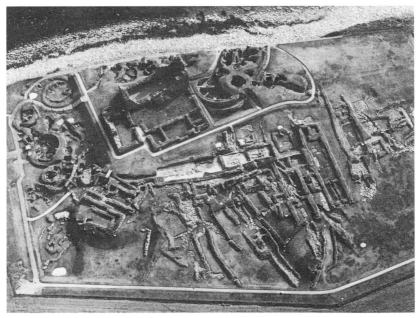

some monuments has been greatly enhanced. In contrast, many dramatic and eminently visitable sites caught the attention of early antiquarians for whom excavation may have involved little more than a weekend's work to seek out a central burial deposit in a cairn or to empty out the interior of a dun. Thus our knowledge about even well-known sites may be imperfect. In some cases, as at Skara Brae and Jarlshof, programmes of early C20 excavation were designed to help present the monument to the public, rather than to address archaeological issues such as stratigraphy. There is often still much to learn from sites that have been partly excavated in the past.

An increasing number of radiocarbon determinations means, however, that the broad chronological framework within which the field monuments of Scotland may be placed is becoming clearer. The technique involves the measurement of radioactive carbon (carbon-14), which is present in all living things, but which decays at a fixed rate on death. This means that the human bones from a burial, the animal bones from a refuse layer, chunks of charcoal from a hearth or destruction layer, or some hazelnuts from a storage pit can all be dated with broad precision. This does not produce a precise calendar date, but a band of time during which the event occurred. As numbers of dates from excavations increase the chronological pegs become firmer, particularly where they can be checked against tree-ring dating. In addition, programmes of dating wood or bones found with artefacts now in museums is helping to link earlier discoveries into the new techniques. But traditional archaeological methods of comparisons between artefacts or classes of monument are still useful. For example, distinctive pottery found on a site many years before the advent of radiocarbon dating is likely to belong to the same broad chronological span as comparable pottery from a well-dated context in a modern excavation. The principle is less readily applied to field monuments, as they are rarely as distinctive, but it is in theory the same. Tree-ring dating coupled with the enormous potential of underwater archaeology in terms of the preservation of artefactual and environmental evidence will undoubtedly add precision to the chronology of Scottish archaeology in the near future.

In the first millennium AD, scientific methods of dating are supplemented by written sources. These are mostly external sources, such as the Roman Tacitus writing about Agricola or Irish monastic annals recording events in Scotland, but two important sources are closer to home. Adomnan of Iona wrote a *Life of Columba*, which has useful information not only about the early monastery on Iona but also about Columba's visits to Pictland, and the Picts themselves have bequeathed a list of kings. Literacy was introduced into Scotland by the Christian Church, but little evidence of its use has survived. For the Viking Age, the Icelandic Sagas provide information, particularly *Orkneyinga Saga*, which records the history of the Earls of Orkney and in so doing records the names of a number of important farms, some of which have been confirmed by excavation. Surviving place-names throughout Scotland are in themselves an invaluable research tool, for they chart the extent of settlement not only by Scandinavian-speakers but also by early English-speakers (Angles) and Gaelic-speakers.

But archaeology remains the most important source of information even for the first 1,200 years of the Christian era. The following sections will trace the various thematic threads of the prehistory of Scotland, as a background to the monuments that survive to be visited and enjoyed.

Exploitation of Natural Resources

Human activities affected the plant record from early prehistoric times. Even before a farming life-style was adopted, introducing cereal crops into the native flora, repeated harvesting of wild foodstuffs and burning woodland altered the natural pattern. These are fugitive traces of change and often difficult to interpret, but there are more positive changes, such as the appearance of wheat and barley and their accompanying weeds of cultivation. Analysis of pollen from soils and sediments has identified in Scotland, as elsewhere in the British Isles, evidence for a dramatic decline in elm trees around 3000 BC. This may reflect an early form of disease such as the Dutch Elm Disease that struck Britain in the C20 AD, but the explanation may be more complex and may involve both disease and the effects of human interference by felling. Not only was timber needed for building, but large areas had to be cleared of forest to allow cultivation and the creation of pasture. There was clearly enough open grassland in some parts of Scotland by about 3000 BC to enable huge quantities of turf and topsoil to be used to build burial-mounds. Another use for timber was involved in burial rites. Cremation rather than inhumation became popular in the second millennium, and the process of cremating an adult corpse requires a lot of fuel. Some idea of how much timber was needed can be gained from the fact that, in the First World War, the standard allowance for the cremation of an Indian soldier was one ton.

In the first millennium BC, vast quantities of timber were used to build protective stockades round settlements and to strengthen the stone walls of hillforts.

Different woods were used for different purposes, and sometimes artefacts made from exotic wood were imported, as in the case of the neolithic longbow of yew from Dumfriesshire, a Bronze Age sword made of yew found in Orkney, and the larch box containing the Pictish treasure of silver found on St Ninian's Isle in Shetland.

Wild herbs, berries, and nuts (especially hazelnuts) have remained part of the basic diet until modern times, and a few excavations have yielded traces of specific herbs used both for culinary and medicinal purposes in Roman times: coriander, dill, celery, linseed, and opium poppies, the latter imported from Europe along with figs. Heather was used for bedding and for making rope—the earliest example of heather rope is from the neolithic settlement of Skara Brae (p. 184).

From the introduction of farming onwards, domesticated cattle, sheep, and pigs were the mainstay of the economy, and they were supplemented by hunting deer, catching birds and collecting their eggs, and fishing in rivers, lochs, and the sea. As well as food, all these species provided other necessities, such as hide for clothing, bedding, and tents, and bone for tools and ornaments and even, in the case of whalebone, furniture and dishes. The hair of primitive sheep was not suitable for textiles, but there is evidence of weaving by the end of the Bronze Age. Flax-growing as a source of fibre for making linen appears to have been introduced by the Vikings.

Exploitation of stone resources from early times can be demonstrated by the use of flint, chert, quartz, and various igneous rocks for tools. The mesolithic site at Kinloch on the island of Rum was closely connected with the exploitation of Rum bloodstone, which was exported to places within a 50 km. radius of the island. Pitchstone from the island of Arran was another coveted stone for small implements, owing to its excellent flaking properties. In many areas of Scotland, the only flint available was in the form of beach pebbles washed up from marine deposits, but the Buchan gravels of NE Aberdeenshire were a valued source of good flint. Deep pits dug to extract the flint have been excavated at Den of Boddam. The makers of neolithic polished stone axes used local igneous stones where possible, but there was also a considerable exchange system in particularly good rocks such as that from Killin in Perthshire, or, farther afield, that from Tievebulliagh in Northern Ireland. Shetland felsite was used both for axes and for an oval type of knife, but they were almost all for local consumption.

Once metalworking had been introduced, suitable ores would have been sought within Scotland. Copper and lead were available in several places, although their exploitation in prehistoric times cannot be proved, but tin to make bronze had to be imported from Cornwall, the only source in Britain, or from Europe. Small amounts of silver and gold could be gleaned for the fine metalwork of the Early Historic period, but analysis has shown that much Pictish silver was in fact melted down from late Roman silverwork.

Travel and Transport

Until relatively recent times, it was infinitely easier to travel about Scotland by water than overland. The great rivers gave access deep into the interior of southern and eastern Scotland, and the sea-lochs of the west not only penetrated far inland but linked the mainland with the islands of the inner

Hebrides. Water transport had to meet two needs, local fishing and travel within rivers and lochs, and sea-travel both for deep-sea fishing and long-distance communications. Logboats and hide boats were perfectly suited to inland travel, but, prior to the development of plank-built boats, only the larger hide boats could cope adequately with the needs of long-distance travel. Logboats hollowed out from large tree-trunks are sufficiently substantial to survive in the right water-logged conditions, and there are extant examples dating from mesolithic times to the medieval period. Hide boats consisted of a wooden or wickerwork frame covered by water-proofed hides, and they are by nature ephemeral, but there are literary references to their use in early medieval Iona.

It is likely that the Picts had plank-built boats as well as logboats and hide boats, and the Vikings certainly used clinker-built vessels with overlapping planks, keels, and sails. During the early part of the Viking Age, both sea-going ships and small rowing boats seem to have been imported from the Norwegian homeland. The 6.3 m.-long boat excavated at Scar in Sanday, Orkney, in 1991 was found to have been caulked (sealing of the overlap between the planks) with material including grit of an igneous rock foreign to Orkney.

The first metalled roads were constructed by the Roman army, creating a network which allowed troops and goods to move quickly and easily. There are well-preserved stretches of Dere Street to visit (p. 49). The network spread north of the Antonine Wall to serve the fortresses guarding the Highland glens and the signal-stations along the Gask Ridge (p. 99). Once the Roman roads fell into disrepair, however, there were again no extensive metalled roads until another period of military activity in the early C18 after the Jacobite risings.

Lack of roads was no bar to the use of wheeled vehicles. A solid wooden wheel from Blair Drummond in Perthshire has been dated by radiocarbon analysis to around 1000 BC (NMS), and there is literary evidence of the use of war chariots among the Celtic tribes of Scotland. Tacitus describes chariots in use before the battle of Mons Graupius in AD 83 (*Agricola*, 35–6). Some seven centuries later, a carved slab from the Pictish church at Meigle (p. 101) showed a horse-drawn vehicle with a pair of spoked wheels (the slab is now lost), although this motif may have been copied from some imported book or artefact rather than from contemporary life. Horses are frequently—and lovingly—depicted on Pictish cross-slabs, their riders mostly engaged in the hunt but also, at Aberlemno (p. 86), in battle.

Domestic Life

Study of the domestic houses of prehistoric times highlights the contrast between the visible evidence surviving in the stone-using north and west of Scotland and the rest of the country. The neolithic period in the

Northern Isles is particularly rich in domestic buildings, some surviving to roof level as at Knap of Howar (p. 195) and Skara Brae (p. 184). Others are represented only by their basal courses but are remarkable for other reasons, for example Barnhouse (p. 190) with its physical hierarchy of buildings and Scord of Brouster (p. 218) for its contemporary landscape of field walls and burial monuments.

In contrast to the ephemeral structures used by mesolithic communities, those erected by the early farmers included substantial, commodious, and apparently well-furnished buildings. But we may not have found the houses of the earliest pioneers. Particularly in the Northern Isles, where sea level is still rising, early coastal settlements may well have been lost through coastal erosion. At present, the archaeological record is certainly skewed, with burial monuments appearing earlier than houses.

Neolithic houses in Scotland were predominantly oblong or square in plan, whether they were built in stone or in wood. One of the earliest was discovered by aerial photography at Balbridie beside the River Dee in Aberdeenshire; this was built around 3600 BC as a great timber hall capable of holding 30 to 50 people. Like the huge building at Stanydale in Shetland (p. 219), Balbridie may have been a meeting-place rather than a normal domestic house. One end appeared to have been used as a granary. All that survived as evidence of the structure were post-holes and bedding-trenches, and these are no longer visible (this would be an ideal candidate for a modern reconstruction). Elsewhere in mainland Scotland, excavation has uncovered traces of smaller and less substantial timber houses, which may be more characteristic of those of the majority of the population.

Neolithic settlements appear not to have been enclosed in any substantial way, but at Loch Olabhat in North Uist two oblong houses were built on a small island, connected to the shore by a narrow causeway. The choice of location here hints at the possibility that social conditions were not always peaceful at this period. Although Skara Brae was not formally enclosed by any barrier, in its final phase the main group of houses opened on to passages which could be closed off by gates, and each house had a single door which could be barred against entry from the passage. Security seems to have been an important element in the life of the community, but the fact that the door into one house could be barred only from the outside suggests that the security was about more than simply safeguarding belongings.

People seem to have lived in small communities ranging from the farms of single extended families, such as Knap of Howar, to settlements of perhaps six to eight families, as at Skara Brae. One of the advantages of farming was the ability to create stores of food and other commodities, and storage facilities are a feature of the houses at Skara Brae and Knap of Howar. They range from alcoves and shelves built into the wall-face, to cells built within the thickness of the wall and small stone-lined pits sunk into the floor. Most of the furniture at Skara Brae is built of stone, presenting an unparalleled picture of a neolithic house-interior, with panelled beds and shelved dressers as well as large slab-lined hearths. Knap of Howar revealed evidence of low benches lining the walls, built both in stone and in timber.

The design of the houses at Skara Brae, Barnhouse, and Knap of Howar is mirrored in that of contemporary chambered tombs in Orkney, suggesting that the latter were seen as houses of the dead. The people who lived at Skara Brae and Barnhouse used pottery known to archaeologists as Grooved Ware; this consists of thick, flat-bottomed, bucket-shaped pots, decorated with grooved patterns or raised designs. This style of pottery is an additional link between the Skara Brae type of square house with side cells and the equivalent Maes Howe type of tomb. In contrast, the people of Knap of Howar made round-based pottery known as Unstan Ware, both plain jars and bowls with decorated collars, and again the pottery is another link between the oblong houses and stalled tombs, both divided into rooms/burial compartments by thin upright slabs of stone. The wealth of information available from these well-preserved sites makes the Orcadian neolithic an absorbing study. But their unique preservation should not obscure their relationship with the rest of Scotland and indeed the rest of the British Isles. Grooved Ware was popular from Orkney to the south of England, and Unstan Ware was used both in the Western Isles and in mainland Scotland. Such links are underlined by the far-reaching exchange of stone axes that can be demonstrated from before 3000 BC. The origin of the stone used can be pinpointed through analysis of the rock types. An axe discovered in a peat bog in Lewis is thought to have been made of porcellanite from County Antrim in Northern Ireland. The axehead was still in its wooden haft, and the latter could be dated by radiocarbon analysis to the century or so before 3000 BC.

For almost two thousand years after about 2400 BC, it is difficult to create as rounded a picture of houses and settlements as in neolithic times. The enigmatic monuments known as burnt mounds belong to this period. They are widespread throughout the British Isles, and they consist literally of heat-shattered stones and black earth, surrounding hearths and sunken cooking-troughs (e.g. Liddle, p. 205). They are normally situated close to a source of water, and they are best interpreted as cooking-places, where meat and fish were cooked in water heated by hot stones. At Jarlshof (p. 211) and Clickhimin (p. 208) in Shetland, the foundations of houses of the first half of the first millennium BC can be seen, and there are unexcavated sites such as Steinacleit in Lewis (p. 228) that may belong to this period. The uplands of mainland Scotland are dotted with the foundations of circular houses, often marked on Ordnance Survey maps as hut-circles, but relatively few have been excavated. In the southern counties, there are equivalent settlements of circular houses visible on hillsides as groups of levelled platforms. Overall, there seems to have been a gradual change in building tradition over the centuries after 2000 BC, with oblong houses being replaced by circular houses.

By the middle of the first millennium BC, a new trend can be seen with the construction of massive stone roundhouses, which appear to embody the emergence once again of an élite in society. These are found in the north and west of Scotland, and they are echoed in the south and west by large timber roundhouses. The latter are visible as post-holes or bedding-trenches during excavation, and they represent a very high standard of carpentry techniques. Stone roundhouses developed not only into brochs (see below, under warfare and defence) but also into the wheelhouses (so-called because of their radial internal subdivisions, like the spokes of a wheel) still visible at Jarlshof. Here they survive to roof level, providing a vivid impression of the comfort and convenience of this house-design. The Pictish houses of the later first millennium AD in the Northern Isles evolved from wheelhouses (e.g. Gurness, p. 181).

Pictish house-design embraced both cellular forms descended from wheelhouses and more strictly rectangular forms. The latter appear to have been used for feasting-halls in mainland Pictland and in British and Anglian southern Scotland (e.g. Doon Hill, p. 68), where their evolution may well owe something to Roman building traditions. Viking settlers also built rectangular houses in Scotland, as they had been accustomed in the Norwegian homeland, although it is possible that the idea of wooden benches lining the walls was adopted from the Pictish population. For the first 300 years or so of the Viking Age, the typical farm consisted of separate dwelling-house and outbuildings, but eventually in the C11 the true longhouse evolved, in which people and cattle lived under one roof, and in the C12 side-rooms were added to the dwelling-house.

Death and Ceremony

The monuments associated with death and the deposition of the dead are among the most enduring, particularly those that were formed by the creation of large mounds of stone. But the rituals and ceremonies involved in their construction are largely lost to us. The massive stones of a burial chamber or the great cairn of stones that covers a cist burial make statements about prehistoric society, religion, and the relationship of people to one another and to the land they occupy—but the techniques of archaeology cannot interpret them. Ethnographic analogy can suggest avenues of research, but it can also offer myriad possibilities, and there are no means of deciding which may be most applicable. The burial monuments of the farming communities of the fourth and third millennia BC include both stone chambered cairns and long barrows and cairns. Chambered cairns consist of a burial chamber and entrance passage built of stone slabs and covered by a round or rectangular cairn; they were designed to be used over and over again. Long barrows and cairns consist of a timber, or stone and timber, chamber covered and sealed by a long mound of earth or stone. In the absence of excavation, the internal arrangements of these monuments are difficult to assess. The constructional techniques involved in the building of a chambered cairn display a high degree of engineering skills both in the manœuvring of large stones and in the manipulation of intractable boulders to form vaulted chambers.

In some cases, the siting of a cairn appears to have an integral relationship with a unit of land around it, as though the cairn is part of the history of the particular community nearby. The classic case-study is that of the Orcadian island of Rousay, where the famous archaeologist, Professor V. Gordon Childe, realized that the distribution of the chambered cairns was mirrored by that of C19 farms. The siting of other cairns offers no such sense of geographical order, but, where two or three sites are found in close proximity, it may be that this is a boundary zone between several communities. What is clear is that there are very different architectural traditions: in Argyll and Arran, for example, the cairns are of Clyde type, in which the chambers have parallel sides and are divided by cross-slabs into a number of compartments. In the Hebrides, the north of Scotland and Orkney, the passage-grave is more standard, a design in which a distinct passage leads to a chamber, sometimes a simple oval on plan, sometimes a structure of considerable complexity. In Shetland and around Inverness there are further local groups. We have chosen representative examples in the Gazetteer and hope that these may serve as an indication of what to look out for at other chambered cairns which the visitor will find marked on Ordnance Survey maps.

The chambers were probably used on many occasions over several centuries, and excavation reveals the latest stage in the burial ritual, with all earlier burials gathered to one side or long disintegrated. It is not known whether burial in a tomb was permitted for all members of the community, but certainly both sexes and all ages are represented when the bones can be identified with any accuracy; in the very few cases where large numbers of bones survived, there is no evidence of any degree of social selectivity. The skeletons are rarely complete, but it is difficult to know whether this is because only parts of the body were buried or whether bones were removed subsequent to burial. Sometimes sherds of pottery, flint tools, and other artefacts are found mixed in with the bones, but they appear to have been part of the burial ritual rather than grave-goods in the sense of personal belongings of the dead. Animal and fish bones are also commonly present, along with soil that was apparently brought deliberately into the tomb.

Ceremonial Centres

Concentrations of monuments provide one of the most telling impressions of cultural stability and social organization in early prehistory. The Clava cairns with the symmetry of orientation of their passages (p. 150) imply both a society that is capable of long-term planning and traditions that may involve an interest in celestial movements. Circles of standing stones sometimes form impressive ceremonial centres, as at Callanish in Lewis (p. 225). Some such circles are associated with great rock-cut ditches with external banks, known obscurely as henge monuments (after Stonehenge, in Wiltshire, where the stones were envisaged as 'hanging', for which the Middle English inflection is 'heng'). Henge monuments may also contain timber circles as at Balfarg in Fife (p. 90) or, unexcavated, they may appear simply as earthen banks as at Normangill in Lanarkshire (p. 84).

At Stenness in Orkney, the architecturally intricate chambered cairn of Maes Howe (p. 187) is close to the stone circle and henge known as the Stones of Stenness (p. 189) and within sight of the complex of burial-mounds around the second henge and stone circle of the Ring of Brodgar (p. 189). The labour involved in building these monuments was on a

▼ Aerial view of Callanish stone circle and alignments (p. 225) (RCAHMS)

grand scale. Whereas the construction of an average chambered cairn might require some 10,000 man-hours, Maes Howe is likely to have needed 100,000 man-hours. It has been estimated that digging the rock-cut ditch at the Ring of Brodgar would have involved some 80,000 man-hours, on top of which the great slabs for the stone circle had to be quarried, transported to the site, and set up in individual holes.

Such ritual centres as Machrie Moor on Arran (p. 73) or the stone rows of Caithness and Sutherland may suggest to the visitor a sense of land-scapes both terrestrial and celestial. For this reason we have not shied away from the notion that one reason for visiting a monument may indeed be the view from it of the surrounding landscape. We reject Dr Johnson's reaction after visiting the cairn of Kinchyle of Dores that 'to go and see one druidical temple is only to see that it is nothing, for there is neither art nor power in it: and seeing one is quite enough'!

The study of stone circles has controversial aspects. It has been argued that, because in plan some circles are ellipses or flattened circles rather than true circles, quite advanced knowledge of geometry was involved in their construction, including Pythagorean triangles. A standard unit of length has also been proposed, the so-called megalithic yard, which is equivalent to 82.9 cm. The function of stone circles and alignments has been attributed to the prediction of astronomical events such as eclipses of the sun and moon, again involving an advanced level of knowledge. Beguiling though these theories are, the major problem for the archaeologist is reconciling the idea of sophisticated understanding of geometry and astronomy with the physical evidence of early prehistoric technology, which was relatively primitive.

There was certainly an interest in the movements of the sun and moon, which were important to the farming calendar. The recumbent stone circles of Aberdeenshire were clearly designed with lunar observation in mind. They consist of a circle of standing stones with a massive slab lying recumbent on the SW arc of the circle; the recumbent is flanked by two particularly tall stones, and the rising or setting moon is framed by these three stones when viewed from inside the circle. Loanhead of Daviot is a well-preserved example (p. 142). Interest in the sun can be demonstrated very clearly at the great chambered tomb of Maes Howe in Orkney (p. 187), where the entrance passage was laid out in such a way that the setting sun at midwinter shines along the passage and into the chamber. Midwinter marks the turning-point of the year, when the days begin to lengthen again and spring becomes a promise of renewed life. The Temple Wood settings in Argyll provide the earliest evidence of an awareness of the movements of the sun, here dated to around 3200 BC (p. 124).

Such monuments and their surroundings are often impressive in rural locations where one can appreciate a sense of continuity with the past. However it is equally important to evoke the long tradition of occupation in densely populated areas of the C20, for the central locations of today

▲ Stone alignment at Dervaig, Mull (RCAHMS)

may for reasons of geography also have been important in the past. One such is the complex at Balbirnie-Balfarg in suburban Glenrothes in Fife (p. 90). Prehistoric monuments in urban settings are important reminders of past societies in contemporary surroundings, and several standing stones and cairns have been included in the Gazetteer to suggest this continuum of settlement.

Sometimes excavation has demonstrated activity on one site over many centuries. At Cairnpapple, West Lothian, for example, a hilltop location was the focus for ritual activity for many centuries (p. 65). In other cases, the sequence of building seems to have taken place in a linear way with one cairn acting as the focus for an adjacent burial. The great cairns of the Early Bronze Age may cover only a single cist, although there may have been other later burials inserted into the same mound. Among the most dramatic today are those in the Kilmartin Valley and on hilltop locations throughout Scotland. Some later burials were covered by small kerb-cairns, where a kerb of large boulders contains a low stony filling (e.g. Strontoiller in Argyll, p. 131).

Later Burials

Only a very few burials of the later first millennium BC and the earlier first millennium AD have been found, perhaps because different forms of deposition were preferred and less formal disposal of the dead was the norm. Classical sources discussing similar Iron Age tribes describe a religion with many gods and traditions of worship in natural surroundings rather than formal temples. There are also very few Roman burials in Scotland.

Orderly deposition of burials in formal graves returns in the Early Christian period, with cemeteries of long cists aligned east and west, which contain inhumation burials without any accompanying gravegoods. Christianity was introduced into Scotland in two main waves, one from Whithorn in Galloway (p. 44) from the late C5 onwards, and the other from Iona (p. 113) from the mid-C6. Pictland appears to have been thoroughly Christian by the early C8, and centres of Christian worship and burial can be identified by collections of sculpture at places such as St Andrews (p. 104), Meigle (p. 101), St Vigeans (p. 105), and Rosemarkie (p. 157).

Particularly in the Moray Firth area but also as far north as Shetland and as far south as Fife, burials beneath square cairns have been identified as Pictish because of their association with distinctively Pictish decorated stones and with appropriate radiocarbon dates in the C4 to C8. These Pictish burials lack gravegoods, whereas the pagan Viking graves of the C9 and C10 contain personal belongings such as dress ornaments, tools, and weapons. Four Viking boat-burials have been excavated in Scotland but none is now visible. Once the Norse settlers had been converted to Christianity, they too dropped the custom of placing personal belongings in the grave. Christian Norse graves can be seen in the churchyard on the Brough of Birsay in Orkney (p. 177), and the massive hogbacked tombstones at Govan in Glasgow (p. 76) reflect Scandinavian influence from northern England in the C10 and C11.

Art, Ornament, and Decoration

Pottery is one of the most diagnostic elements in the archaeological record, and many excavated monuments can be dated only by distinctive types of pottery vessels that have been discovered in the course of excavations. This is particularly true of neolithic and Bronze Age burial monuments, but recognizable pottery styles are also present at later periods. The description of the gravegoods accompanying a burial in a cairn may include the conventional names for such pottery styles as Beaker and Food Vessel, which refer to archaeological types rather than to functional groups—although analysis of residues in beakers suggests that they held alcoholic beverages. The elaborate decoration of many vessels allows archaeologists to group them into various styles, and this may permit the creation of regional groups or may help to demonstrate widespread fashions. Prehistoric pottery in Scotland was coil-built rather than wheel-thrown, the coils being added one on top of the other and the junctions carefully smoothed over; before firing, while the clay was still malleable, the surface might be decorated in many ways. Patterns could be incised;

ornament could be impressed, perhaps by twisting a cord round the vessel, or perhaps by jabbing the surface with a tiny bone. After firing, the decoration is still crisp and could be used as a basis for colourful encrustation, though evidence for this is hard to find. Whether such decoration has any religious or social meaning, or whether it represents a delight in designs is impossible to tell.

Considerable skill was also employed in the carving of ceremonial stone balls, decorated by patterns of knobs or intricate spirals, which are particularly common in Aberdeenshire. Carved balls and spiked objects were found at Skara Brae (p. 184), along with decorated stone knives and bone ornaments. The balls are surely prestigious artefacts, expressing status or perhaps some aspect of tribal tradition, and other artefacts have also been seen as symbols of power, such as maceheads carved from naturally attractive stone or the jadeite axeheads imported from the Alps. These are the trappings of a society with the ability to organize the labour required to build great public monuments such as stone circles.

Only rarely was carved decoration used to adorn the chambered cairns of the first agricultural communities, but at the Holm of Papa Westray South there are distinct eyebrow motifs (p. 196), and in Tankerness House Museum, Kirkwall, there is an elaborately decorated slab from Pierowall, Westray, with crisply carved spirals and concentric arcs. Decorative motifs can help to link different sites; for example, incised linear designs at Maes Howe (p. 187) are comparable to those on slabs in the settlement at Skara Brae (p. 184). Slabs with simple cup-markings have been found in the neolithic long burial-mound at Dalladies, Kincardineshire, the earliest dated example, and also on structural slabs in the Clava cairns.

Rock Art

Great expanses of this simple style of carving make a considerable impact on the visitor, particularly where the cup-marks are surrounded by multiple rings. The superb displays at Achnabreck and Cairnbaan in Argyll (pp. 126, 127) stimulate a sense of surprise at the effort involved, together with unanswerable questions about purpose and connections. Of all types of prehistoric monuments, such expanses of rock carvings prompt many questions in an attempt to understand them. Over how many decades were the markings cut? Does the location of the rocksheet have a relationship to likely settlement sites or routeways? Are there other monuments close by, such as cairns or standing stones? Could involvement with natural or celestial worlds have had a part to play in the ceremonies of carving? Scottish rock art is relatively simple in comparison with that of Sweden or Spain, but the scale of many cup-and-ring markings demonstrate a degree of planning and commitment that underlines the importance of these decorated rock surfaces in the creation of landscapes of ritual and intercession with nature.

▲ Cross-slab at Cladh a' Bhile, Ellary, Argyll (RCAHMS)

Several standing stones and stone circles also bear decoration with cup-marks and cup-and-ring markings; there are a few more elaborate carvings, such as the double spiral at Temple Wood, Kilmartin, in Argyll (p. 124). Some motifs may be a deliberate expression of power or authority over resources, though in some cases these were designed to be hidden as part of the rituals of death. The slabs of several cists in the Kilmartin Valley are decorated with axe-markings (Nether Largie North and Ri Cruin) and this may reflect the importance of trade in bronze to this community. Others make impressive exhibits in museums, notably the side-slab of a cist from Badden, Mid Argyll, now in Glasgow Art Gallery and Museum, Kelvingrove; this is decorated with lozenge patterns, the slab having grooves pecked at either end to receive the end slabs, rather in the manner of tongue-and-groove carpentry. The find is important on several counts: first it is a reminder in stone of the undoubtedly sophisticated and highly decorated objects that would have existed in wood and other perishable materials from the prehistoric past; secondly, it has been suggested that comparable continental examples represent the patterned textile hangings of a contemporary house.

Later Stone Carving

Highly ornate upright stones are not found in Scotland in Iron Age contexts, though these are known from Ireland, and the art of the later first millennium BC and early first millennium AD is represented in bronze-work and pottery decoration. Celtic tribes used nature as the backdrop to ceremony, often a loch or grove, rather than a timber or stone construction. Personal ornaments made in bronze, such as torcs and armlets, denote the outward trappings of rank. It is not until the Roman occupation that public statements in stone are again found. The most important are the distance slabs on the Antonine Wall and these are now housed in the National Museums of Scotland and especially in the Hunterian Museum of the University of Glasgow. Several of the stones make moving statements about the supremacy of the Roman legions over the native tribesmen, with the naked torsos of headless barbarians, their weapons strewn around them, depicted cowering beneath the victorious cavalryman. Such overtly political statements are something new in the repertoire of decorated stones in Scotland, but, along with a single Roman milestone, they show a different approach to the ordered landscape and its inhabitants than anything that can be sensed in earlier times.

Stone monuments are, however, an important part of Early Christian commemoration, and Scotland has an important series from the beginnings of Christianity in the C5 to the high crosses of Iona and Kildalton of the later C8 and the late Pictish cross-slabs of the C9. The sculptural styles also help us show the traditions of the various peoples of early medieval Scotland: Picts, Scots, Britons, and Angles. In the north and east there are the Picts whose decorated stones are among the most startling expres-

▲ St Madoes Pictish cross-slab (RCAHMS)

sions of tribal vitality within a Christian artistic framework. The earliest stones show a variety of incised motifs with arcane archaeological names enshrined in modern scholastic tradition—double disc and Z-rod, crescent and V-rod, and the like. Combinations of symbols clearly conveyed a message that was intelligible to the Picts but is quite obscure today. Many theories have been proposed for the meaning of the symbols, but none can be proved. They include political statements about marriage alliances, records of territorial boundaries, and memorials to dead dignitaries. These possibilities should be explored not only in the open air as at Aberlemno (p. 86), Strathmiglo (p. 107), and elsewhere, but in museums such as those at Forfar, Dundee, Inverness, and Dunrobin. Symbols have also been found on the walls of caves as at East Wemyss in Fife, and bulls were carved on the walls of the great Pictish fort at Burghead in Moray (p. 134).

On art-historical grounds, these early symbol stones are dated to the C6 and C7, and this has been supported by a mid-C6 radiocarbon date for material from a domestic context in which a very crude symbol stone was found at Pool in Sanday, Orkney. Symbols may have been used even earlier on organic materials such as wood and leather. No trace of paint has yet been found on these stones, but it seems likely that colour would have been used to emphasize the designs.

Rather later in date are cross-slabs with Christian motifs alongside Pictish symbols, which show that Pictish carvers had access to Christian iconography of international complexity in the C8 and C9. The biblical stories of David were particular favourites, of which the slab-built shrine at St Andrews is the most impressive embodiment (p. 104), but other biblical motifs include Daniel in the lions' den (Meigle, p. 101), and Paul and Anthony breaking bread in the desert (Nigg, p. 156). Rather than create free-standing crosses, the Picts chose to carve the cross in relief on large slabs of stone, which allowed the addition of elaborate decoration on the background to the cross. Although Pictish symbols were clearly compatible with Christianity, they were never placed on the cross itself.

Cross-slabs were also favoured by the Britons of Strathclyde and Galloway, whereas both the Scots of Argyll and the Angles of SE Scotland preferred free-standing crosses. The high crosses of Iona (p. 113) and Kildalton in Islay (p. 116) reflect links with Pictish, Northumbrian, and Irish sculpture, while the superb Ruthwell Cross in Dumfriesshire (p. 40), with its Latin and runic inscriptions, is one of the high points of early medieval European art.

Warfare and Defence

There are few glimpses of the aggressive element in society before the late Bronze Age, apart from weapons. Bronzesmiths were certainly producing increasing numbers of weapons after about 1000 BC, most of which are known from hoards buried for safety or deposited in wetlands or lochs to placate the gods. One site where it is possible to see the shelter in which a bronzesmith worked is Jarlshof in Shetland (p. 211), and fragments of moulds demonstrate that swords were one of the products commissioned there. The climatic deterioration that had already begun before 1000 BC led not only to the formation of blanket peat and consequent contraction of arable areas, but also to crop failure, particularly where constant farming over the centuries had impoverished the soil. Good land would have been at a premium, and there would have been fierce competition between warlords to accumulate enough wealth through land and cattle to maintain bands of warriors and demonstrate their status in society.

Competition for land and livestock is reflected in the archaeological record first by timber stockaded enclosures built around settlements and then by hillforts. Scotland has an immense variety of hillforts, some on surprisingly low-lying situations as at Chesters in East Lothian (p. 68) and most on naturally defensive hilltops, of which the sky-high fort on Tap o' Noth in Aberdeenshire is pre-eminent (p. 149). Equivalent in natural defence are some coastal promontory forts, but these are a speciality of the Early Historic period, by which time boat technology had advanced to the point that naval strength was very important (e.g. Burghead, p. 134).

Hillfort defences can take several forms. There may be a stone wall, sometimes strengthened originally by a timber framework; in some cases this timber-lacing caught fire, either accidentally or as a result of enemy attack, and the result is a vitrified wall with fused masses of partly molten stone, as at Carradale in Argyll (p. 121). There may be a series of earthen ramparts and ditches as at Whiteside Hill in the Borders (p. 62). In many cases, hillfort defences were modified and improved over the centuries of their use, and without excavation it can be difficult to unravel the sequence. These forts enclosed round timber houses, traces of which are often visible on the surface. In the case of very large forts containing many houses, it is reasonable to assume that these were tribal capitals with an important role in the economy of the area. An excellent example is the great fort on Eildon Hill North, above Melrose in the Borders (p. 52), where, although they were probably not all contemporary, traces of some three hundred houses can be seen. The importance of this Iron Age community may be gauged from the fact that the Roman army established a legionary fortress on the level ground below the native fort.

Very small stone forts in the west of Scotland are often known as duns, and some are small enough to have been roofed over entirely as fortified houses. This was part of a trend apparent throughout the Western and Northern Isles from the middle of the first millennium BC towards massive stone roundhouses, and the trend culminated in the broch, the ultimate in chieftains' fortified residences. Brochs were multi-storey stone towers with a single entrance and no windows, the tallest of which could be in double figures of metres—Mousa in Shetland (p. 215) survives still to about 13 m. and may have been the tallest ever built. As an architectural response to a social need, brochs are the equivalent of the lairds' towerhouses of the C16 in Scotland. Brochs belong to the last two centuries BC and the first two centuries AD, after which the need for them, whatever it was, seems to have passed. The main distribution of brochs was beyond those areas of southern and eastern Scotland involved in the Roman attempt to occupy northern Britain, but a few outliers may have been encountered by the Roman army (e.g. Torwoodlee in the Borders, p. 59).

An entirely new style of fortification was introduced by the Roman war machine. The Roman army built rectangular earthwork enclosures to protect its tents and personnel while on the march (temporary or marching camps), and more substantial versions to act as long-term legionary fortresses. The latter enclosed timber-built barrack-blocks and stone-built commanders' houses and granaries, and an annexe to the main fort would contain the stone-built and intricately plumbed bath house (the only visible example in Scotland is at Bearsden near Glasgow, p. 79). An extensive road-system was engineered to facilitate movement between forts, and signal-stations were established to aid long-distance communications.

The design of Roman forts seems to have made no impact on indigenous ideas about fortification, although Roman influence may well have encouraged the development of rectangular rather than circular buildings amongst the Britons and Picts. Early Historic fort-builders favoured hilltops and coastal promontories, as had their Celtic forebears, and in some cases existing forts were refurbished at this period. It was probably Northumbrian influence that led in the C8 and C9 to the evolution of fortified royal residences amongst the fertile farmlands of river plains, as at Forteviot in Strathearn, known only from historical evidence, surviving sculpture, and crop-marks on aerial photographs. Several sites of Early Historic forts, or of concentrations of Pictish sculpture that imply centres of power, were later used for medieval castles. This may simply reflect the natural defensive qualities of the site, but it may also indicate some degree of continuity in secular administration.

Inverurie in Aberdeenshire (p. 141) is one place where a motte was built in a location that boasts a number of Pictish symbol stones. The motte was a timber castle set on a great earthen mound surrounded by a ditch and sometimes, as at Motte of Urr in Galloway (p. 39), set within a bailey or outer enclosure in which domestic buildings and stables could be placed. Mottes were an innovation brought into Scotland by Anglo-Norman settlers in the C12, and the idea was adopted by Scottish lords in SW, central, and NE Scotland. They were replaced by stone castles from the C13 onwards. The earliest stone castle in Scotland is well beyond the area of influence of the motte—Cubbie Roo's Castle on the Orcadian

▲ Aerial view of Motte of Urr (p. 39) (RCAHMS)

island of Wyre (p. 205) was built in the C12 by one of the leading families of the Norse earldom.

Who Looks after Scottish Monuments?

This book includes both monuments in State care and less well-known monuments, some of which are protected by legislation. The task of looking after archaeological sites on behalf of the Secretary of State for Scotland falls to the government agency, Historic Scotland, who are also charged with scheduling sites for protection under the law. Some monuments are situated on land belonging to the National Trust for Scotland, some are in the care of local authorities and many are on privately owned land. Scotland is exceptionally well endowed with visible archaeology—the choice of monuments presented here aims to give a rounded impression of the prehistory and early history of this beautiful land.

Archaeological sites arranged by region

Dumfries and Galloway (Map, p. xv)

There are some remarkably well-preserved earthworks in this area, from the defended farmstead of Iron Age times at Rispain to the numerous C12 mottes on which timber castles once stood. Rock-art is a special feature of the prehistoric landscape of Galloway. At Whithorn, Christianity not only survived the demise of the Roman province of Britain but flowered afresh with the bishopric of St Ninian.

Barsaloch Point Fortified farmstead, Monreith

NX 347412. On the N. side of the A747, 1 km. W. of Monreith (Historic Scotland, but there is no formal access route).

This stretch of coast along the east side of Luce Bay is an excellent example of how the coastline has changed since early times. The road runs along a raised beach and the steep escarpment to the landward side was once a sea-cliff against the waves. Traces of the activities of the earliest hunters and fishermen have been found along the raised beach, and the old cliff provided the ideal location for a small fortification probably built sometime in the last centuries BC.

The enclosure is D-shaped, with its back against the scarp and its entrance on the landward side. Its defences consist of a massive ditch, 10 m. wide and still 3.5 m. deep despite silting over the centuries, with a rampart on either side. The enclosed area covers about a tenth of a hectare, just large enough for the residence of a minor chieftain, but there has been no excavation and nothing is known of any internal buildings. A later field-bank obscures the entrance.

Birrens Roman fort, Ecclefechan

NY 219751. Beside a minor road off the B725 NE of Ecclefechan.

The Roman name for this fort was Blatobulgium, and it was built as an outpost for Hadrian's Wall on the Roman road from Carlisle into western Scotland. Its history is well documented from campaigns of excavation in the 1890s and 1960s, in which an important collection of inscribed stones was recovered. The fort lies on flat ground at the point where the Middlebie burn flows into the Mein Water, and the modern road runs along the east side of the fort. None of the recorded internal buildings is visible, but the main rampart appears as a low bank, and the six outer ditches are clear at the north end of the fort, with a causeway leading to one of the four entrances into the fort.

There was a long sequence of fort-building here, from a fortlet of the late C1 to a Hadrianic fort of 1.65 ha. and an Antonine fort of 2.1 ha., the

latter destroyed and rebuilt in AD 158. Blatobulgium was finally abandoned around AD 184.

Burnswark Fort and Roman siegeworks, Ecclefechan   ★★

*NY 186787. Just after the railway bridge on the B725 E. of Ecclefechan, a minor
road on the left runs N. to a plantation on the S. flank of Burnswark Hill.*

To explore this complex of earthworks is physically arduous but quite
fascinating, for this is a landscape redolent of the Roman military occupation of northern Britain. Burnswark Hill itself was fortified with a
timber-laced rampart with an outer stone face by Celtic tribesmen around
600 BC—its area, some 7 ha., suggests that this may have been a tribal
centre of power, perhaps for the Novantae. Prestige rather than defence
appears to have been paramount here, for there are three entrances along
the south side of the fort. Was this great hillfort still occupied when the
invading Roman army arrived in its vicinity? Evidence from excavation
suggests that people were still living there in the C2 AD, but that it had
been abandoned by the time that the Roman siegeworks were built
and used.

The Roman presence is indicated by two rectangular earthwork
camps, one to the north and one to the south. That on the south has three
projecting platforms for artillery, each directed to one of the entrances of
the native hillfort just 120 m. or so uphill. Lead sling-bolts and stone balls
from Roman siege-engines have been found within the fort, and it would
seem that the old fort was used by the Roman army for target practice,
presumably by soldiers stationed at nearby Birrens.

A burial-cairn and stone cist within the hillfort indicate that
Burnswark Hill was the scene of earlier prehistoric activities, and excavation has revealed that the fort defences were preceded by a timber stockade enclosing the hilltop. At the SW end of the fort is a platform for later
artillery action, probably dating from the mid-C17.

Cairnholy Chambered cairns, Gatehouse of Fleet   ★

*NX 517538, 518540. Signposted on the A75 between Gatehouse of Fleet and
Creetown, a minor road leads up Kirkdale Glen to a car-park beside the first cairn;
a track leads uphill to the second cairn (Historic Scotland).*

The hills between Gatehouse of Fleet and Creetown are sprinkled with
early prehistoric monuments, from cairns and cup-and-ring marks to
standing stones and stone circles. They imply that this was a favoured area
for settlement, overlooking the wide expanse of Wigtown Bay.

The two Cairnholy tombs are among the earliest monuments, and
their appearance today is very different from that 5,000 years ago. Stones
have been robbed from their cairns to build field-walls, and the burial
chambers, once dark and womb-like, are now open to the sky. These were

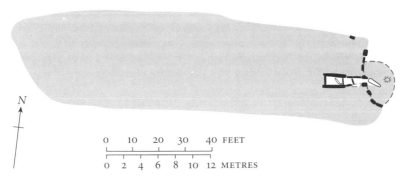

0   10   20   30   40 FEET

0   2   4   6   8   10   12 METRES

▲ Plan of Cairnholy lower cairn (after A. S. Henshall)

major enterprises in terms of labour, and they underline the importance of ancestors to the community that built them.

Despite excavation in 1949, little is known about the people buried here, because acid soil conditions had dissolved the bones, but some of the objects left with them in the tomb survived. Most notable is part of a ceremonial axe made of green jadeite imported from the Alps, a mark of the high status and wealth of the chief or community who could afford it. Even as a fragment, this would have considerable heirloom value.

The first cairn was originally some 43 m. long, extending the other side of the modern track, and the great mound of stones would have risen in height towards the east in order to cover the burial chamber. Entrance into the tomb was between two tall portal stones, and the curving façade of eight slabs would have formed a striking backdrop to the ceremonies carried on in front of the tomb. Evidence of small fires has been found, and there was a hole for a stone pillar in line with the entrance. The burial chamber appears to have two separate compartments, and it is thought that originally there was just the inner box-like chamber within a small cairn, and that the outer compartment with its elaborate façade was added later. At that stage, the cairn was enlarged and elongated. When the tomb was sealed for the last time, stones were strewn over the sacred forecourt.

Sherds of late neolithic pottery were found in both chambers. A stone carved

▼ Plan of Cairnholy upper cairn (after A. S. Henshall)

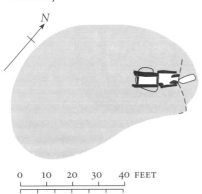

0   10   20   30   40 FEET

0   2   4   6   8   10   12 METRES

with a cup surrounded by six concentric rings lay in the inner compartment, and a flint knife and the fragment of jadeite axe in the outer.

The second cairn was built about 150 m. uphill from the first, but not necessarily at the same time, although the use of the two tombs must have overlapped. One of the entrance portal stones is broken, but the other is curiously pointed in shape, and it may have been this remarkable landmark that led to local tradition attributing the tomb to Galdus, a mythical Scottish king. Again there are two compartments to the burial chamber, and the inner box still has its huge capstone in place.

Castle Haven Dun, Borgue

NX 593482. From Borgue, on the B727 between Kirkcudbright and Gatehouse of Fleet, a minor road runs W. to Corseyard. A footpath leads to the shore of Castle Haven Bay.

This is a unique outlier of a type of fortification favoured in Argyll and the Western Isles—some tale of dynastic intrigue in the Iron Age may lie behind its appearance on the Galloway coast. It is also unusually well preserved, but that is the result of enthusiastic restoration by the landowner in the early C20. The restoration was faithful to the original structure, however, and it is well worth a visit.

The dun is D-shaped, with its straight west wall along the rocky cliff and its main entrance at the north end; another entrance at the south end led down to the beach. There is a concentric outer wall but it is uncertain whether this is contemporary or later in date. The feature that links this small fort with those in western Scotland is the use of hollow-wall construction, providing three galleries, presumably for storage, within the thickness of the dun wall. Six doorways lead into the galleries, which may imply the former existence of six dwellings built against the main wall. Projecting slabs acted as steps up to the wall-top.

▼ Plan of Castle Haven dun (after RCAHMS)

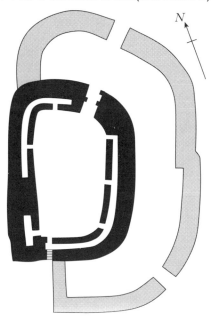

N

0 10 20 30 40 FEET

0 2 4 6 8 10 12 METRES

Artefacts found during the clearance of the dun suggest that its occupants were relatively wealthy, for they include two spiral finger-rings made of bronze, and a blue and white glass bead. There were also fragments of a mail tunic and a medieval brooch, and it has been suggested that the dun may have been used as a refuge for the Balliol family in the C14.

Castle O'er Fort, Eskdalemuir

NY 241928. From Eskdalemuir, NW of Langholm on the B709, a minor road leads S. along the W. side of the White Esk. A Forestry Commission car park at NY 246928 offers easy access westwards to the fort (Forestry Commission).

Not only are the defences of this fort still very impressive, but it has the added interest of being the focus of a system of linear earthworks. The whole complex represents a long history of occupation which is only partially understood. The fort itself appears to have had two major phases of building, beginning with twin ramparts with a medial ditch which enclose an oval area measuring 120 × 60 m. The inner rampart was later replaced by a wall enclosing a smaller area 95 × 53 m., in which several house-platforms are visible. There is an entrance at either end of the fort.

An outer annexe was attached to the south side of the outer defences, and the linear earthwork boundaries appear to be contemporary with the annexe and the later occupation of the fort.

Druchtag Motte, Mochrum

NX 349466. A minor road leading N. from Port William towards Wigtown passes through Mochrum; the motte is beside the road NE of the village (Historic Scotland).

This is a fine example of the steep-sided mound on which a timber castle would have stood in the C12. The flat top of the mound is about 20 m. in diameter, and a deep ditch encircles its base, with an outer bank. Druchtag was the first motte to be taken into State care in 1888.

Dumfries and Galloway are particularly rich in mottes, probably because feudal settlement there was based on relatively small baronial fiefs. The most massive example in southern Scotland is somewhat north of the modern Galloway boundary at Dinvin in Ayrshire, about 6 km. south of Girvan on the A714 Girvan to Newton Stewart road (NX 200931). It stands prominent on the hillside, a great oval mound with two huge outer ditches and ramparts.

Drumtroddan Cup-and-ring marked rocks and standing
stones, Monreith

NX 362447, 364443. From the A714 Wigtown to Port William, Drumtroddan farm is signposted to the E. some 4 km. from Port William; monuments in fields to S. of farm (Historic Scotland).

Drumtroddan is just one of several outcrops of greywacke rock in this area which were considered suitable some 4,000 years ago for decoration

with cup-and-ring marks. Here there are cups, cups with one or more
concentric rings up to 70 cm. in diameter, and radial grooves. To the SE,
two 3 m.-high stones survive of what was once a three-stone row, but the
middle, slightly shorter stone is now fallen. Set on a SE-facing slope, this
row is thought to have been aligned on the SW midwinter sunset.

Durisdeer Roman fortlet, Durisdeer

*NS 902048. Durisdeer is E. of the A702, some 20 km. S. of Crawford. A track
from the N. end of the village leads to the fortlet.*

One of the Roman roads running south from the fort at Crawford follows
the Potrail Water into Nithsdale, and the fortlet near Durisdeer was placed
here to control the pass through which the road descends into the valley.
It is a very well preserved example of the small outposts built in the 140s
and 150s to strengthen communications and military control in southern
Scotland. Durisdeer is likely to have been garrisoned by a unit of eighty
soldiers from the fort at Crawford.

The main rampart, 9 m. thick, encloses an area about 31 × 18 m., in
which traces of wooden barrack blocks have been found. Outside the
rampart is a deep ditch and an outer bank, and the entrance at the NE end
has the additional protection of a ditch across the ridge along which the
fortlet is most easily reached.

High Banks Cup-and-ring marked rock, Kirkcudbright

*NX 709489. From the A711 between Kirkcudbright and Dundrennan, a minor
road runs N. and passes the track to High Banks farm to the E.; the rock outcrop
lies to the SE of the farm.*

There are several groups of cups and cup-and-rings carved on this
30 m.-long rock-exposure. The largest cup-and-ring design is 45 cm. in
diameter, and some are surrounded by dense clusters of plain cups. The
overall effect is stunning.

Kirkmadrine Cross-slabs, Sandhead

*NX 080483. Signposted from the A716 S. of Sandhead in the Rhinns of Galloway
(Historic Scotland).*

Somewhere in the vicinity of Kirkmadrine in the late C5 AD, there must
have been a major Christian cemetery. The inscribed cross-slabs that
survive are a moving memorial to the Christian community in Dark Age
Galloway. They are preserved in a glass-fronted porch attached to a C19
burial chapel, but they and the later fragments were all found around the
churchyard; the two tallest pillars were in use as gateposts, hence the pairs
of holes in them.

The three earliest stones each bear an encircled chi-rho cross, the
crook-like symbol attached to the upper arm of the cross showing that the
cross was to be seen as the sacred monogram of Christ (a combination of

the first two letters of Greek *Christos*). In addition, above the chi-rho on the stone with six lines of inscription, there is an A for alpha and E for et (and), and the O for omega has presumably been broken off, meaning 'the beginning and the end'. The inscription, also in Latin, reads 'Here lie the holy and outstanding bishops Ides, Viventius, and Mavorius'. It has been suggested that, after the death of Ninian in the late C5, the seat of the bishopric moved temporarily from Whithorn to Kirkmadrine. Another stone, now lost, commemorated a deacon named Ventidius and supports the idea of a centre of church administration in the area.

The inscription on the other tall pillar reads, somewhat enigmatically, 's and Florentius'—presumably an abbreviated memorial in which 'Here lies' is understood and the name ending in s was left unfinished. The smaller pillar is inscribed 'The beginning and the end' and is thought to have been a prayer-cross dating to around AD 600.

Mote of Mark Fort, Rockcliffe

NX 845540. From the A710 about 7 km. SSE of Dalbeattie, a minor road leads SW to Rockcliffe; take the signposted path at the N. end of the village (National Trust for Scotland).

The rich birdlife of the Urr estuary may have been a factor in the choice of location for this fort. The hill itself was not ideal, for its natural defence is limited—low in height, it is steep and rocky only on the west side. It appears to have been strongly fortified, however, with a timber-laced stone wall 3 m. thick encircling the twin summits, and an inner wall round the hollow between them. The main wall had been set on fire in the early C7 AD, resulting in distorted lumps of fused stone, but occupation continued after that date, and an attempt was made to repair the destroyed rampart.

The association of this fort with King Mark of Arthurian times is purely a matter of legend, but it may reflect local memory of the fort's history, for it was certainly occupied in the Early Historic period. Scientific dating of the firing of the main rampart to the C7 suggests that this was a stronghold of some warlord of the British kingdom of Rheged, and its destruction may have been the work of Northumbrian Angles intent on territorial expansion westwards. Excavation in the interior has produced evidence of fine metalworking and of pottery imported from France, both of which are appropriate to a chief's residence.

Motte of Urr Dalbeattie   ★

NX 815646. From the B794 about 3.5 km. NNW of Dalbeattie, a minor road to the W. crosses the Urr Water and the motte is to the N.

Despite its low-lying situation beside the Urr Water, the magnificent scale of this earthwork makes it memorable even today. In its own day, when the angles of mound and ditch were steeper, and when the motte was crowned with a timber tower and a great stockade rose above the outer ditch, this must have been a breathtaking sight. The motte is set at one end of a large outer enclosure known as a bailey, in which there would have been domestic buildings such as stables, barns, and bakehouse.

The bailey ditch is 15 m. wide with an outer bank, and there are two entrance causeways on the SE and NW. There has been some excavation on the top of the motte, indicating that the original C12 structures had been destroyed by fire and that subsequent occupation had continued into the C14.

Rispain Camp   Fortified farmstead, Whithorn

NX 429399. Beyond Rispain farm, NW of the A746, 1 km. SW of Whithorn; park at farm (Historic Scotland).

This is a most impressive rectangular earthwork, so well preserved that, prior to excavation, it was thought to be either a Roman military post or a medieval moated homestead, and it was one of the earliest monuments to be taken into State care in the late C19. It is now known from radiocarbon analysis and artefactual evidence to date from between 100 BC and AD 200 and to be a fortified Celtic farm, latterly contemporary with the Roman occupation of southern Scotland. Its location was well chosen on the slope of a ridge with wide views to the north, east, and south, and its 4 m.-deep surrounding ditch probably had a dual function from the start, both defence and drainage. (The truncated cone of stonework on the west rampart is relatively modern.)

Like the smaller fortified farm at Barsalloch Point, the ditch has a rampart on either side, creating a formidable defence. The entrance is on the downslope side and traces of a wooden gateway were uncovered by excavation; this may have been linked with a wooden parapet along the crest of the inner rampart. Only a small part of the interior was excavated, revealing traces of two substantial timber round houses. One was 13.5 m. in diameter with a plank-built wall and an internal ring of posts to help support the roof. There is space inside the defences for several such dwellings and their ancillary buildings and open-air work-areas, and the whole site is likely to have been a prestigious family farm. Bone remains indicate that cattle, sheep, and pigs were kept and that deer were hunted, and grains of barley and wheat suggest that these crops were cultivated in the surrounding fields.

Ruthwell Cross   Ruthwell   ★★

NY 100682. Inside the parish church at Ruthwell, about 9 km. W. of Annan on the B724 (Historic Scotland).

The enigma of this superb stone cross is its location. It ought to be a prayer-cross on an important pilgrim route, perhaps from the Solway Firth to the Anglian monastery at Hoddom, yet there is no suitable harbour in the vicinity. In truly splendid isolation, the Ruthwell Cross is a monument to the strength of early Christianity and to the stonecarver's craft—but one would dearly like to know who commissioned it and why it is here. Its precise original location is uncertain, but it was in the church around 1642, when it was deliberately toppled and broken. In 1802 the cross was re-erected in the manse garden and in 1887 it was moved into the church.

Even in its own day the cross must have been an object of wonder as well as devotion. Thought to date from the early C8, it stands 5.2 m. high and is carved on every face (the original centre and horizontal arms of the cross-head are missing and have been replaced). Not only are there figural panels with biblical scenes and decorative panels of vine-scroll, but there is also text on the margins of the panels, some written in Old English in the runic alphabet and some in Latin in Roman script. The vine-scroll on the sides of the shaft is particularly fine, inhabited on one side by birds and on the other by animals.

The largest panel on the front of the cross depicts Christ in Majesty, with his feet resting on two animals, surrounded by a Latin text reading 'Jesus Christ the judge of equity. The animals and the serpents recognized the Saviour of the world in the desert'. The panel above shows St John the Baptist holding the Lamb, and what survives of the text reads 'we worship'. The two panels below illustrate first St Paul and St Anthony, 'St Paul and A[nthony] broke bread in the desert', and then Mary and the Child on an ass fleeing into Egypt. On the back of the cross, the panels show, from the top of the shaft down, the Visitation surrounded by a runic text which includes the phrase 'Mary Mother of the Lord'; Mary Magdalene washing the feet of Christ, and in Latin 'She brought an alabaster box of ointment; and standing behind his feet, she began to moisten his feet with tears, and with the hairs of her own head she wiped [them]'; the healing of the blind man, 'And passing by [He] saw [blind] from birth'; the Annunciation, 'The angel came in . . .'; and finally the Crucifixion, which is very worn. At the base of the cross-head on this side is carved an archer, and at the top St John with an eagle as his symbol, while on the other side there are two seated figures at the base of the cross-head and an eagle in the top panel.

All these Latin texts relate to the Bible, whereas the runic inscription on the sides of the shaft is part of an Old English poem known from a later manuscript as 'The Dream of the Rood'. The rood is the cross on which Christ was crucified, and here the narrator is the cross itself:

Almighty God stripped himself as he prepared to climb the gallows, valiant in men's sight . . . I raised up a great king, Lord of Heaven. I dared not bow down. Men reviled us both together. I was drenched in blood . . . Christ was on the cross. Yet to him in his solitude came noble men, eager, from afar. I beheld it all. I was

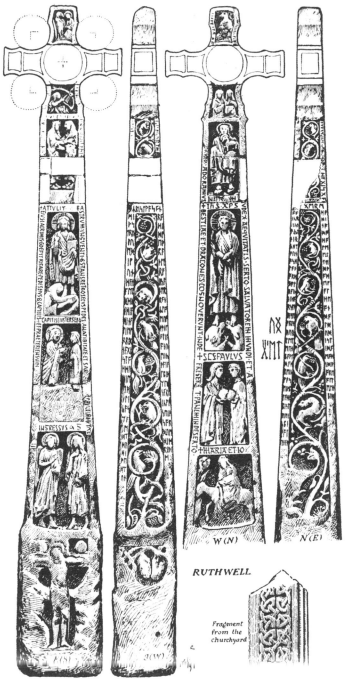

RUTHWELL

Fragment
from the
churchyard

▲ Ruthwell Cross (drawing by W. G. Collingwood)

bitterly troubled with griefs. I bowed . . . wounded with arrows. Down they laid that limb-weary one. They stood at the corpse's head. There they beheld . . .

Anglo-Saxon runes

The runic alphabet was invented in Scandinavia before the end of the C2 AD as an easy method of inscribing on wood and stone. The letters consist of combinations of vertical and oblique strokes. Runes were widely adopted in NW Europe and used in several languages. In southern Scotland there are inscriptions in Old English using Anglo-Saxon runes at Ruthwell and Whithorn, whereas in northern and western Scotland there are Norse runes used for inscriptions in Old Norse (e.g. IONA, MAES HOWE in Orkney).

Torhousekie Stone circle, Wigtown

NX 382564. Signposted on the B733 5 km. W. of Wigtown (Historic Scotland).

Although its stones are relatively low, this is a powerful and spacious circle, built of solid granite boulders. The circle is in fact a ring, 21.4 × 20 m., and its nineteen stones are graded in height, with the lowest to the NW and the highest towards the SE. This grading suggests a link with the recumbent stone circles of Aberdeenshire, although here the celestial interest seems to be in the midwinter sunrise rather than the movements of the moon. Another echo of recumbent stone circles is the inner setting of three stones, where two large boulders flank a low stone and are backed by the remains of what may be a ring-cairn.

On the other side of the road, some 127 m. east of the circle, is a row of three standing stones, graded in height to the SW and aligned on the midwinter sunset.

Trusty's Hill Fort and Pictish symbols, Gatehouse of Fleet

NX 588560. From the first bend in the B796 at the SW end of Gatehouse of Fleet, a minor road leads NW; a footpath to Anwoth Church passes to the N. of Trusty's Hill.

The popular idea that there were Picts living in Galloway is a myth that arose from a misunderstanding by C12 English historians. But there were contacts between the Britons of SW Scotland and the Picts, of which the symbols carved on a rock-face on Trusty's Hill are a tangible reminder.

The dun encloses an oval area about 24 × 15 m. on the summit of the hill, with an entrance at the south end. At the other end, there is an outer rampart and ditch controlling access along the ridge. The main rampart was originally a stone wall laced with a timber framework, but this was set on fire, causing collapse and vitrifaction of the stone. Excavations in 1960 indicated that the dun belonged originally to the C1 or C2 AD and that it had been refortified in the C6 or C7. It was presumably during this later occupation that the Pictish symbols were carved beside the entrance. A raid by Pictish forces has been suggested as an explanation, but the dun and its occupants were far from Pictland and Pictish interests, and there may well have been quite different reasons. The symbols consist of a double disc and Z-rod and three motifs which are not strictly symbols, in the sense that they do not appear elsewhere: what may be a monster with a spiral tail, a design which looks like a paper knife, and an absurd 'face' with antennae.

Twelve Apostles Stone circle, Newbridge, Dumfries

NX 947794. From the A76 about 4 km. NNW of Dumfries, take the B729 W. for almost 0.5 km., and a minor road SE towards Newbridge. Circle in field to N. of road.

This is one of the largest stone circles in Britain, an oval fully 86.5 × 79 m. across. One of the 'Twelve Apostles' had been removed before 1837, but in fact it is thought that originally there may have been eighteen stones, regularly spaced at about 14.5 m. apart. Opposite a 2 m.-tall slab on the NE is a huge fallen slab more than 3 m. long, suggesting that the circle was aligned on the midwinter sunset in the SW. Ploughing round the circle has turned up unusual quantities of white quartz pebbles. Old records and air photographs indicate that this may have been just one element in a ritual landscape consisting of another circle and two cursuses.

Whithorn Early Christian centre   ★★

NX 444403. Signposted in main street (Whithorn Trust and Historic Scotland).

'Ninian's own episcopal see, named after Saint Martin, and famous for its stately church, is now used by the English, and it is here that his body and those of many saints lie at rest.' This passage from Bede's *History of the English Church and People*, written in the early C8, encapsulates the story of Early Christianity at Whithorn. Ninian's bishopric in the C5 was based here and by Bede's time Whithorn had become an important place of pilgrimage. But by then the Britons in SW Scotland were subject to English rule, and the monastery had been absorbed into the Northumbrian Church. Bede records that Ninian's church was, unusually for the Britons, built of stone and known as the White House, Candida Casa in Latin but hwit erne in Early English, hence the modern Whithorn.

The earliest visible building at the Priory is the C12 Romanesque church, but excavations have uncovered traces of the Northumbrian monastery and the outline of some of the buildings, including the church, are marked out on the ground. The museum and visitor centre provide an absorbing visit. Artefacts reflect not only everyday life but trade contacts with France in the C6 to C8, importing costly items such as glass beakers. Among the large collection of carved stones is the earliest Christian inscription known from Scotland; it is a pillar stone bearing a faint chi-rho, and it reads 'We praise thee Lord. Latinus, aged 35, and his daughter, aged 4. The grandson Barrovadus set up the monument here'. It implies three generations of Christians in the area by the mid-C5, and it is thought that Ninian was sent to care for an existing community of Christians.

Other stones of particular interest include a C7 cross-slab inscribed in Latin 'The place of Peter the Apostle'; the fine lettering is of Merovingian type and reinforces the link between Whithorn and France. The splendid Monreith Cross represents a Whithorn school of stone-carving in the C10 and C11.

Places associated with St Ninian

Ninian's Whithorn was not ideally located, some 5 km. from the sea, for the later development of trade and pilgrimage, but there are other places on the coast associated with the saint and with Whithorn. Tradition would have St Ninian's Cave at Physgill (NX 422359; Historic Scotland) as his retreat for meditation, following the example of St Martin of Tours to whom the church at Whithorn was dedicated. As well as crosses carved on the rock-face, excavations have yielded a number of cross-slabs dating from the C8–C11, and it is clear that the cave was used by pilgrims from the C8 onwards. The Isle of Whithorn shelters a natural harbour to the SE of Whithorn itself, and St Ninian's Chapel was built on the island around AD 1300 to service pilgrims bound for Whithorn. An earlier chapel was built in the C10 or C11, perhaps for the benefit of Irish pilgrims, on the coast near Mochrum (NX 278489; Historic Scotland). This is known as Chapel Finian, after an Irish saint who was educated at Whithorn in the mid-C6.

Borders (Map, p. xv)

The Border counties encompass great natural beauty, from the sweeping valley of the River Tweed to the breathtaking range of the Cheviot Hills. The valleys are famous for their medieval abbeys and castles, whereas the hills take the visitor back into prehistoric times, when Celtic tribesmen fortified almost every hilltop. Roman engineers laid out the great arterial Dere Street across the hills and moors between the two Roman Walls, and there are well-preserved camps and forts to mark the army's progress.

Addinston Fort and settlement, Lauder   ★

NT 523536. Addinston village lies a little to the E. of the A697, NE of Lauder; the fort is on the hillside N. of the village.

Its situation on a slope suggests that the massive ramparts of this fort were designed more to impress than to fulfil any real need for defence. The two ramparts survive up to 4.5 m. in height. They and their accompanying ditches enclose an oval area some 85 × 49 m. In the interior are traces of stone-built houses which may be of later date. Across the valley to the NE is another fort at LONGCROFT (see below).

Blackbrough Fort, Hownam

NT 808177. From Morebattle on the B6401, NE of Jedburgh, take the minor road S. to Hownam and fork left along the valley of the Heatherhope Burn; a little beyond Greenhill, a footpath leads NE beside a subsidiary burn and up on to Craik Moor.

The sequence from a timber palisade to an earthwork is very clear at Blackbrough, despite lack of excavation. A sunken groove marks the bedding trench in which the timber uprights stood, enclosing an area about 35 × 26 m., with a metre-wide gap on the south side where there was a gateway. The earthwork fort with its well-preserved rampart and ditch takes in a larger area around the palisade trench, and both phases are likely to date to the first millennium BC.

Bonchester Hill Fort, Bonchester Bridge

NT 595117. From Bonchester Bridge, take the B6357 N. for almost 2 km.; just the other side of the bridge over the Rule Water, take the minor road E. to Gatehousecote, park, and follow the track S. up the gentler flank of Bonchester Hill.

On the way up the hill, you will pass a complex of earthworks consisting ⸺⸺⸺⸺⸺⸺⸺⸺⸺⸺⸺⸺⸺⸺⸺⸺⸺⸺⸺⸺⸺⸺⸺⸺⸺⸺⸺⸺⸺⸺⸺⸺⸺⸺ sions. Their date and purpose are unknown, but medieval or later stock-pens are a likely guess.

Solidly astride its isolated hill, the fort commands wide views in all directions. There were small-scale excavations in 1906 and again in 1950, which established a basic sequence. In its earliest phase, the fort was enclosed by a stone wall more than 3 m. wide, which enclosed an area some 100 × 85 m. on the summit. Two additional walls provided extra defence on the gentle north slope. There were three entrances to the NE, NW, and south. At a later stage, an outer rampart was added, greatly increasing the area enclosed. Stone foundations of houses are visible,

▼ Plan of Cademuir I fort (RCAHMS)

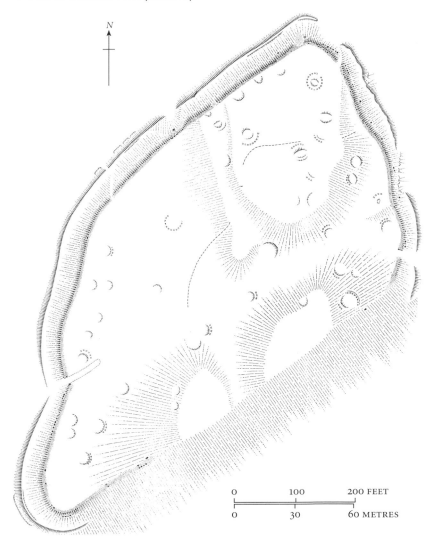

N

| 0 | 100 | 200 FEET |
| 0 | 30 | 60 METRES |

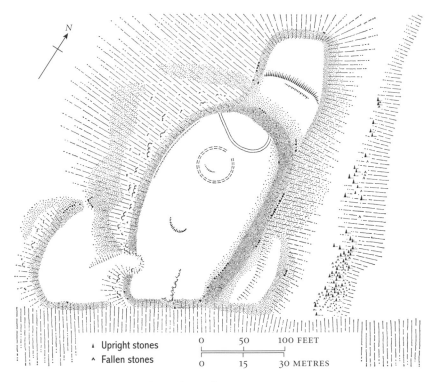

▲ Upright stones
▲ Fallen stones

0   50   100 FEET

0   15   30 METRES

▲ Plan of Cademuir II fort (RCAHMS)

eight inside the primary fort and another sixteen in the space between it and the outer rampart, but it is not known to which phase any of these houses belong.

Cademuir Hill   Forts, Peebles

NT 230374 (I), 224370 (II). From the A72 about 2.5 km. SW of Peebles, a minor road crosses the River Tweed for Kirkton Manor; a little beyond Kirkton Manor, fork left over the Manor Water and round the foot of Cademuir Hill for just over 2 km., park and walk up the track to the NE.

Two forts crown the western summits of this spectacularly steep hill. The higher and larger fort (I) has a strong stone wall, about 3 m. wide, and two entrances to east and west. An outer bank runs along the west side. In the interior there are traces of at least 35 houses marked by ring-grooves in the turf. Fort II, though smaller, was even stronger, surrounded by a massive stone wall of which facing stones can be seen along the east side, showing that it was fully 6 m. wide. Three terraces to north and south were also enclosed by stone walls, one protecting the entrance to the fort on the

SW. Additional defence was achieved along the east side by a band of upright stones forming a chevaux de frise. The ring-groove of one large house is visible inside the main fort.

Dere Street Roman road, Soutra

NT 450580. From the A68 between Edinburgh and Lauder, take the B6368 S., signposted Galashiels, for 1.5 km. (Historic Scotland).

This major road through southern Scotland was named Dere Street not by the Romans but by the later Anglo-Saxons. The line chosen for the road by Roman engineers is followed for much of its course by the modern A68, but there are still good stretches to be seen. It crosses Soutra Hill at the west end of the Lammermuirs, west of the A68, and a well-preserved section is easily accessible on the southern flanks of the hill. The road is about 6 m. wide and there are clear quarry-pits, from which the gravel for the road-surface was dug, on the west.

Roman roads were often used for centuries after the Romans left. At Soutra medieval use of Dere Street is particularly clear with the location

---

Roman roads in Scotland

A vital ingredient in the Roman military endeavour in Scotland was the road-system created by the army's excellent engineers. It enabled the swift movement of soldiers, equipment, and provisions—and there was nothing to match it until the C18. North of Hadrian's Wall, there were two main arterial routes into Scotland, one on the west from Stanwix up Annandale and Upper Clydesdale (*see* BIRRENS, p. 33), and another (known as Dere Street), which was probably the main route, from Corbridge through the Cheviot Hills, both heading for the Firth of Forth. The fertile plain south of the Forth has been extensively culti-vated over the centuries, and unfortunately there the precise route of the two roads cannot even be traced on air photographs.

There were other roads as well, including one up Nithsdale (*see* DURISDEER, p. 38) and one from Corbridge to the mouth of the River Tweed, where, although the physical evidence has yet to be found, it is assumed that there must have been a harbour servicing the Roman fleet (like CRAMOND on the Forth, p. 70). Major rivers would have played a part in the overall pattern of communications, and a hint of this was found at Newstead in the form of a wooden steering-oar. North of the Forth, a single road has been traced as far as the River Tay at Bertha, but no farther, and it appears that the more northerly forts were aban-doned before the road caught up with them.

Just one Roman milestone has been found, at Ingliston near Edinburgh (now in the National Museums of Scotland); it records the repair of part of Dere Street in about AD 139.

beside it of Soutra Aisle, a C17 burial vault that utilizes the only upstanding remains of the hospital of Soutra, founded in the C12 (NT 452584).

Dreva   Fort, settlement and field-system, Broughton ★

NT 126353. From Broughton on the A701, take the minor road SE towards Stobo and park after about 2 km.

The fort is on the crest of Dreva Craig above the confluence of the Biggar Water with the River Tweed. As you walk along the spur, look out for the field-walls and foundations of small stone houses that represent farmsteads probably of Roman Iron Age date. There is a group of such houses with yards close to the north end of the fort, almost certainly built of stone from its ramparts, as well as several houses inside the fort itself. Despite all this robbing, the two stone ramparts are still impressive, and the entrance is clear on the east. The south end of the spur narrows beyond the fort and was evidently thought to be a hazard to its defence, solved by the provision of a chevaux de frise. This is an excellent example of the device whereby angular stones were embedded in the ground as a painful obstacle to any massed assault on the fort.

Earn's Heugh   Forts, Coldingham

NT 892691. Just NE of Coldingham on the A1107, a minor road leads N. to Westerside Farm; walk along the field edge to the cliffs (great care is needed on this dangerous coast).

Much of these twin forts has probably been lost through coastal erosion, but it is likely nevertheless that the cliff-edge, 150 m. high, was used as the seaward line of defence. Each fort appears to have been built in at least two phases, first a single rampart and then the addition of two more. The outer pair of the western fort clearly overlie the outer defences of the eastern fort. Traces of stone-built houses are visible inside the western fort, and excavation in 1931 yielded Roman artefacts.

Edin's Hall   Fort, broch, and settlement, Preston   ★★

NT 772603. Signposted from the A6112 about 5.5 km. S. of Grantshouse; a round walk of about 4 km. (Historic Scotland).

This is an absorbing monument that raises many questions. It lies on the lower slopes of Cockpen Law above the Whiteadder Burn, amidst good farmland, and the complexity of the remains suggests a long occupation during which the character of the settlement changed (some excavation took place in the C19 but with little gain). The earliest element is the oval fort enclosed by twin ramparts and ditches. The original entrance was on the east (the other breaks in the defences are later). There were probably timber round houses within the fort, but these have yet to be found.

A broch was added, set within its own walled enclosure in the NW corner of the fort. This is unusually large for a broch, with an internal

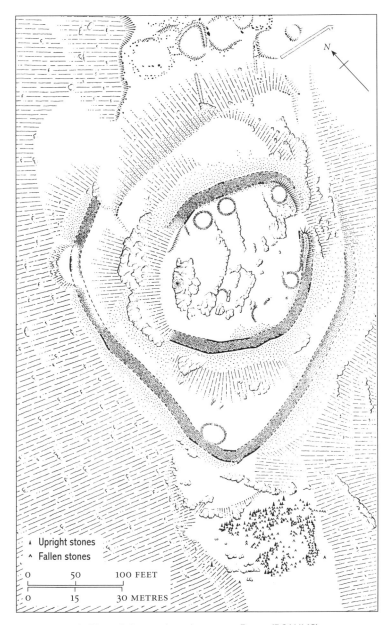

▲ Plan of fort and settlement at Dreva (RCAHMS)

diameter of almost 17 m., but its structure shows several design features of northern brochs. There are guard-cells on either side of the entrance passage and other cells within the 6 m.-thick wall, one of which gives access to a mural stair. As restored, the wall stands almost 2 m. high, and its original height can only be guessed, but the diameter of the broch suggests that it was not of tower-like proportions. It was surely the prestigious residence of the local Votadinian chieftain, built perhaps in the C1 AD.

There are clear remains of circular stone houses and subdividing walls in the rest of the interior, some of which overlie the fort defences. These are likely to belong to a non-defensive phase of settlement late in the history of the site.

Eildon Hill North   Fort and Roman signal station, Melrose

NT 555328. A signposted footpath leads from the B6359 on the S. outskirts of Melrose up to the col between the N. and middle summits of the Eildon Hills.

Ideally, any visit to Melrose and the Eildons should be preceded by a long gaze at their landscape from Scott's View, named after Sir Walter Scott's fondness for the spot (on the B6356 at NT 593342, signposted from the A68). From here, high above the Tweed, you can appreciate how the river meanders, almost encircling a promontory on which the original abbey of Melrose stood in St Cuthbert's day, and then making a broad sweep west-wards round a gentle slope on which the Roman army built the major fortress of Trimontium (literally 'Three Hills', now more prosaically known as Newstead). And looming above them, the great Iron Age fort on the broad summit of the northernmost of the three Eildon Hills.

Small-scale excavation on several occasions has provided little more than a basic chronological framework for the fort. There was extensive occupation on the hill both in late Bronze Age times and in the Roman Iron Age, both leaving traces of house-platforms which cannot be differ-entiated without excavation. About 300 house-platforms are visible, lead-ing to the idea that this was a veritable walled 'town', but in reality the platforms are not all contemporary. The same ambiguity applies to the defences. Almost 18 ha. of the hilltop are enclosed by triple ramparts, a remarkable exercise in terms of labour, for each rampart runs for 1.5 km. but, as yet, it is not certain whether they were built early or late in the first millennium BC. There is also a smaller enclosure round the summit-plateau, but again its date and relationship to the larger fort are unknown.

There was undoubtedly a thriving community on the hill when the Roman army marched into the area in the late C1 AD. A series of tempor-ary camps is known to have existed on the slopes below the hill, and a permanent fort was established around AD 80 and remained in use until soon after AD 200. Eildon Hill North was an obvious spot for a signal-station, for the beacon could be seen over a wide area. Traces of this station survive among the house-platforms at the west end of the summit-plateau in the form of a circular ditch enclosing an area 10.75 m.

N

| | | | |
| 0 | 200 | 400 | 600 FEET |

| | | | |
| 0 | 60 | 120 | 180 METRES |

▲ Plan of fort and Roman signal station on Eildon Hill North (after RCAHMS)

in diameter. Excavation uncovered evidence inside of a square building with a stone floor and a tiled roof, built sometime in the late C1 or early C2. Perhaps the most intriguing aspect is that there was still native occupation on the hill at the time that the signal-station was in use, for this implies that there was a stable political relationship between the local tribe and their military overlords.

Hownam Law Fort, Kirk Yetholm

NT 796220. From Kirk Yetholm, SE of Kelso, take the B6401 S.; after about 3 km., take a minor road S. towards Sourhope, and Hownam Law rises high on the right.

The location and size of the fort and the number of visible house-platforms within it make this a likely candidate for a tribal stronghold of the Votadini. At 449 m. OD, it is one of the highest forts in southern Scotland, and its single stone wall encloses not only the summit of the hill but also a lower terrace, a total area of some 8.5 ha. The wall is at least 3 m. thick, with an entrance at the west end. House-foundations are scattered about the interior but appear to respect a 'street' leading eastwards from the entrance. About 155 houses have been identified, either as hollows or as levelled platforms, but they may not all have been in use at the same time. At the east end of the fort is a later enclosure, the stone wall of which overlies the original fort wall.

Innerleithen Cross-shaft

NT 332369. Beside the parish church on the B709 at the N. end of Innerleithen.

This is a curious piece of sculpture, quite unlike other early cross-shafts in its decoration. It is the lower part of a sandstone shaft and was dug out of the foundations of the earlier church in 1871, along with the stone base in which it had originally stood (the base was broken up). All four faces bear a pecked design of small hollows surrounded by two concentric circles and linked by double lines. Despite the naïvety of the design and

▼ Innerleithen cross-shaft (RCAHMS)

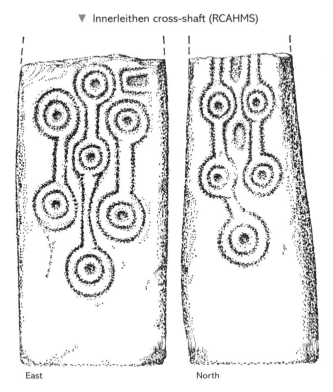

East   North

its technique, the carving is well executed, and a date in the C9 has been suggested.

Longcroft Fort, Lauder

NT 532543. Some 9 km. N. of Lauder, a farm road leads N. from the A697 beside a bridge to Longcroft; the fort is on the hill NE of the farm.

A steep-sided spur rises between two burns and is crowned by a fort with well-preserved defences of two periods. Initially there were two strong ramparts with a ditch between them, enclosing an area some 98 × 85 m.; at a later stage, two more ramparts were built within the earlier defences, reducing the area for habitation. Later still, round stone houses and enclosures were built in the interior (see photograph, p. 6).

Lyne Roman fort, Peebles

NT 187405. On the N. side of the A72 about 7 km. W. of Peebles.

Set in a bend of the Lyne Water, this fort has been shown by excavation to have been built in the late AD 150s and probably abandoned after only a few years. It was linked by road to the forts at Newstead to the east and Castledykes to the west. The defences survive well on the east and west, particularly the main rampart and ditch. There were originally annexes to north and south, and excavation revealed both stone and timber buildings within the fort, but these are not visible. Aerial photography has revealed traces of a fortlet a short distance to the north, a temporary camp to the NE, and another fort on the other side of the Lyne Water to the SE, and the latter has been dated to the late C1 AD.

Milkieston Rings Fort, Eddleston

NT 248459. From Eddleston on the A703, 7 km. N. of Peebles, walk along the track that runs SE towards Burnhead Farm; at the point where the track crosses a burn, follow the burn uphill to the S.

The fort consists of several lines of defence which appear to represent at least two major phases. Initially there were two stone walls, and subsequently these were replaced and the area of the fort enlarged by two pairs of ramparts with median ditches. An outer bank and ditch on the north side controlled access to the fort. The slopes of the spur on which this fort stands are relatively gentle and bear two further lines of linear earthwork, which were probably designed to control cattle in pasture below the fort itself.

Mutiny Stones Long cairn, Gifford

NT 622590. From the B6355 about 9 km. SE of Gifford, a minor road leads to

Longformacus; take the track at NT 635612 southwards past Killpallet for about 2.5 km. over moorland.

This is a visit for serious devotees of prehistoric burial cairns! It is a long cairn, rare in this part of Scotland and reasonably well preserved despite robbing to build sheep enclosures. Some 82 m. long and 21 m. wide at the east end, this is a classic example of a neolithic long cairn, its bare stones bleak against the moor. Nothing is known of the burials for which it was built.

▼ Plan of Lyne Roman fort (RCAHMS)

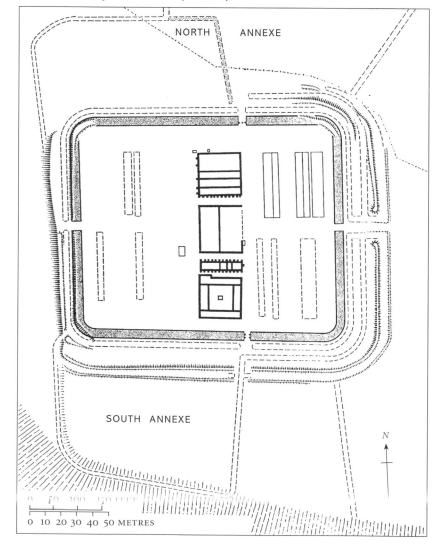

NORTH   ANNEXE

SOUTH   ANNEXE

N

0 10 20 30 40 50 METRES

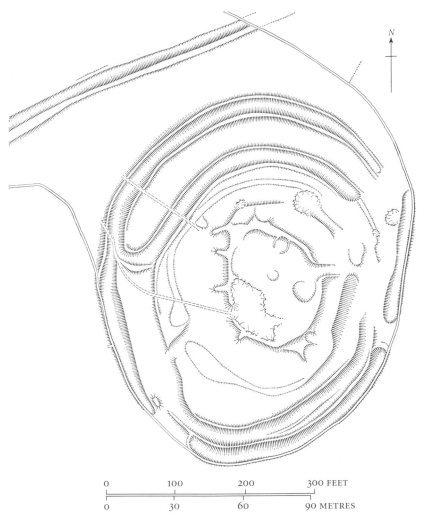


```
0          100          200          300 FEET
├────────────┼────────────┼────────────┤
0           30            60          90 METRES
```

▲ Plan of Milkieston Rings fort (RCAHMS)

North Muir Cairn, West Linton

NT 105503. From the A702, 5.5 km. SW of W. Linton, take the minor road W. to Garvald and Medwynbank; a track leads NE from the latter, and the cairn lies to the N. after about 0.7 km.

Known as the Nether Cairn, this is a notable example of a round burial cairn, 15 m. in diameter and surviving to a height of 3.6 m. There are traces of a surrounding ditch. It is one of a number of cairns scattered along the eastern edge of North Muir, suggesting that this was a special burial place in the second millennium BC.

Rubers Law Fort and Roman signal station, Denholm

NT 580155. From the A6088 7.5 km. E. of Hawick, a minor road leads N. towards Denholm on the A698; after about 3 km. a track opposite the farm of Whitriggs leads E. to plantations on the flanks of the hill. Skirt these and continue to the top (a strenuous round trip of 4 km.).

The imposing summit of Rubers Law reaches 424 m. OD and affords magnificent views of the Border country. It is very rocky with restricted terraces suitable for habitation. The outermost wall enclosing both summit and lower terraces, an area of about 2.8 ha., is thought to represent the original fort. The summit was later enclosed by a stone wall, as were

▼ Plan of Torwoodlee fort and broch (after RCAHMS)

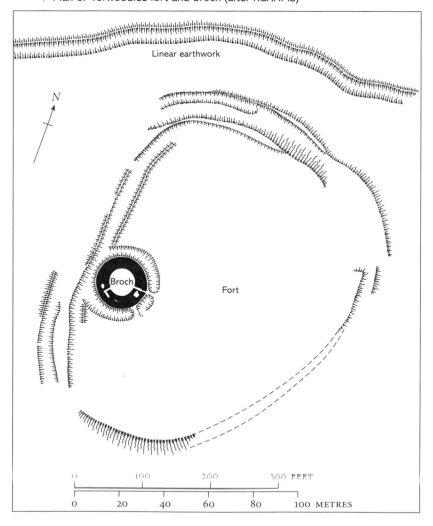

N

Linear earthwork

Broch

Fort

0	100	200	300 FEET	

0	20	40	60	80	100 METRES

the large terrace below it to the south and a small terrace to the north. This arrangement of citadel and terraces is a classic design favoured in Early Historic times, and here that date is reinforced by the discovery in the walls of dressed sandstone blocks, which can only be Roman workmanship. The theory is that there was a Roman signal-station on the hill (as on Eildon Hill North, see p. 52), the walls of which were demolished and the stone used to build a new fort after the departure of the Romans.

A hoard of Roman bronze vessels and scabbard-mounts of C2 date was found on the hillside well below the fort in 1863 (now in Hawick Museum).

Torwoodlee Fort and broch, Galashiels

NT 465384. From the A72 about 3 km. W. of the centre of Galashiels, take the farm road N. to Torwoodlee Mains; follow the track beyond the farm uphill.

Set on a spur in a bend of the Gala Water, this multi-period monument has yielded rare evidence of deliberate destruction. The fort is now barely visible, but excavation has shown not only that the broch was built partly over the filled-in ditches of an earlier fort, but also that the broch itself was systematically demolished. The presence beneath the broch wall of Roman artefacts of late C1 date suggests that it was built around AD 100 or later.

The broch wall survives to a height of less than 1 m., but there are several interesting features visible. The entrance passage shows the check against which a stout wooden door would have been barred. The interior is 12 m. in diameter within a 5 m.-thick wall, and a doorway leads both to a mural cell and to the foot of the stair that led up within the thickness of the wall.

Unusually, the broch is surrounded by a ditch, and excavation showed that this had been filled with rubble from the demolition of the broch wall—and that this had happened soon after the ditch had been dug, for there had been no time for any silt to gather at the bottom.

It is always hazardous in Scotland to try to relate archaeological events with historical events, but in this case it seems reasonable to relate the fortunes of the broch with the presence of the Roman army. Was the broch destroyed by the Romans as a demonstration of their military strength? Were the owners of the broch obliged to demolish it as a token of their compliance with Roman rule?

White Meldon Fort, Peebles

NT 219428. From the A72 about 5 km. W. of Peebles, a minor road leads N. towards Eddleston; White Meldon is to the east of the road after about 2.5 km.

The modern road along the valley of the Meldon Burn passes between two prominent hills, both of which bear the remains of summit forts. The

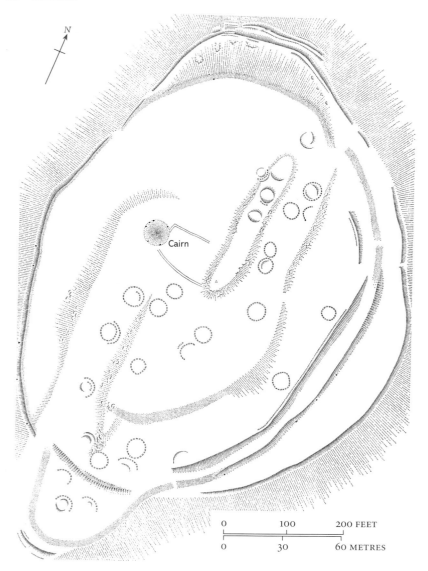

N

Cairn

| 0 | 100 | 200 FEET |
| 0 | 30 | 60 METRES |

▲ Plan of White Meldon fort (RCAHMS)

larger and more complex fort is that on White Meldon, and the steep climb
is well worth the effort for the view as well as the archaeology. There are
four lines of defence, which probably represent a long history of occupation, but there has been no excavation to determine their relationship.
Innermost is a stone wall, now only visible on the south, and a second
stone wall lies a little farther downslope on the east. Better preserved is a

▲ Plan of Whiteside Hill fort (RCAHMS)

wall which encloses traces of about 29 houses, visible as ring-grooves in the turf. The outermost rampart appears to be unfinished.

The fort on Black Meldon (NT 206425) is enclosed by a stone wall with a second wall on the west where the approach is easier and traces inside of at least seven houses. The area around the Meldons is full of interest, from unenclosed settlements of house-platforms, of which there are two groups of nine on the west (NT 216434) and NW flanks of White Meldon (NT 218436), to the Roman works described under LYNE. A track through the forestry plantation on the west side of the Meldon Burn leads past another platform settlement at Green Knowe (NT 212434) to a fort and unfinished linear earthwork on Harehope Hill (NT 196445).

Whiteside Hill   Fort, Romannobridge

NT 168461. From Romannobridge on the A701, take the B7059 S. for 1.5 km. and park near the church; follow the track to Whiteside and thence walk uphill.

The fort lies on a spur overlooking the confluence of the Flemington Burn with the Lyne Water, with its entrance facing upslope. There are three concentric ramparts enclosing an oval area with traces of house-platforms, and outworks or annexes at either end. At some later date, a walled enclosure was built partially on top of the earlier innermost rampart, and later still a smaller earthwork enclosure was inserted into the SE corner of the walled enclosure.

Woden Law   Fort, and Pennymuir, Roman camps   ★

NT 768125 (fort), NT 755140 (camps). From the A68 SE of Jedburgh, take a minor road NE towards Hownam and Morebattle.

Here, perhaps better than anywhere else in Scotland, it is possible to envisage the Roman impact upon the native Celtic population from the monuments that survive. Perched on the NW edge of the Cheviot Hills is the native fort of Woden Law, while below lie Roman temporary camps and alongside runs the great Roman road known as Dere Street.

The fort on Woden Law encloses the northern end of the summit, overlooking a burn and the easiest descent from the massif of the Cheviot Hills to the Kale Water and the lower ground to the NW. In pre-Roman times, access along the ridge from the SE both to the Law and to this route down to the Kale Water was controlled by a series of short earthworks (NT 771121–772120). The same route was taken by the builders of Dere Street, which is particularly well preserved on the ridge as a raised ribbon some 8 m. wide.

The oval fort consists of an inner stone wall and two outer ramparts which were added on the east and south sides. Three bands of earthworks east of the fort were formerly interpreted as Roman siegeworks, built to provide training exercises for troops living temporarily in the Pennymuir

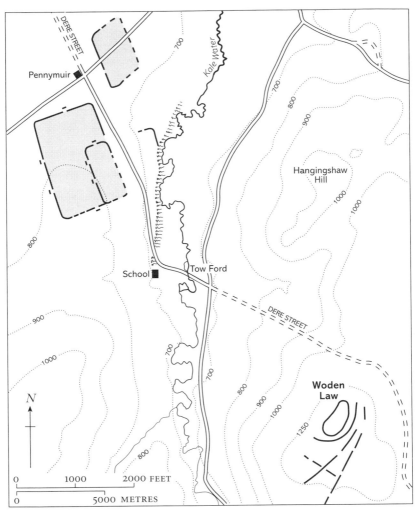

▲ Map showing Woden Law fort and Pennymuir Roman camps (contours in feet) (after RCAHMS)

camps, but it is now thought more likely that these outer earthworks relate to the fort.

After its descent past Woden Law, Dere Street crosses the Kale Water and runs northwards, beneath the modern road from the crossing to the Pennymuir junction, and thence over moorland to Whitton Edge, where another good stretch may be seen (NT 740189). On the left before Pennymuir it passes close to two well-preserved temporary camps, one enclosing 17.5 ha. within a rampart still more than 1 m. high, and a

▲ The Yarrow inscription (RCAHMS)

smaller camp of 3.65 ha. built within the SE corner of the earlier camp. Two more camps are known from air photographs on the other side of the road.

Yarrow Early Christian stone, Selkirk

NT 348274. From the A708 Selkirk to Moffat road, about 1 km. SW of Yarrow, a track on the right leads to Whitefield and the stone is about 150 m. up the track.

This stone is one of the most important physical testimonies to early Christianity in Scotland. It is in approximately its original position, having been discovered lying prone below the turf during ploughing early in the C19. There were said to have been bones beneath it, and its inscription certainly implies that it was set up as a gravestone. Carved in the early C6 to judge by the lettering, the vertical Latin inscription reads: 'This the everlasting memorial. In [this] place [lie] the most famous princes Nudus and Dumnogenus. In this tomb lie the two sons of Liberalis.' It commemorates a British ruling dynasty in southern Scotland who were Christian, perhaps owing their Christian traditions to the missionary efforts of Whithorn.

Lothians and Edinburgh (Map, p. xvi)

The fertile coastal plain along the south side of the Firth of Forth still offers some spectacular sites, despite intensive land-use over the centuries. A long cycle of prehistoric ceremonies can be traced on Cairnpapple Hill, and there are standing stones even within the city of Edinburgh. There are forts perched on volcanic hills, such as Traprain Law and Arthur's Seat, and along the northern edge of the Lammermuir Hills, and remains of the roads and forts built by the Roman army on its way northwards. Near Dunbar can be seen the defended residence of some of the Anglian invaders who overcame the native British population in the C7 AD.

Abercorn Carved stones, South Queensferry

NT 081791. From the A904 W. of South Queensferry, take a minor road to the N. signposted Abercorn.

There has been a church here, above the shore of the Firth of Forth, since at least as early as the AD 680s when the presence of a Northumbrian bishop is recorded. Most of the fabric of the present church dates from the C16 and later, apart from a Norman doorway of the C12 incorporated into the south wall, but there is an important collection of earlier sculpture in the building beside the churchyard gate.

None is as early as the C7, but there are several large fragments of C8 cross-shafts decorated with interlace designs and part of a cross-head. There is also a fine example of a C11 hogback tombstone with arched back and carved 'roof-tiles', as well as parts of two C12 hogbacks with flat ridges.

Black Castle Fort, Gifford

NT 580662. From the B6355 almost 5 km. SE of Gifford, a minor road leads S.; just under 1 km., park near Newlands farm and walk SE along the track beside the Newlands Burn for 1 km. and then N. uphill to the fort.

Shrouded in a plantation of trees, this is a well-preserved circular fort, some 110 m. in diameter with twin ramparts and a ditch between them. It lies on a spur of the Lammermuir Hills, between two burns, and the two entrances into the fort reflect the natural route along the spur.

Cairnpapple Hill Henge and burial cairns, Torphichen   ★

NS 987717. About 10 km. S. of Linlithgow by the A706, B792, and a minor road, signposted (Historic Scotland).

The view from here on a clear day is surprisingly far-ranging in all direc-

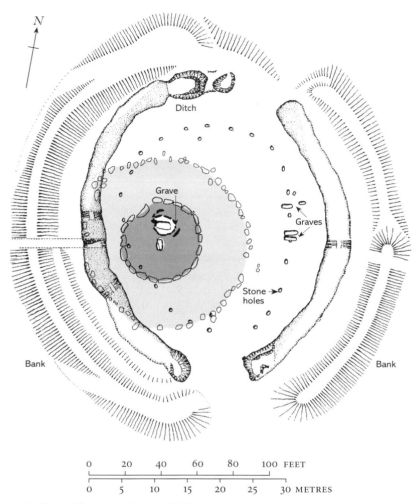

N

Ditch

Grave

Graves

Stone ➤ o
holes

Bank

Bank

| 0 | 20 | 40 | 60 | 80 | 100 | FEET |

| 0 | 5 | 10 | 15 | 20 | 25 | 30 | METRES |

▲ Plan of Cairnpapple (after S. Piggott)

tions—surprising because the hill does not appear to dominate the local landscape. But it was chosen as the appropriate place for a ceremonial centre that lasted some 1,500 years from around 2800 BC.

After excavations in the late 1940s, the various elements of the site were laid out in such a way that almost its entire history can be seen. The earliest activity involved a setting of three upright stones at the centre of an arc of small pits in which token deposits of cremated human bone were placed, in two cases along with bone pins. This little cemetery was then enclosed within the ditch and bank of an oval henge monument, and a ring of twenty-four standing stones was set up inside the henge. A burial with a beaker pot was later inserted beside one of the standing stones. In the centre of the circle was another burial beneath a small kerbed cairn with a fine standing stone at one end (the kerb and the monolith are still visible). This grave was clearly the resting place of someone important, for the body was laid out with some kind of mask over the face, a wooden club alongside, and two beakers, probably containing liquid, one at the head and one at the feet.

Later still, a burial in a large cist with a Food Vessel was set beside the little cairn, and a large cairn with a kerb of massive boulders was built over both. A modern dome recreates the effect of this mound, and the visitor can climb down a ladder to see the various graves inside. Subsequently this cairn was enlarged to cover two cremations in cinerary urns.

Castle Greg Roman fortlet, West Calder

NT 050592. Close to the B7008 between the A71 at West Calder and the A70 Edinburgh to Lanark; just over 1 km. NW of the latter junction.

This neat little fortlet has survived in extraordinarily good condition, probably because it was formerly surrounded by peat-bog (now rough pasture). The internal area is about 38 × 20 m. and could have housed a unit of eighty soldiers, surrounded by a rampart and two outer ditches. The entrance is in the middle of the east side. Although this was the first Roman monument to be excavated in Scotland in the mid-C19, its precise date is uncertain. The absence of a Roman road in the vicinity suggests a date in the late C1 AD, before the road construction programme was under way in this part of Scotland.

▼ Plan of Castle Greg Roman fortlet (RCAHMS)

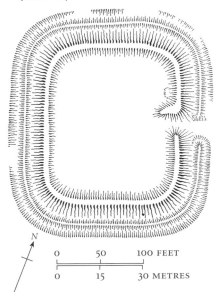

N

| 0 | 50 | 100 FEET |
| 0 | 15 | 30 METRES |

Castle Law Fort and souterrain, Penicuik

NT 229638. Signposted from the A702 5 km. S. of Edinburgh (Historic Scotland).

Set on the lower slopes of the Pentland Hills, this fort has been shown by excavation to have begun life as a palisaded enclosure in the first millennium BC. The stockade was later replaced by a rampart reinforced by an internal timber framework on either side of a substantial timber gateway. An outer pair of ramparts and ditches was added at a later stage, and finally, after the defences were no longer needed, a souterrain was constructed within the inner ditch. It curves along the old ditch for about 20 m. and survives up to 2 m. in height; halfway along the passage, there is an entrance between two upright slabs into a large corbelled cell. The roof over the main passage was probably timber-framed. Artefacts found in the souterrain included Roman pottery and glass of C2 date.

Chesters Fort, Drem

NT 507782. About 1 km. W. of Drem on the B1377, a minor road leads S. to Camptoun; after 1 km., a signposted track on the left (Historic Scotland).

The surprising aspect of this fort is its location, which shows a total disregard for defensive strategy. It lies at the foot of a ridge at the mercy of attackers on higher ground with the advantage of overlooking the interior of the fort. This apparently suicidal choice of location must imply that prestige rather than defence was the major concern. With the economic wealth of this fertile coastal plain at their command, the Chesters community may have had no fear of attack.

The fort would certainly have looked impressive, with two main ramparts and a series of outer ramparts at either end covering the entrances. The interior of the fort, an oval area some 115 × 45 m., shows traces of many circular house foundations, some of which overlie the innermost rampart and imply a long history of occupation.

Doon Hill Early Historic settlement, Dunbar

NT 686755. Signposted from the A1 S. of Dunbar (Historic Scotland).

A natural harbour attracted settlement at Dunbar from early times, and the incoming Anglian warlords of the C7 and C8 not only secured a stronghold at Dunbar but established control over the fertile coastal plain east and west of Dunbar. Place-names such as Tyninghame to the west and Whittinghame to the SW mark early Anglian settlements, while on Doon Hill south of Dunbar there are traces of a high-status warlord's residence. Both the great feasting hall and the surrounding defensive stockade were built of timber, leaving only post-holes and bedding trenches, but the outlines of the buildings are marked in the turf by concrete and reconstruction drawings on the information board convey an impression of the settlement.

Within the polygonal enclosure of split logs was originally the hall of a British chieftain, perhaps in the C6. It was 23 m. long and had been repaired on several occasions before it was finally destroyed by fire. Unfortunately, Doon Hill is not mentioned in historical records, but the

British stronghold at Edinburgh was captured by Anglian forces in AD 638 and Doon Hill's destruction may have been part of the same campaign. Certainly a new hall was built in Anglian style, on the same spot as the earlier hall, as a large feasting-hall and a smaller room at one end. A small cemetery was found outside the entrance into the enclosure.

Hare Law   Fort, Gifford

NT 546630. From the B6355 on the SW outskirts of Gifford, a minor road leads S. to beyond Longyester and a track up into the Lammermuirs; walk up to the head of the Harelaw Burn and E. along the ridge.

Set on a rocky spur of the Lammermuirs, high above the Lothian plain, this fort is highly defensible and commands an extensive view of its tribal farmland. The innermost wall is relatively modern, perhaps built as a sheepfold, and stones from the ancient rampart have been robbed for its construction. Nevertheless, the rampart is still an impressive band of stone which was once a solid timber-laced wall, enclosing a summit area

▼ Map of monuments in Holyrood Park (after RCAHMS)

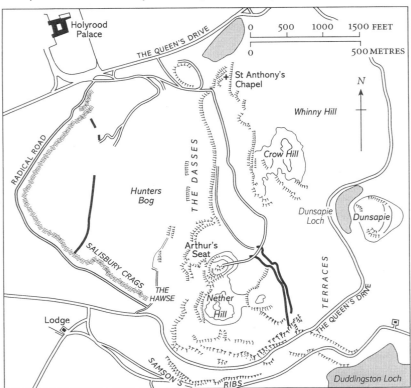

of about 61 × 31 m. Traces of fused stone show that at least part of the wall was set on fire. The entrance faces west and access would have been from the main ridge along the west flank of the spur, controlled by outer defences in the form of a pair of ramparts and ditches.

Holyrood Park Forts, Edinburgh

NT 2773. In central Edinburgh, the Park is accessible from several sides and there is plenty of parking space.

The major eminences are crowned with fortifications, and the slopes and terraces bear traces of settlement and cultivation, all adding up to a history of activity spanning the last 3,000 years. Bronze Age burials have been found on Arthur's Seat and a large hoard of bronze artefacts was retrieved from Duddingston Loch, suggesting activity in the later second and early first millennia BC. The visible monuments range from the foundations of circular stone houses on the hillside east of Hunter's Bog to the 8-ha. fort defended by two stone ramparts on Arthur's Seat, but there is very little dating evidence. A small fort perched above Samson's Ribs has yielded a Roman finger-ring, but this was a stray find and there has been no excavation. Another fort lies on the hill beside Dunsapie Loch, and a stone wall forms a large enclosure on the flank of Salisbury Crags.

The prehistory of a city

There is a surprising amount of visible prehistory in Edinburgh. Before major drainage work took place, there were lochs and marshes between the hills and settlement was restricted to the higher ground. Many discoveries of prehistoric burials and hoards of bronze artefacts were made during the building developments of the last two centuries. In Caiystane View at Oxgangs, beside the modern road, is a large standing stone decorated with cup-marks, while beside the busy Newbridge roundabout on the west of the city, at the junction of the motorways to Glasgow and Stirling, is a Bronze Age ritual centre known as Huly Hill. Here a large cairn is surrounded by standing stones, and an outlying standing stone survives to the east. There are forts of the first millennium BC on Wester Craiglockhart Hill and at Hillend on the nearest of the Pentland Hills. Traces of a Roman fort may be seen at Cramond, and a rare statue of a lioness devouring a man was found in the mouth of the River Almond. A Pictish symbol stone was found reused as a footbridge in Princes Street Gardens (the Scandinavian runestone still to be seen below the Castle Esplanade came from Sweden in the ('19). The medieval archaeology of the city can be explored in Huntly House Museum in the High Street.

Traprain Law Fort, Haddington

NT 581746. From the A1 at East Linton, take a minor road S. through Traprain to a junction with a side-road to Haddington which passes Traprain Law.

The distinctive whale-backed hill rises from a flat plain and is a landmark visible for many miles—even from Edinburgh. An obvious and ideal location for a fort, the steep sides of this volcanic extrusion could be defended with relatively minor ramparts. Excavations have produced a wide chronological range of artefacts, from neolithic times until the C5 AD, and the hill has clearly played many roles over a very long period which is only partially understood.

The two most visible lines of rampart belong to the Iron Age, one halfway down the north and west sides of the hill enclosing some 16 ha., and one taking a higher line along the north flank which encloses about 12 ha. The smaller fort is thought to be the later of the two, contemporary with excavated traces of sub-rectangular buildings on either side of a 'street' on the terrace at the west end of the hill. The scale of the fort and its rich assemblage of artefacts imply that this was the tribal capital of the Votadini during the Roman period; a vast hoard of Late Roman silver found buried on the hill has been interpreted as a bribe from the Roman authorities to ensure native co-operation (all the finds are in the National Museums of Scotland in Edinburgh).

White Hill Fort, Garvald

NT 613686. From Garvald a minor road runs SE to join the B6355; about 3.5 km. from Garvald, the fort is beside the road on the left.

Set on a small promontory above a burn, this oval fort is defended by triple ramparts and is easily appreciated from the road. It is one of a series of forts along the NW flanks of the Lammermuir Hills, none of which has been excavated.

From the Clyde to the Forth
(Map, p. xvi)

Two great rivers straddle Britain's narrowest point and between them create a natural means of communication from sea to sea. This was the point chosen by Roman engineers for their second mural frontier, the Antonine Wall, and, in post-Roman times, the chief stronghold of the British kingdom of Strathclyde was Dumbarton Rock in the Clyde estuary, complementing the Gododdin capital at Edinburgh on the Forth estuary. Here, the monuments are arranged in groups from west to east, beginning with those on the beautiful island of Arran.

ARRAN

Almost 900 m. high above the sea, Goatfell in the Isle of Arran beckons from afar, guiding travellers of old into the great Firth of Clyde. Arran is an island of contrasts, from sheltered sandy bays to bleak and rocky hill-tops, and its archaeology is equally absorbing and diverse.

Auchagallon Cairn

NR 893346. Signposted on a minor road from the A841 on the W. coast (Historic Scotland).

A low cairn of stones, some 13.5 m in diameter, lies on a terrace with wide views across the sound to Kintyre. It is a curious monument, a cross between a stone circle and a regular cairn. Its kerb of upright stones are graded with the higher stones along the seaward side, where a low broad stone is flanked by two taller stones, reminiscent of the recumbent and flankers in Aberdeenshire stone circles. Here the 'recumbent' and its opposite number on the other side of the circle are pale grey granite, whereas the rest of the kerb-stones are red sandstone. Excavation would probably reveal that a complex history lies behind the present appearance of this monument.

Carn Ban Chambered tomb, Kilmory

NR 991262. From the A841 about 1 km. E. of Kilmory, walk N. up the Forestry Commission road and follow the signposted Forest Walk to the cairn; a round trek of about 12 km. (Historic Scotland).

A spectacular spot for a picnic on a fine day, for the neolithic builders chose to commemorate their ancestors high in the hills. Below the cairn a burn runs south to feed the Kilmory Water, a lifeline that links Carn Ban with the tombs on either side of the mouth of the Water far below (*see* TORRYLIN). Its remote location has helped to preserve Carn Ban, indeed

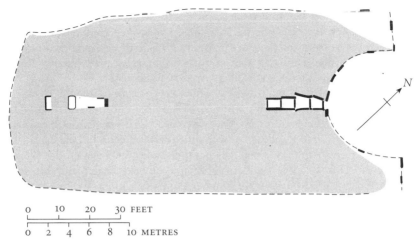

```
0      10      20      30  FEET
0    2    4    6    8    10  METRES
```

▲ Plan of Carn Ban chambered cairn (after A. S. Henshall)

its main chamber was intact when it was excavated in 1902, and the great cairn is still up to 4.5 m. high.

The chamber (no longer visible) is at the uphill end of the long cairn, opening off a semicircular forecourt lined with 2 m.-high orthostats. The chamber was filled in after the excavation, but it was a fine example of a Clyde-type tomb, some 5.6 m. long and divided into four compartments. The floor of the chamber was lower than that of the forecourt, with the result that the chamber was unusually spacious with its roofing slabs at a height of 2.7 m. Unfortunately acid soil conditions had destroyed all but a couple of fragments of bone, and the only artefacts recovered were a flint flake and an Arran pitchstone flake.

Visible within the cairn at the other end are hollows and large slabs suggesting the presence of a second chamber, but this has not been excavated.

Machrie Moor   Ceremonial landscape   ★★

NR 900325-912323. Signposted from the A841 about 6 km. N. of Blackwaterfoot on the W. coast of the island; a walk of some 5 km. (Historic Scotland).

There are many prehistoric monuments in the moorland on either side of the lower reaches of the Machrie Water, but this area on the south side was clearly the focus of the early ceremonial complex. There are stone circles and chambered tombs of neolithic date, and cairns and hut-circles probably of Bronze Age date. The first monument encountered along the track is a large cairn with a kerb of huge granite boulders (10 on the plan), reminiscent of the AUCHAGALLON cairn to the north (see above). Farther along there are low circular foundations known as hut-circles on both sides of the track, and a standing stone to the north, before the track passes over the remains of a chambered tomb (9). Part of the chamber is visible between the track and the fence on the south. Two more chambered tombs lie in the moorland south of the track, including a reasonably well-preserved Clyde tomb some 200 m. west of tomb 9.

Beside the deserted Moss Farm lies the first of six stone circles (5). There are two rings of low granite boulders, an inner ring 11.5 m. in diameter and an outer ring, not quite concentric, which appears to be a kerb rather than a free-standing circle. A stone cist was found in the centre of the monument in the C19, suggesting that it may well have a multi-phase history. Only four low boulders survive of the next circle (4), and it may have been a four-poster setting rather than a true circle. Again a central cist was dug out in the C19, and it contained a Food Vessel, a bronze pin, and some flint tools.

The next circle (3) is sadly mutilated; there were originally nine stones, but five have vanished and three are merely stumps, leaving just one standing (the stones were probably broken up to use in the farm buildings). Two cists are known to have existed inside the circle. In contrast to this sorry monument, the next dominates the landscape (2). Only three stones are still standing, but they are elegant pillars of red sandstone, soaring to a height of 5.5 m. Other stones lie prone, and the circle appears originally to have had seven or eight stones (an attempt has been made to reuse one of them as millstones). Two cists have been found inside the circle, one containing a cremation and a Food Vessel and the other an inhumation.

Circle 1 is the designer version—tall sandstone slabs alternate with low granite boulders. There were probably twelve stones at one time.

▼ Map of monuments on Machrie Moor (after A. Haggarty)

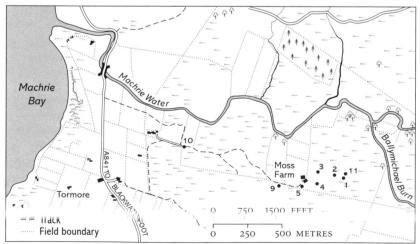

Excavation has revealed that the stone circle was preceded by timber setting. At the same time another stone circle was uncovered (11), its ten stones previously hidden in the peat; here too there was an earlier timber phase.

Monamore Chambered tomb

NS 017288. From the A841 just S. of Lamlash, take the Ross road and after about 0.5 km. park in the Forestry Commission car-park; a signposted track leads uphill to the SE to 'Meallack's Grave' (Forestry Commission).

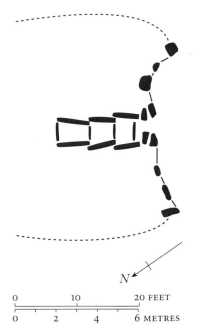

▲ Plan of Monamore chambered cairn (after A. S. Henshall)

Like Carn Ban, this Clyde tomb lies on a terrace above a small glen. The cairn is much robbed but was originally about 14 m. long, and the entrance to the chamber is between two tall stones in the middle of a concave façade. Excavation in 1961 revealed evidence of fires and feasting in the forecourt, and radiocarbon dates suggest that the tomb was used for about a thousand years from early in the fourth millennium BC. Earlier excavation of the chamber yielded a few scraps of pottery and some flakes of Arran pitchstone, but all trace of the burials had dissolved in the acid soil.

Torr a' Chaisteil Dun, Blackwaterfoot

NR 922233. Almost 8 km. S. of Blackwaterfoot, signposted from the A841 (Historic Scotland).

Perched on a grassy knoll above a burn, this small dun has a delightfully domestic air despite its pretensions of defence. It is enclosed by a thick stone-faced wall, of which two courses of very large stones can be seen, and a substantial outer earthwork gives added protection to the entrance on the landward side.

Torrylin Chambered tomb, Kilmory

NR 955211. Signposted on the A841 at Torrylin (Historic Scotland).

There is a well-marked raised beach along this southern shore of the island, and two chambered tombs and a cairn are located on it either side of the Kilmory Water. Both the tombs belong to the Clyde group and both have been excavated, but only Torrylin is now visible. The stones of its covering cairn have been robbed, but most of the upright slabs of the chamber survive, forming four rectangular compartments. Remains of at least four people were found in the third compartment and at least six adults and two children along with a pottery bowl and a flint knife in the fourth compartment.

Dumbarton Rock   Fort, Firth of Clyde

NS 400744. Signposted from the A814 S. of Dumbarton (Historic Scotland).

This spectacular volcanic plug rises abruptly from the shore of the River Clyde, the perfect sentinel to guard that great waterway into central Scotland. This is also the point at which the River Leven runs into the Clyde, giving easy access northwards into the Highlands, and a little to the east was once the lowest crossing on the Clyde. Most of the visible fortifications on the Rock relate to the C16 and later, but there are some traces of the earlier medieval stone castle and of the Dark Age fortress known from historical records to have existed here from the C6. This was the major stronghold of the British kingdom of Strathclyde, captured by Vikings for a time in the late C9.

Excavations have identified the remains of an early rampart on the east side of the Rock, overlooking the access route from the mainland, together with artefacts dating to the C6 to C9. In the Governor's House there are two carved gravestones of C10 date, similar to those at Inchinnan (*see* box p. 77) and GOVAN.

Govan   Early Historic carved stones, Glasgow   ★

NS 553658. In Govan Old Parish Church, Govan Road, in the centre of Govan, signposted from the A8.

The present church was designed by Robert Rowand Anderson and built in the 1880s, but it stands on an important early Christian site that goes back into the C9 with the foundation of a church dedicated to St Constantine. The shape of the modern churchyard wall is likely to preserve much of that of the original enclosure, although it is difficult now to envisage the peaceful spot beside the Clyde in which the early church was built—indeed Govan was rural until its industrial development began in the early C19.

Inside the church is preserved the largest collection of early medieval sculpture in Scotland, reflecting the importance of Govan in the C9 and C10. Thirty-one stones have survived, and another sixteen have been recorded in the past (presumed to be buried somewhere in the churchyard), making a total of forty-seven. They include cross-shafts and standing cross-slabs, and a large number of recumbent grave-slabs, all with

▲ The Govan sarcophagus (P. Chalmers)

carved decoration. The stars of the collection are five hogbacks and a sarcophagus. The latter is a solid stone coffin, now unfortunately lacking its cover which was probably richly carved to match the sides of the surviving base. It bears panels of interlace, animals, and a mounted warrior with a clearly depicted sword at his side. The hogbacks are classic in their humped shape and decoration, and they show strong links with similar monuments in Cumbria in NW England.

Early sculpture around Glasgow

There are several other places in the Glasgow area with interesting early sculpture. The weathered but still impressive C8 cross from Barochan is preserved in Paisley Abbey (NS 485639; Historic Scotland), and a C10 cross stands in the churchyard of Hamilton Parish Church (NS 723555). At Inchinnan, outside the New Parish Church, are three impressive stones, all now lying flat but one, with panels of interlace, is in fact part of a standing cross-shaft, although it was subsequently used as a grave-slab. All three are closely related to the Govan collection and date probably to the C10 and C11. The earliest stone is a recumbent grave-slab with corner knobs like some at GOVAN; this is carved with animals and, at the foot of the upper surface, Daniel in the lions' den. Farther north, on the banks of Loch Lomond at Luss, there are two cross-slabs and a hogback tombstone in the churchyard (NS 361928).

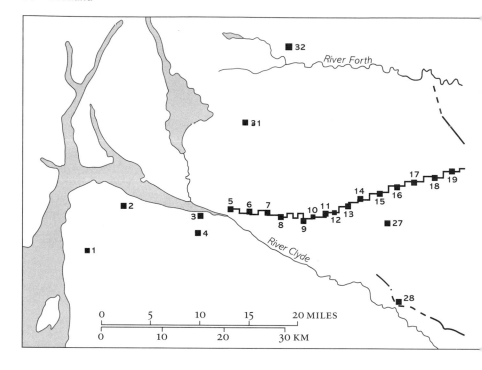

THE ANTONINE WALL

It takes more imagination to appreciate the Antonine Wall as a substantial barrier than its predecessor farther south, Hadrian's Wall. The latter was obviously a massive stone wall, whereas the Antonine Wall was built of turf on a stone base and survives today mostly as a low bank. But it would have looked very impressive in its day, a solid turf rampart some 3–4 m. high with a timber stockade along the top. In front, there was a steep-sided ditch, 6–12 m. across and 2–4 m. deep, often cut through bedrock. At intervals through this double barrier rose the timber gateways of forts and fortlets, the means by which traffic through the mural frontier could be controlled. A road, the Military Way, ran along the south side of the Wall, linking the forts and enabling both troop movements and transportation of vital goods. The native population was confronted by the physical expression of an entirely new concept, built with all the efficiency and precision of the alien Roman army, to the Celtic tribesmen the equivalent of a war-machine.

The Antonine Wall was built in the AD 140s across the narrowest part of mainland Scotland from Old Kilpatrick on the Clyde to Bo'ness on the Forth, a distance of 40 Roman miles. Well-preserved stretches of the Wall can be seen at ROUGH CASTLE (see below), Watling Lodge near Falkirk

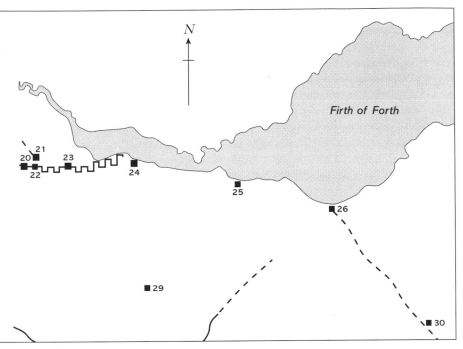

N

Firth of Forth

▲ Map of the Antonine Wall (after G. and A. Ritchie). 1. Outerwards; 2. Lurg Moor; 3. Barochan; 4. Old Bishopton; 5. Old Kilpatrick; 6. Duntocher; 7. Castle Hill; 8. Bearsden; 9. Balmuildy; 10. Wilderness Plantation; 11. Cadder; 12. Glasgow Bridge; 13. Kirkintilloch; 14. Auchendavy; 15. Bar Hill; 16. Croy Hill; 17. Westerwood; 18. Castlecary; 19. Seabegs; 20. Rough Castle; 21. Camelon; 22. Watling Lodge; 23. Mumrills; 24. Carriden; 25. Cramond; 26. Inveresk; 27. Mollins; 28. Bothwellhaugh; 29. Castle Greg; 30. Oxton; 31. Drumquhassle; 32. Malling.

(NS 863798; Historic Scotland), and Croy Hill near Cumbernauld (NS 725762-743770; Historic Scotland).

Bearsden Roman fort and bath house, Glasgow   ★

NS 546720. Signposted from the A809 in Roman Road, Bearsden (Historic Scotland).

Despite being overlain by houses and gardens, much of the fort survived and has been excavated. It appears to have been planned as a large fort of 1.4 ha., but a rampart across the interior reduced it to 0.9 ha., with the rest used as an annexe, and it was within the annexe that the bath house was found, the only part of the fort now visible. This fascinating building is remarkably well preserved and gives a good impression of a vital element in Roman military life. The baths were built in stone because of the fire

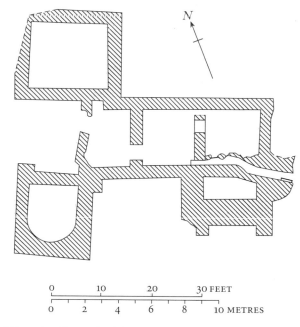

▲ Plan of Bearsden Roman bath house (after D. J. Breeze)

▼ Plan of Bearsden fort (after D. J. Breeze)

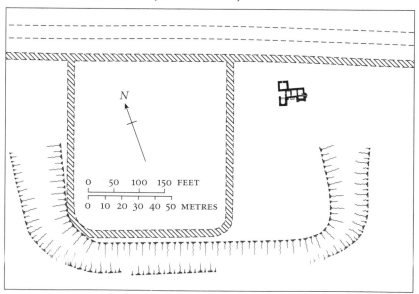

risk, whereas the changing rooms at the west end of the complex were built of timber (now marked by modern posts).

From the changing rooms, the bather could turn left into the hot and dry room (now partially paved and the hypocaust and flue system can be seen), emerging to take a cold plunge in the bath opposite, or he could cross the hall to the hot steam suite opposite the changing rooms. Here the temperature increased in each of the three rooms, and a hot plunge bath opened off the farthest and hottest room. He would then return through the steam rooms and finish with a plunge into the cold bath. The whole process was as much a social experience as a means of cleansing—most excavated bath houses have yielded gaming pieces.

Ingeniously, drains from the bath house allowed the water to be re-cycled to flush the latrine, remains of which can be seen against the wall of the fort a short distance away (the effluent exited along a drain through the wall into the ditch outside).

Rough Castle Roman fort and Antonine Wall, Falkirk ★

NS 843798. Signposted from the A803 in Bonnybridge SE on the B816 (Historic Scotland/National Trust for Scotland).

Both the fort and the Antonine Wall are excellently preserved here, sand-wiched between the railway and the Forth and Clyde Canal. The fort was laid out after the Wall was built, in the angle between the Wall and a steep-sided burn. The Military Way crossed the burn on a timber bridge and ran through the fort and its annexe, although it was also possible to bypass the fort on a road that skirted its outer defences. The area of the fort is rela-tively small at 0.4 ha., but the space available is more than doubled by the addition of the annexe on the east. Excavation has revealed buildings in the fort and a bath house in the annexe, but these are no longer visible. The north gate of the fort leads through the Wall and across a causeway in the ditch, and, slightly to one side, the approach is guarded by closely massed pits; known as lilia or lilies, these pits were originally spiked with sharp-ened stakes.

Kinneil Roman fortlet and Antonine Wall, Falkirk

NS 977803. Kinneil Park is signposted from the A993 in Bo'ness; from Kinneil House, follow the signs for the fortlet some 500 m. to the SW.

The original design of the Antonine Wall included fortlets between the larger forts, although only a third of them have been located on the ground. Kinneil lies 2.6 Roman miles from the east end of the Wall, and it was probably garrisoned by soldiers from the fort at Carriden. It was exca-vated in 1977 and has been partially reconstructed, along with part of the Wall to which it was bonded. From the evidence of distance slabs and the layout of the fortlet, Kinneil was built by the II Augusta legion. The in-terior is 21 × 18 m. and contained two timber barrack-blocks to house a

▲ Plan of Rough Castle Roman fort (RCAHMS)

detachment of eighty men. It was enclosed by an earth and turf bank on a stone foundation, and there were stout timber gateways, one to the north through the Antonine Wall and one to the south giving access from the Military Way.

A museum in C18 farm buildings to the east of Kinneil House has a collection of Roman artefacts.

Arbory Hill Fort, Abington

NS 944238. From Abington (bypassed by the A74) take a minor road E. across the River Clyde and turn N. to the foot of Arbory Hill.

This superb fort overlooking Clydesdale consisted originally of two concentric ramparts and ditches enclosing the summit of the hill. The existence of five entrances suggests that prestige rather than real defence was paramount in its design. At a later period, an inner stone wall with two entrances was built. There are traces of round-house foundations

▼ Plan of Arbory Hill fort (after RCAHMS)

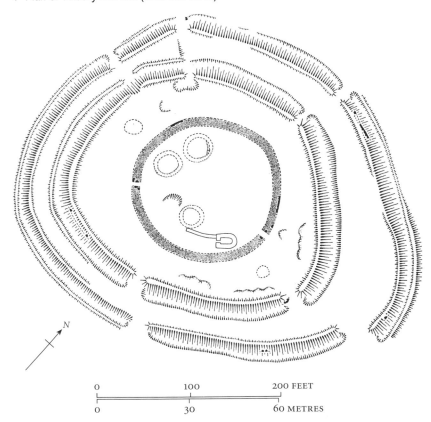

N

| 0 | 100 | 200 FEET |

| 0 | 30 | 60 METRES |

within the walled enclosure, between it and the innermost rampart, and built into the collapsed rubble of the stone wall, indicating a long history of occupation. On the higher ground to the east, there is a linear earthwork barring access to the fort, but it is not known to which period this belongs.

Black Hill   Cairn, fort, and settlement, Lesmahagow

NS 832435. From the B7018 between Lesmahagow and Lanark, a minor road runs W. across the S. end of the hill, whence a track leads to the summit.

At the summit is a large Bronze Age burial cairn, 18 m. in diameter with a stone kerb visible on the west (an Ordnance Survey triangulation point has been built on top of the cairn). The fort consists of a stone wall enclosing an oval area of about 1.67 ha. At a later period, a settlement was established on the ridge at the south end of the fort, enclosed by two banks with a ditch between them which are attached to the fort wall at either end. There are traces of house foundations inside the settlement, and it is likely that the fort interior was used as a stock enclosure.

Ballochmyle   Cup-and-ring carvings, Catrine   ★

NS 511255. From the A76 about 2 km. SE of Mauchline, take a minor road S. opposite Ballochmyle Golf Course and park after about 180 m.; a stile and a foot-path lead W., passing below the rock-face to the N.

Incredibly, this major display of rock-art was discovered only in 1986 when trees masking the vertical rock-face were felled. There are two areas of carving, including cups with multiple rings, cups within squares or lines, and plain cups. The sandstone surface is very fragile and visitors are requested not to touch the carvings.

Carnwath   Motte

NS 974466. Close to the A70 just W. of Carnwath, NE of Lanark, on a golf course.

Easily visible from the road, this grassy mound rises from flat ground beside a burn, surrounded by trees. There is a ditch at its base, and it rises some 9 m. to a flat summit on which the timber tower would have stood in the C12 (there has been no excavation).

Normangill   Henge, Crawford

NS 972221. From Crawford (bypassed by the A74) a minor road leads NE to Camps Reservoir; the henge is just E. of the entrance to Normangill farm.

Sadly bisected by the road, this is, nevertheless, worth visiting as a rare upstanding example of a henge. Its oval interior is surrounded by the usual ditch and external bank, and there is an entrance at either end (the south end of the west bank is overlain by a sheepfold, itself now an antiquity of the more recent past). Nothing is known of the internal features of this henge.

Fife, Angus, Stirling, and Perthshire (Map, p. xvii)

The archaeological monuments of east-central Scotland are more scattered than those to the north and west as intensive agricultural improvement has changed the landscape more radically than in other areas. However, there are well-preserved hillforts, at heights above the Improvers' interest, and underground souterrains, or storehouses, which are often discovered as a result of ploughing and which testify to the agricultural importance of the area in Iron Age and Roman times. In the middle of the first millennium AD, this was the heart of the Pictish kingdom to the south of the Grampians, and their carved stones are vital

Pictish symbol stones and cross-slabs

An important aspect of the landscape in this area is Pictish sculpture dating from as early as the mid-C6 until the mid-C9, when in AD 843 Kenneth mac Alpin, the king of the Scots to the west, established political supremacy over his eastern neighbours. The stones and their decoration are one of the most distinctive elements of the archaeology of eastern Scotland from the Forth to Orkney and yet they are one of the least understood. In part, this is because the symbols on the stones are not susceptible to ready, or at least universally acceptable, interpretation; in part it is because obviously Christian motifs are juxtaposed to imaginary figures and animals that we cannot explain in religious terms. When visiting the individual stones and the museums where they have been gathered together, such as Forfar, Meigle, and St Vigeans, it is worth identifying the recurrent symbols, crescent and V-rod, double disc and Z-rod, mirror and comb, all of which had a contemporary meaning that eludes us today. The cross-slabs date from the beginning of the C8, and include elaborate Christian symbolism as well as ornate crosses, for example those at ABERLEMNO. Some stones have been included as individual monuments to visit, but others, equally interesting to see, are mentioned here more briefly. Cossans (NO 400500); a cross-slab remarkable for the representation of a boat, it also bears a crescent and V-rod and double disc and Z-rod symbols. Eassie (NO 352474) has been preserved within the ruined Eassie Old Parish Church; the scenes include a variety of animals, figures, and angels. Glamis (NO 385468), set up in front of the manse, is a very powerful stone visually, with unusual scenes and crisply carved symbols.

archaeological evidence of the cohesion of this territorial grouping and of its wide-ranging contacts at what is for Scotland the beginning of history.

Abdie Churchyard   Pictish symbol stone, Lindores

NO 259163. The stone is set up in a little building at the entrance to the churchyard, some 3 km. SE of Newburgh.

The stone is not in its original position, but it is worth seeking out as a good example of the monumental carving of the Picts in the C7 AD. The stone bears three instantly recognizable Pictish symbols: at the top a symbol comprising three circles, the central one very much larger than the flanking two, with a horizontal bar cutting across the centre of all three; below there is a crescent and V-rod symbol, and on one side there is a representation of a mirror. The front face of the stone has been used much later both as the base for a sundial and as a bench-mark for the Ordnance Survey. The triple circle symbol has been interpreted as a cauldron with suspension rings, and there is certainly a cauldron on a stone at Glamis, Angus.

Aberlemno   Pictish symbol stones and cross-slabs   ★★

There are four stones at Aberlemno, a dispersed farming parish to the NE of Forfar; one stone stands in the churchyard at the heart of the parish (NO 522555), and the other three are to the side of the minor, but busy, Forfar to Brechin road

▼ Abdie Pictish symbol stone (Historic Scotland)

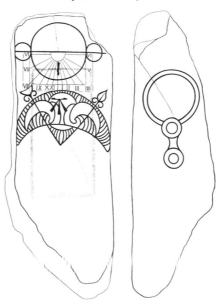

(B9134) (NO 522558). At the time of writing the stones are protected by wooden covers during the winter; in due course they may be taken under cover locally (Historic Scotland).

Two of the stones have been moved in recent times into the recesses in the field-wall in which they now stand, but the impressive cross-slab is in its original position. The earliest stone is a simple slab bearing carefully incised Pictish symbols: serpent, double disc and Z-rod, mirror and comb. On the reverse there are several cup-marks, but these are very faint. Between this stone and the cross is another upright which bears traces of a crescentic marking. The cross-slab has great presence, with an imposing cross on the front flanked by areas of panels of interlaced and key-pattern ornament, two angels, reptile and animal figures. On the back can be seen, from top to bottom, a crescent and V-rod symbol, double disc and Z-rod symbol, a spirited hunting scene with men on horseback, some on foot, two blowing long hunting horns, stags and dogs; below this scene on the left side there is a centaur apparently carrying a branch and an axe; to the right there is a representation of David, identified by the sheep and harp, in the process of rending the lion's jaws. It may be that no single 'meaning' should be sought in the juxtaposition of the symbols and scenes, but that to the carver and his patron there was a range of statement that included both secular and religious ideas.

The cross-slab in the churchyard is better preserved than that at the roadside. The interlaced cross stands in high relief and is flanked by imaginary animals, some intertwined and biting others; an elegant pair of sea-horses face each other with forelegs raised and fish-like tails. At the top of the back of the cross there are two symbols, the first with the arcane description of notched rectangle and Z-rod, the second the triple disc symbol, surely a cauldron. The remainder of the back is filled by a battle scene, almost certainly recalling the battle of Dunnichen in AD 685 between the Picts, who were ultimately victorious, and the Angles. The Anglian warriors are depicted wearing helmets with a distinct nose-guard, a type that can readily be paralleled among contemporary finds. Both mounted and foot soldiers of the Picts confront the foe.

Abernethy   Fort, round tower, and Pictish symbol stone

NO 183153 (fort), NO 189163 (symbol stone and round tower; Historic Scotland).

The confluence of the Rivers Tay and Earn has long been an important centre of communications and thus power in central Scotland; in Pictish times there was a royal seat at Forteviot, and at Abernethy an Iron Age fort, symbol stone, and round tower bear testimony to the continuing importance of the area.

The fort is on the nose of the ridge of Castle Law to the SW of the village and is approached from the narrow road between Abernethy and Strathmiglo; it was excavated between 1896 and 1898 and the inner wall was found to be built with neatly coursed facing stones with timber-lacing to increase its stability. Some traces of the inner and outer facing stones can still be seen, and the site is worth visiting in order to appreciate its strategic location overlooking the valley floor.

The attractive village of Abernethy probably has its origin as a seat of Pictish rulers, perhaps with an episcopal see in the C8. The village is dominated by a round tower, probably of early C11 date; it is about 22 m. high and now has a modern spiral stair leading to the top. Round towers were as much belfries with hand-bells being rung from the top as they were treasuries, where the precious books and ecclesiastical metalwork of the religious community could be stored, and refuges in times of trouble.

At the bottom of the tower there is a fragment of a Pictish symbol stone dug out of the foundation of a house nearby; it had been cut down to form a building stone, but still bears symbols known as a tuning-fork (perhaps a broken sword), hammer and anvil, and a fragmentary crescent and V-rod.

Ardestie Souterrain

NO 503344. The souterrain is situated on the N. side of the A92 Dundee to Arbroath road; it is best to park in the lay-by on the B962 Mains of Ardestie to Monikie road a little to the E. of the footpath to the site (Historic Scotland).

The souterrain was found in 1949 and was excavated by the doyen of souterrain studies, Dr F. T. Wainwright, in 1949 and 1950. The underground element of the complex is particularly well preserved with corbelled drystone walling forming the sides of a curving underground structure originally some 24 m. in length. The site was not ideally chosen as the surrounding soil formation meant that water gathered in the souterrain; although a drain was inserted, even this did not prove sufficient to ensure dry conditions and the site was eventually filled in. This gives an insight into the purpose of such sites, however, for long-term storage would demand constant

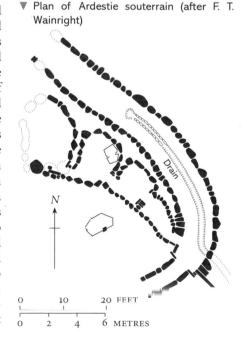

▼ Plan of Ardestie souterrain (after F. T. Wainright)

N

0   10   20 FEET

0   2   4   6 METRES

dry conditions. The above-ground structures at Ardestie are also of interest, as they illustrate a range of domestic and industrial use not normally found. Recent excavations have shown that souterrains were probably intimately connected with substantial timber houses, and at Newmill, the most recent to be fully excavated, the underground element was interpreted as a food-store.

Ardoch   Roman fort, Braco   ★

NO 839099. The fort is situated at the N. end of the village of Braco; it is best to park in the village and go on foot across the bridge that takes the A822 N., as parking closer to the fort is very restricted. The entrance to the fort is signposted.

The photograph in the Introduction shows the magnificent preservation of the earthworks, laid out in the classic playing-card shape of the textbook Roman fort. It is likely that the fort belongs to the Roman occupation of this part of Scotland in the AD 150s. The principal ramparts visible today enclose an area of some 2 ha., but nothing of the internal arrangements of streets and garrison buildings can be seen on the ground.

Souterrains in Angus

The readily accessible souterrain at Ardestie is the best known example of a class of monument that is known throughout lowland Angus. Early antiquaries thought of these underground passages as 'Picts' houses', and thus the name earth-houses, by which they are sometimes known, gained currency. There is little doubt, however, that they are storage cellars associated with the timber farmhouses of the C1 and C2 AD, and the often curving passage may reflect the position of the contemporary circular farm house above and to one side of its cellar. Grain and farm produce could readily be stored in the cold and normally dry conditions; the waterlogging of Ardestie was a mischance in choice of location. The distribution of known souterrains in Angus and Perthshire has been greatly extended in recent years by the realization that they can be identified as crop-markings on aerial photographs on which they appear as dark banana-shaped markings.

There are other souterrains that are well worth visiting not far from Ardestie. **Carlungie** is situated 1.7 km. to the NE and has a more complex and less readily understood series of passages (NO 511359). It too was associated with paved areas at ground level and it appears to have been filled in, in antiquity, after its usefulness had passed. At **Tealing** to the north of Dundee (NO 412381) another souterrain may be seen. In this case the entrance passage is well preserved and the corbelled technique of wall-building is particularly clear. Near the entrance is a large boulder decorated with cup-and-ring markings, perhaps a relic from a much earlier construction.

Balfarg and Balbirnie Prehistoric ceremonial complex, Glenrothes

Impending road realignment and urban expansion of Glenrothes New Town resulted in a series of excavations that demonstrated the importance of this area as a centre for ceremony and burial ritual between the fourth and second millennia BC. *The archaeological trail that has been laid out to link the preserved or reconstructed remains may seem incongruous as it weaves through modern house developments, but it helps to remind visitors and residents alike of the importance of the past in shaping the present, if only through postal addresses like 97 The Henge, Glenrothes. The ceremonial complex lies either side of the A92 Kirkcaldy to Cupar road, NW of Markinch. The henge (NO 281031), from which the trail begins, is to*

▼ Map of Balfarg ceremonial complex (after G. J. Barclay)

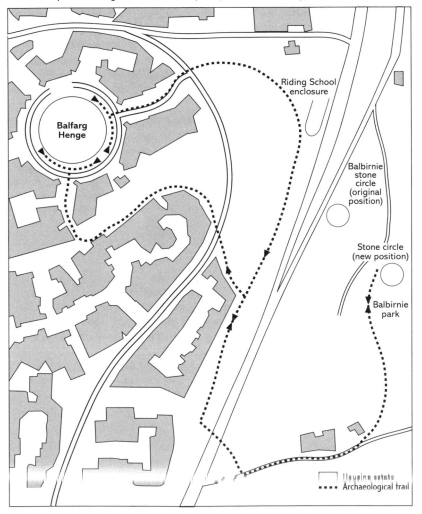

be found to the SE of the B969 from a roundabout which has a modern stone circle as a feature; then left and right.

The henge comprises a massive ditch about 60 m. in diameter, originally with a substantial external bank of which there is now no trace. In the interior there were several periods of use including circles of upright timbers and wooden posts. The layout of the timber circle is now indicated by low modern posts. The two surviving standing stones are all that remain of the megalithic period. At the centre of the henge a large flat slab is the capstone of a burial-pit of a young person, whose gravegoods included a beaker vessel and a flint knife.

The archaeological trail leads the visitor to a reconstructed setting of upright posts which represents one of the timber enclosures and platforms that appear to have been in use in the fourth millennium BC as part of the ritual of death and burial.

The little **stone circle of Balbirnie** (NO 285029) has had the indignity of having been moved after excavation and then relandscaped because of further road-works. It is, however, of interest as one of the few such sites in eastern Scotland to have been excavated in recent times. The setting of stones is in fact deliberately elliptical in shape, with a square arrangement at its centre. This can readily be compared to features at CAIRNPAPPLE in West Lothian and at the STONES OF STENNESS in Orkney. Several burials in cists were deposited within the circle, and finally the interior was covered by a cairn of stones in which cremation

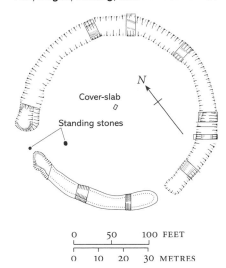

Cover-slab

Standing stones

0   50   100 FEET

0   10   20   30 METRES

▲ Plan of Balfarg henge (after R. J. Mercer)

▼ Plan of Balbirnie stone circle (after G. Ritchie)

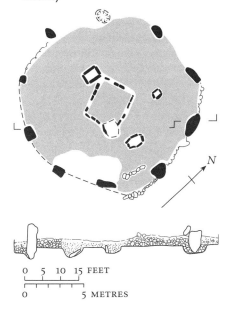

0   5   10   15 FEET

0   5 METRES

burials were interred. A replica of the decorated side-slab of one of the cists was prepared by the Glenrothes Town Artist, D. Harding, and a modern sculpture evoking the idea of upright stones today with contemporary themes can be seen in Falkland Court behind Glenrothes House.

Brechin   Round tower and carved stones

NO 594601. Brechin is now bypassed by the A94 Dundee to Aberdeen road, but the turn-offs are clear. Adjacent to the Cathedral at Brechin (Historic Scotland, tower only).

The round tower is all that survives of an earlier monastery; it is probably of C11 date, but the carved stones now preserved in the Cathedral show that the site was an important ecclesiastical centre at least two centuries earlier. The round tower is 26 m. in height and internally was subdivided into seven floors, which were reached by ladders. The interior is not currently accessible. The doorway is an impressive piece of Romanesque sculpture, surmounted by a crucifix, and flanked by ecclesiastics, one bearing a crozier, the other a book. At the base of the doorway there are two beasts, while at the top of each side there are two panels that lack the decoration which was presumably intended.

Within the Cathedral there is a group of early carved stones, including an unusually ornate hogback stone and a well-preserved Pictish symbol stone from Aldbar. An important fragment of what must have been an impressive cross-slab is mounted on a nearby wall; it depicts the Virgin Mary and Child with an encircling inscription that reads 'St Mary, the mother of Christ', one of the very few Latin inscriptions of this period in Scotland, flanked by angels and accompanied by two saints and what may be interpreted as the symbols of the Evangelists, the lower pair, representing the eagle of St John and the lion of St Mark, being the more readily recognizable.

Brown and White Caterthun   Forts   ★

NO 555668 and NO 547660. The twin forts are situated on adjacent summits 7.5 km. NW of Brechin and 5.5 km. SW of Edzell. The road leads to a car-park in the col between them at NO 552660. The approaches to the forts are not arduous (Historic Scotland).

The **Brown Caterthun** exhibits several lines of defence of differing phases pierced by an unusually large number of entrance gateways. The principal summit fortification was a wall some 7 m. in thickness which encloses an area of about 140 × 190 m.; there are now nine breaks in the wall, although there are not always corresponding breaks in the external ditch. Within this line of defence there are the remains of a further wall, which encloses an area of some 88 × 55 m., and now has five breaks across it, though not all of these need be original. There are further suites of

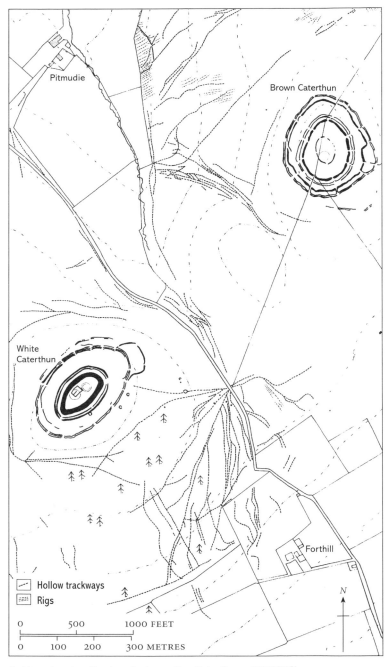

Pitmudie

Brown Caterthun

White
Caterthun

Forthill

Hollow trackways

Rigs

| 0 | 500 | 1000 FEET |

| 0 | 100 | 200 | 300 METRES |

N

▲ Map showing the two forts on the Caterthuns (RCAHMS)

defensive ramparts rather lower down the slopes, but in the absence of excavation the structural sequence of the various elements is difficult to determine. It is likely that the inner pair is the earlier and the outer the later, perhaps with the innermost wall being robbed to provide building material for its successor.

The **White Caterthun** is crowned by a great stone-walled oval fort, the mass of rubble measuring some 20 m. in thickness, up to 4 m. in height, and enclosing an area of about 150 × 70 m. The rubble probably represents a major inner wall and a second wall rather lower down the slope set within an encircling ditch with counterscarp bank. The mass of rubble is so great that it conceals the position of the entrance. At the SW end of the interior there is a rock-cut cistern.

Lower down the flanks of the hill there are remains of at least three periods of construction; a possible interpretation is that the most severely denuded line of defence, now little more than a band of quarry-scoops, is in fact the earliest fort, but that it was swept away to form the stone-walled fort we see today. The outer line is formed by double banks and median ditch broken by many entrances. It may be that this is a later line of defence for the central fort.

On the SW side of the fort amid the rubble of the collapsed wall there is a cup-marked boulder bearing about seventy simple cups.

The sequence of construction implies that the hilltops were centres of authority in Strathmore over long, though not necessarily continuous, periods, perhaps extending into the Pictish times.

Croft Moraig Stone circle

NN 797472. The circle is situated on the S. side of the A827 Aberfeldy to Kenmore road at the entrance to the farm of Croftmoraig. Parking is restricted on this busy road.

The stone circles and settings of Perthshire offer a variety of shape and scale, with the most intimate being small settings of four stones, known as four-posters. Larger and more complex settings such as Croft Moraig are often difficult to interpret if unexcavated, and even then it can be difficult to disentangle different periods amid upright stones and stone-holes. At Croft Moraig, excavation revealed that the earliest period was a timber one, with uprights forming an irregular circle about 9 m. in diameter. This was replaced by an oval setting of eight upright boulders, perhaps associated with the band of stones and boulders that acts as the perimeter of the site. There is a large cup-marked boulder on the south side; twenty-three cup-markings and two rings can be seen. The circle of stones between the outer oval and the innermost stone setting belong to the third period of construction. The sense of construction and rebuilding over a long period underlines the importance of sacred places or centres perhaps of communal ritual in the third and second millennia BC.

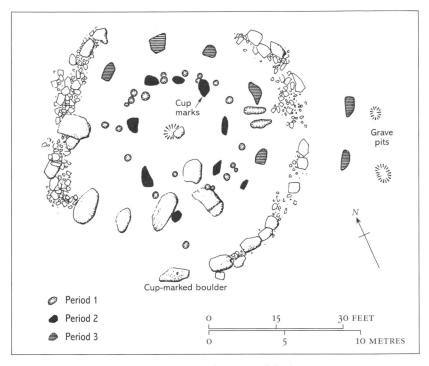

Cup marks

Grave pits

Cup-marked boulder

🦠 Period 1

● Period 2

🍪 Period 3

0   15   30 FEET

0   5   10 METRES

▲ Plan of Croft Moraig stone circle (The Stationery Office)

Dumyat Fort, Bridge of Allan

NS 832973. The footpath to the summit starts at about NS 813980 on the minor road between Bridge of Allan and Sheriff Muir.

The location of this fort is as important as the surviving remains, for it occupies a position that affords extensive views over the valley of the Forth and the surrounding hills. From here the stategic position of Stirling is immediately apparent—there must surely have been an important prehistoric fort on the rock now occupied by the magnificent castle.

Perched on the edge of the ridge, Dumyat fort is protected by nature on the south and east and by once impressive stone walls on the north and west, where there is an entrance. In the interior there is a second defensive structure of a type that is comparable to the stone-walled duns of the west; it measures about 27 × 16 m. and the stone wall may originally have been 4 m. in thickness. Without excavation the relationship of the various features is not known.

This is one of very few sites to retain a name that can be linked to the recorded names of the Celtic-speaking peoples of this part of Scotland, for Dumyat is interpreted as Dun Myat or the fort of the Maeatae, a name for the people recorded by Dio in the C3 AD as living by the wall that divides

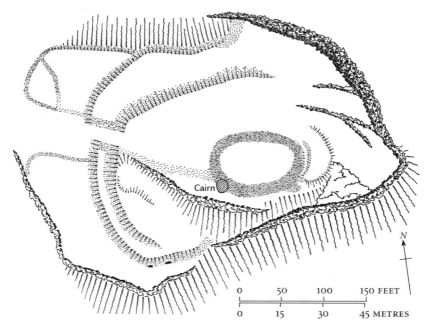

▲ Plan of Dumyat fort (after RCAHMS)

the island in half, with the Caledonians beyond them. 'Both inhabit wild and waterless mountains and desolate swampy places, and possess neither walls, cities, nor cultivated land.' Dumyat is a good place to ponder the clash of cultures between Roman and native peoples. The main Roman road from the Antonine Wall to Ardoch crossed the Forth at Stirling, and cropmarks of Roman temporary camps have been recorded at Dunblane and Craigarnhall, a little to the west.

Dundurn Fort, St Fillans

NN 708232. At the E. end of the village of St Fillans, on the Crieff to Lochearnhead road (A85), take the track signposted to Wester Dundurn farm and seek permission; go back down the track, fork E. to St Fillan's Chapel, and continue to the more gentle W. flank of the massif.

The long inland lochs of Perthshire are vital routes of communication between east and west. They must have been of great strategic importance in the third quarter of the first millennium AD, when the Scots from what is now Argyll and the Picts of eastern Scotland dispatched raiding parties and warrior bands into each others' territories. The fort of Dundurn occupies an isolated massif that rises from the valley floor at the east end of Loch Earn, at a point where several routes from Argyll and the Clyde join lines of communication from Pictland. Dundurn is known to have been a stronghold in the C7, for the *Annals of Ulster* for the year 683 record 'the siege of Dun At and the siege of Dun Duirn' (DUNADD and Dundurn); in the tantalizing manner of such elliptic accounts, we do not know who held the strongholds nor who was victorious.

The rocky terraces of the craggy summit offer natural defence that might be additionally strengthened by timber stockades or walls faced with stone. The first phase saw the summit of Dundurn defended by a stout timber palisade; later it was enclosed by a stone wall, doubtless with timber strengthening; finally the lower terraces were brought into the defensive plan. The situation of the fort, its irregular interior, and the rich finds recovered in the restricted excavations that have so far been undertaken, help to illustrate the nature of frontier society and defence in the C6 to C9 AD.

Dunfallandy Pictish symbol stone, Pitlochry

NN 946565. This well-preserved stone is protected in a glass cover, in a position close to the Dunfallandy Hotel (Historic Scotland). From Pitlochry cross the River Tummel to Ballinluig to the SW of the town following the minor road to Logierait under the new A9; from the A9 take the turning to the Festival Theatre and continue towards Logierait.

Both sides of this cross-slab have intricate ornament. The front has a cross with rectilinear arms and dominant bosses, the cross itself infilled with spiral ornament, key-pattern, and interlace. In the panels around the cross are animals and angels, with at the bottom right a sea monster either swallowing or disgorging a man, possibly illustrating the biblical story of Jonah and the whale. On the back, several scenes are enclosed within a border formed by two sea-serpents, licking a man's head at centre top. Below this are three symbols: a double disc, a Pictish 'beast', and a crescent and V-rod; there are also two ecclesiastics seated on elaborate thrones. A man on horseback rides towards a crescent and V-rod and a second beast. Beneath that there are the symbols representing the hammer, anvil, and tongs of the blacksmith, the first two symbols very reminiscent of the fragmentary stone at ABERNETHY (see p. 87).

East Lomond Fort, Falkland

NO 244062. The fort on the summit of E. Lomond is approached from the A912, and it is possible to drive almost to the summit; it is signposted midway between New Inn and Falkland.

As so often with the fortifications of southern Scotland, it is as much the situation as the surviving remains that commands respect. Nevertheless the ramparts are clear, and a large burial cairn can be seen on the highest point. It is a site well worth visiting for the views over a rich and densely settled area of Iron Age and Pictish Scotland (a slab carved with a figure of a steer in Pictish style was found on the hill in 1920).

Fairy Knowe Cairn, Bridge of Allan

NS 796981. This splendid cairn is situated on the Bridge of Allan Golf Course on the N. side of the town. Turn N. at Westerton on the A9 (NS 778977); check at the club house (NS 793983) for permission to walk on the course and be careful not to impede play.

The mound, which measures about 18 × over 2 m. in height, was dug into in 1868. The seqence of burial cannot now be appreciated from the visible features, but a central cist was surrounded by a small cairn of stones. The mound visible today was built over the top of this earlier cairn and more burials inserted. A fine Beaker vessel found in the top layers of the mound suggests that the burial sequence begins in the mid-to-late third millennium BC.

Finavon Fort, Aberlemno

NO 506556. NE of Forfar, a minor road links the A94 at Finavon (NO 489564) to the B9134 Forfar to Brechin road to the SW of Aberlemno (NO 516553).

The fort is situated on the top of a low rocky ridge and is well worth visiting, both because of its situation and because of the mass of vitrified material that shows it to have been totally destroyed by fire. The fort measures 150 × 36 m. within a wall about 6 m. in thickness. The only visible feature in the interior is the rock-cut cistern at the east end. The excavations in 1933–4 and 1966 did not reveal dramatic finds, although scientific dating has suggested that the fort may have had its origin sometime in the mid-first millennium BC and may have been reused in Pictish times. The carved stones at Aberlemno underline the importance of this area to the Picts.

Fowlis Wester Pictish carved stones

NN 927240. The village is situated to the N. of the Perth to Crieff road (A85) 5 km. E. of Crieff. (Large prehistoric mound to NW of turn-off.) The two stones are displayed in the church, and there is a cast of the larger cross in the centre of the village.

The taller stone is over 3 m. in height, with an elaborately decorated cross on the front face, now rather worn, but with the arms of the cross extending beyond the main slab. The back is worth examining closely as there are several unusual features, including a man leading a cow with a bell. At the top of the stone there is a double disc and Z-rod; below are horsemen in two tiers with a beast between. One of the lower horsemen seems to have a hawk on his arm. The man with his cow head a procession of six bearded men. At the bottom of the panel there is a crescent and V-rod and a worn figure that has been interpreted as a man being devoured by a beast.

The second slab, found during the restoration of the church in the early 1930s, is in superb condition. It bears a fine ring-headed cross with a square central boss, square-ended arms, and a highly ornate base, the whole decorated with crisp interlace, spirals, and key-pattern. The right hand of the pair of scenes at the top of the slab has been interpreted as the biblical story of Jonah being swallowed by, or spewed forth from, the whale. The two clerics who sit opposite one another on either side of the shaft have elaborately decorated chairs, a reminder of the fittings of ecclesiastical establishments for which we have little other evidence. These may be representations of St Paul, the first hermit, and St Anthony; the former's symbol is the date palm and perhaps this is suggested by the tree behind the figure on the left. St Anthony was sustained by visions and it may be that the figure behind the right-hand figure is an attempt to represent this. The vestments of the two saints and the clerics on the lower register give a good impression of the detailing that was possible on such stones, but that because of erosion is often no longer visible.

Gask Ridge Roman signal stations

The Gask Ridge is a bluff of higher ground on the N. bank of the River Earn to the SW of Perth. The watch-towers of the Roman frontier-system along the Ridge offer an insight into control and communication in the newly conquered territory in the first millennium AD. The sites are on the line of a minor road between Crossgates and Kinkell Bridge, the former on the A9 some 3.5 km. SW of Perth.

The best-preserved signal station is at Arduine (NN 946187); park at a bend in the minor road between Trinity Gask and Madderty (NN 960188) and then walk west for 1.3 km. The watch-tower is on the south side of the track. Such towers comprised a two-storeyed wooden structure, set within an earth bank and an outer ditch with a single causeway. Where excavated the four massive post-holes for the corner-posts of the tower have been found. The line of the Roman road from Ardoch north to the river crossing at Innerpeffray (near the Roman fort of Strageath, but there are no visible remains) is indicated on the Ordnance Survey map, as is the Gask Ridge line, which the road follows to Bertha (Perth) on the Tay. The other watch-towers on the frontier are at distances of between 0.8 km. and 1.5 km. apart, for reasons relating to the lie of the land rather than strict measurement.

Laws of Monifieth Fort and broch, Dundee

NO 491349. Laws farm is approached from the B961 Lower Whitfield to Drumsturdy road, with the turning-off at NO 491355. Seek permission at the farm.

The hilltop has been fortified by a massive wall taking in an area about 120 × 60 m., the best-preserved portion of which survives at the east end. When the fort was excavated in 1859, parts of the wall were about 2 m. in height and 9 m. thick. The fine masonry of the wall-faces can still be seen;

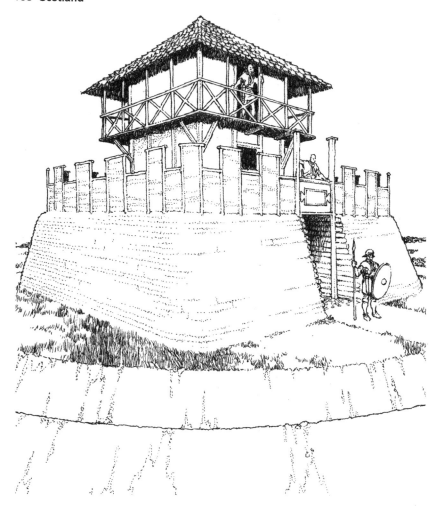

▲ Artist's reconstruction of a signal station on the Gask Ridge (M. Moore; Historic Scotland)

there were also patches of vitrified stone, but whether this represents the burning of this fort or perhaps of an earlier defensive work on the same site is not known.

The broch was cleared out in 1859, and apart from the wall and the entrance there is little to see. It is one of the few brochs in eastern Scotland and may date to around the C1 AD.

The views from here across the Tay to Fife and along the Angus coast are impressive—they also account for landscaping of the hill in the C19, including the creation of several ornamental stone mounds using stones from the fort walls.

Lundin Links

Standing stones ★

NO 404027. At the W. end of Lundin Links to the N. of the Leven to Largo road (A915), on the fairway of the Lundin Links Ladies Golf Course. Park at the club house to seek permission, but they are in fact readily seen from the road.

These are three of the most impressive standing stones in Scotland. The technical skills involved in their erection can instantly be appreciated. The single stone is some 5.5 m. in height and the pair set closer together are 4.1 m. and 4.6 m. high respectively.

Meigle Pictish and later carved stones ★

NO 287445. The village lies on the Perth to Forfar road (A94). No archaeologically- or historically-minded visitor to Pictland should miss the collection of carved stones gathered in the former school, situated a little to the S. of the centre of the village on the A927 to Newtyle; the tall windows planned for educational purposes provide a luminous setting for over thirty carved stones.

The carved stones were formerly set up in the churchyard or were found in the church and buildings round about. In date they belong to the C8–10. The most impressive in terms of scale are the great cross-slabs, but the smaller or more fragmentary stones have a wealth of decorative detail in their illustra-

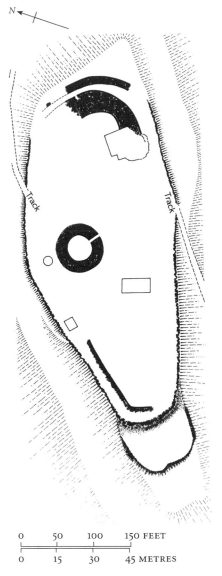

| 0 | 50 | 100 | 150 FEET |

| 0 | 15 | 30 | 45 METRES |

▲ Plan of the fort and broch on the Laws of Monifieth (after RCAHMS)

tion of Pictish horsemen and clerics. The stones are numbered, and those of particular interest include those listed briefly here. No. 1 is a cross slab with some of the animals of fable like the hippocamp and sea-horse; Pictish symbols on the back include a serpent and Z-rod, mirror and comb. No. 2 is a tall cross-slab with unusual animals at either side of the

▲ Meigle No. 26 (RCAHMS)

shaft; on the back there is a hunting scene above a rendering of Daniel in the den of lions (look out for the lion cubs). The symbolism of the axe-bearing centaur is not known. There are fine horsemen with details of their arms and saddlecloths on Nos. 3, 5, and 6. The clerics on Nos. 14 and 29 have elaborate vestments, the latter clasped by a pair of brooches. The skills of the Meigle craftsmen in carving animals is well illustrated on Nos. 12 and 26; the slot at the head of the latter was designed to hold an upright cross or perhaps a relic. Do not miss the fine Pictish 'beast' on the side of No. 5. The unusual recumbent monument (No. 25) is of C10 date and is carved in the style of a hogback tombstone with roof tiles; the animal on the ridge is finely detailed. No. 22 was part of an architectural frieze and bears a siren, a hybrid creature that was half-woman and half-fish, with a beast on either side.

Norman's Law Fort, Newburgh

NO 305201. The fort occupies the summit of the Law, an isolated massif over-looking the middle reaches of the Firth of Tay. Approach from the A913 Newburgh to Cupar road, seeking permission at Denmuir (NO 302188).

The summit has been defended by an oval stone-walled fort measuring about 50 × 30 m., with a gap for the entrance on the NE. This is probably the latest phase of fortification on the hill, for the lower terraces have also been enclosed by stout walls, although these are now more ruined. Look out for the traces of domestic settlement on the summit for there are the foundations of small stone-walled roundhouses and agricultural structures.

Queen's View Ring-fort, Loch Tummel

NN 863601. The small stone-walled fort at Queen's View is part of a Forestry Commission trail at the E. end of Loch Tummel, on the Killiekrankie to Tummel Bridge road. Park at the Forestry Commission centre, walk F. along the B8019 and follow the blue track after Allean Cottages. The ring-fort is about 250 m. to the W.

The small stone-walled forts of Perthshire with some outliers in Angus

▲ Meigle No. 1 (RCAHMS)

and Fife are among the archaeological conundrums of eastern Scotland. The small number of brochs in the east very clearly share the architectural characteristics of their western or northern cousins. The ring-forts of Perthshire seem to be related to the duns of Argyll, yet are not altogether duns. Often they are set on the valley floor, and the excavated example, at Litigan, has provided a rather later radiocarbon date than might be expected for duns. Queen's View is a well-preserved ring-fort or strongly defended house measuring about 17 m. in internal diameter within a wall almost 4 m. thick in places. The doorway on the west is the major feature.

St Andrews St Rule's Church and carved stones ★

The pilgrim to St Andrews will find much of interest, from the great cathedral, the castle with its famous mine and counter mine to the medieval layout of the town itself, to say nothing of the British Golf Museum. The earliest remains are those of St Rule's Church and the many fine carved stones in the Cathedral Museum.

The **Cathedral**, the building of which began in 1162, is the latest in a sequence of ecclesiastical establishments on a terrace overlooking the North Sea, at the eastern apex of the medieval town (NO 513166). An earlier church, however, is that now dedicated to **St Rule** (or Regulus), the most notable feature of which is its tower, some 33 m. high. It was built to house the relics of St Andrew, and its architecture is comparable to Northumbrian buildings of the C11. It was apparently extended in the C12, and the arch on the west side of the tower is an insertion of that date, leading to a now-demolished nave. The east wall has a round-headed arch and the grooves of three roof-lines cut into the masonry.

There are the foundations of another C12 church, known as **Blessed Mary on the Rock**, to the east of the cathedral (NO 515166); this was demolished in 1559. Many Early Christian stones, including fine cross-slabs, were found in the vicinity of the church, suggesting that this

▼ St Andrews Sarcophagus (I. G. Scott, Historic Scotland, RCAHMS)

spot was the focus of earlier activity (the stones are displayed in the **Cathedral Museum**).

An early monastery was in existence here in the first half of the C8, but no trace of its structures survive. It is likely to have been laid out in a similar way to contemporary monasteries at Iona and Jarrow, with church, communal buildings, and perhaps individual cells for meditation. Prominent in its church would have been the stone shrine known as the **St Andrews Sarcophagus**, carved sometime around AD 800 and one of the most important examples of late Pictish sculpture. It was constructed like a box with four carved panels which slotted into grooved corner-posts. The lid does not survive, but it is likely to have been either gabled, like the current reconstruction, or flat. The long panel is a remarkable piece of high-relief sculpture, depicting scenes from the Old Testament story of David. The large figure on the right shows David rending the jaws of a lion, with a woolly sheep and a monkey on either side of his head. To the left a griffin (half-eagle, half-lion) savages a mule, and David with spear and shield follows some animals. The horseman fighting a lion is yet another depiction of David—notice the falcon on his left wrist, which underlines David's royal status. Pairs of monkeys on one of the end-panels emphasize the exotic influences apparent in the art on the shrine.

The museum also contains fine cross-slabs with interlace decoration and fragments of the shafts of free-standing crosses, all of which testify to the wealth of the monastery and the skills of its craftsmen.

St Vigeans Pictish carved stones

NO 638429. The museum is signposted from the A933 Arbroath to Friockheim road a little to the NW of Arbroath. The key is held locally.

The collection of carved stones at St Vigeans offers many insights into the religious, secular, and mythological life of the Picts. The village is dominated by a church perched on a steep-sided knoll, and all the stones were found in the graveyard or built into the walls of an earlier church. They range from symbol-bearing cross-slabs to fragments of free-standing crosses and recumbent tombstones, and they date from the C8–10. Their presence implies that there was a major monastery here from at least as early as the C8, with a church dedicated to St Vigianus, a C7 Irish monk. Look out for the early C9 cross-slab No. 1, which bears one of the rare Pictish inscriptions in Hiberno-Saxon script and a depiction of an archer with a cross-bow. No. 11 shows the vestments and accoutrements of two clerics seated on a bench, and an engaging figure in baggy shorts. No. 7 was once a splendid cross-slab but it has been ruthlessly trimmed in antiquity; to the right of the cross-shaft, beneath two seated figures, is a curious scene with an emaciated little person apparently letting blood from the throat of a calf. A wonderfully arrogant fowl with its feathers interwoven graces the side of the recumbent tombstone No. 8.

Sandy Road Scone, stone circle, New Scone

NO 132264. On the W. side of New Scone, to the W. of the A94 Perth to Cupar Angus road.

This little circle of standing stones was excavated in 1961 and recreated as a feature in a housing development. Originally there were seven stones in a ring with a diameter of some 5.4 m.; the stones were carefully graded in height, with the tallest to the SW. At the centre of the circle there was a cinerary urn with the remains of a cremation deposit, set upright in a small pit. Although now marooned within modern housing, this circle gives a good impression of the scale of some of the smaller ceremonial monuments that were created to serve the needs of local communities in the second millennium BC.

Sir John de Graham's Castle Motte, Fintry

NS 681858. The Fintry to Denny road (B818) skirts the N. side of the Carron Valley Reservoir. This splendid square motte is situated on a tongue of ground in a forestry clearing at the N. end of the reservoir. A minor road leads to a picnic area which includes the motte to the E. of the N. dam.

The central motte mound is about 23 m. square with a surrounding ditch at least 11 m. across and 3 m. deep. At the NE angle of the mound is a length of mortared wall, which is likely to be the remains of a building, but there has been no excavation and even the date of the motte is uncertain. Only a little is known about Sir John de Graham of Dundaff, who fell at the battle of Falkirk in 1298, but the site is included as a remarkably well-preserved medieval monument of a type rare in central Scotland.

▼ Plan of Sir John de Graham's Castle (RCAHMS)

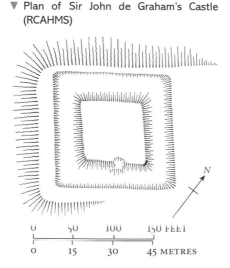

Strathmiglo Pictish symbol stone

NO 216102. The village is situated to the W. of Auchtermuchty on the Kinross to Cupar road (A91).

The original location of this Pictish stone is unknown, for it had been reused as a gatepost, but it is now set up at the entrance to the churchyard. It is a simple pillar bearing the head of a deer and the symbol described as a disc with notched rectangle, and it is likely to have been carved in the C7. There are relatively few symbol stones in Fife.

Wemyss Caves Pictish carvings, East Wemyss

NT 340970. Park at the front at E. Wemyss and walk along the track to the NE of the village; the series of caves is cut into the red sandstone cliff (take a torch).

The caves can be depressing to visit because it is difficult to distinguish the Pictish carvings from more modern graffiti, and the soft sandstone is prone to natural erosion of the incised lines. Nevertheless, as some of the few examples of Pictish symbols not on stones, they offer an interesting contrast to the better-known medium.

Not all the caves have symbols. The first cave the visitor comes to is the **Court Cave** (NT 342969). Inside there are two distinct areas of carving; the smaller has a spear-carrying figure and an animal. On the wall of the main cave look for the double-disc symbols amid the clutter of more recent markings. A little farther on the **Doo Cave** (NT 343970) formerly had an interesting array of symbols, but these are in part of the cave that has collapsed. Look at the rows of compartments cut into the walls of the cave to act as nesting boxes for pigeons. The **Well Caves** (NT 344971) have no carvings, but look up to the C16 part of McDuff's Castle, all that remains of a work begun in the C14.

Jonathan's Cave is the most profusely decorated (NT 345972); the animals are interesting to compare with those on cross-slabs, and the

▼ Location of the caves at East Wemyss (RCAHMS)

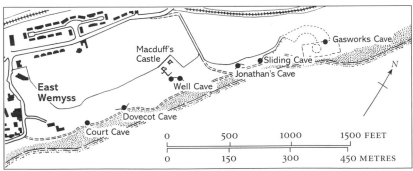

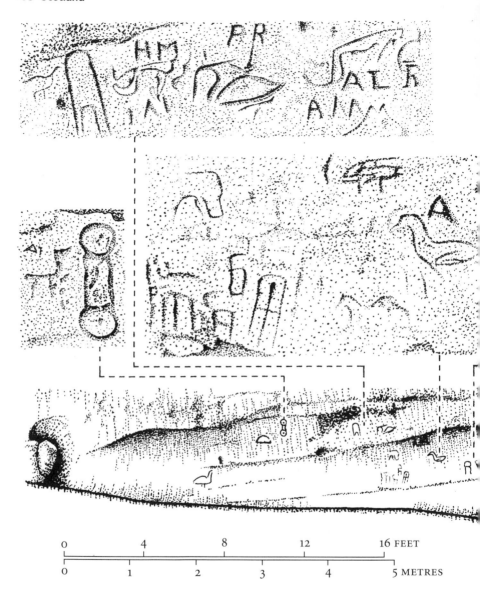

0	4	8	12	16 FEET

0	1	2	3	4	5 METRES

double-disc symbols are clearly authentic. An upright fish with a medial line is Pictish. There is also a rare carving of a boat with oars. The **Sliding Cave**, only a little farther on at a slight bend in the track, and hidden behind the talus (NT 346972) is more difficult to spot and slithery to get into (a torch is essential); there are rectangular symbols on the north wall, perhaps reminiscent of shields, and a double-disc on the other.

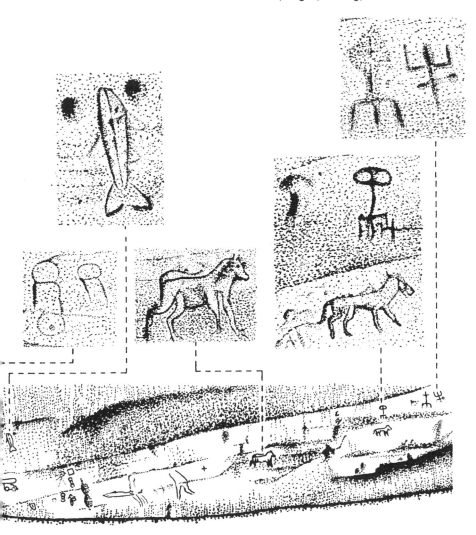

▲ Carvings in the East Wemyss caves (RCAHMS)

The Pictish interest in these caves is clear, even if their use for them is not understood today. There are more caves which were used in Early Christian times further along the Fife coast, and it is reasonable to think that caves have always had a special place in the mythology of local folk. The caves at East Wemyss are among the few where this can be demonstrated by evidence still visible today.

Argyll and Bute (Map, p. xvii)

The ancient monuments of Argyll and Bute offer a chronological range from early chambered cairns, spectacular Iron Age fortifications, to Early Christian crosses of great iconographic and artistic interest. The coastal waters and long sea lochs were the highways of the past and the location of many sites underlines this; cairns or duns can often be envisaged in relationship to an adjacent parcel of land. A site that may seem remote today may be only a day or two's sailing from a relatively major settlement. The Early Christian monuments particularly show Argyll and Bute to be part of a much wider framework of contacts, and are reminders of the trading and exchange contacts that were important factors in earlier times.

Achnacree Chambered cairn, North Connel

NM 922363. To the S. of the minor road that crosses the N. side of the Moss of Achnacree. Park about NM 923364 and walk across the moss to the massive cairn.

The cairn is now in a hollow in the moss, for the peat does not appear to have grown over the perimeter. The cairn is over 24 m. in diameter and 4 m. in height and is surrounded by a low platform of cairn material that increases the diameter to about 40 m.; it is thus one of the largest neolithic cairns in Argyll. It is not surprising that it attracted the attention of early antiquaries and it was entered in 1871 by Angus Smith, a pioneer in public health in Manchester who explored the archaeology of the Loch Etive area. The central crater by which he gained access can still be seen. Smith found that the chamber had comprised three compartments built of upright stones and drystone walling, which had been entered along a passage from the SE side of the cairn and the upright stones of the shallow forecourt at the entrance to the passage can still be seen. Within the chamber Smith found neolithic pottery as well as a number of white quartz pebbles which appeared to have been deliberately laid on two ledges formed by the drystone construction of the upper part of the chamber. The size of the cairn, even in its ruined state, bears testimony to the ordered nature of neolithic society.

There are several other monuments on or around the Moss of Achnacree, at least one other neolithic cairn (NM 929363) and several of Bronze Age date. Land divisions which have been found beneath the peat and have been shown to be of Bronze Age date indicate that the moorland scape that we see today may result from soil and climate conditions in the first millennium BC.

St Blane's Church Kingarth, Bute

NS 094534. Situated near the S. tip of Bute (Historic Scotland).

For some sites the feeling for the location and the sense of setting can be almost as important as the surviving remains, and this is particularly true for Early Christian monuments where the spirituality of the early Church is difficult to evoke from the slight archaeological evidence. Here, however, is the traditional location of the monastery of St Blane, who was born on Bute in the C6 and educated in Ireland, and who returned to found a community that flourished, so tradition says, until Viking raids around AD 800. The secluded setting is exactly appropriate to the contemplative life, enjoying a closeness to natural surroundings; it is also well suited to an involvement with trade and exchange by its proximity to the sheltered bay of Dunagoil. The church and cells of the community no longer survive, but there are several simple Early Christian crosses which were the grave-markers for the early community. A large circular stone-built foundation known as the Cauldron or the Devil's Cauldron has also been attributed to the earliest ecclesiastical use of the site. A drystone foundation, it measures some 10 m. within a wall 2.5 m. thick, and there is an entrance on the SE. It is not likely to be a defensive structure, and it is most improbable that it is the base of a round tower. Excavations undertaken at the end of the C19 produced workshop debris that indicated that fine artistic objects were being made here in the C9.

The church itself is of C12 date with fine Romanesque carving; it comprises a nave and chancel.

The rocky headland about 1 km. west of St Blane's Church is dominated by the remains of a spectacular Iron Age fort known as Dunagoil; the track to the shore runs along the edge of a field from a point a little to the north of Dunagoil farm (NS 088535). First pass Little Dunagoil, a fortified site in prehistoric times, later occupied in the medieval period by longhouses. The finds from the excavations are in the Bute Museum, Rothesay. Between Little Dunagoil and the main massif there is a large stone cist or burial chamber, which would originally have been covered by a cairn of stones. While there are examples of comparatively simple chambered tombs of neolithic date, equally are there examples of large cists of Bronze Age date; it is better to suspend judgement on the date of this little structure.

The larger fort is situated on the highest point of the promontory and measures about 23 × 90 m. with what was formerly a thick timber-laced wall. The burning of the wall created such intense heat that the stones of the wall fused together; such vitrified material is particularly clear in the NW angle of the fort. The main entrance appears to have been at the SW. Excavations between 1913 and 1925 produced a rich array of finds, including metalwork of Iron Age date, pottery, and evidence of metalworking. These are in the Bute Museum, Rothesay. The views from the fort

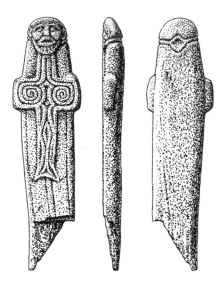

▲ Riasg Buidhe, Colonsay (RCAHMS)

are spectacular. From the site ponder on the possibilities of a trading-station near Dunagoil Bay with a wide market around the Firth of Clyde and beyond.

Colonsay House Riasg Buidhe cross-slab, Colonsay

NR 395968.

Situated at the rear of Colonsay House, the gardens of which are open to the public, the cross was moved to its present position beside a well known as Tobar Odhrain in about 1870. The cruciform slab bears a solemn face with pronounced eyebrows and ears. The chin may be intended to represent a beard. The cross has two spirals on the arms and a splayed fish-like tail. It is thought to be of C7 or C8 date; although there are no close parallels in Scotland, it may be compared to examples from Ireland from this period.

Crarae Chambered cairn, Furness

NR 985972.

Within the beautiful gardens of Crarae Lodge on the east side of Loch Fyne where the Crarae Burn has formed a small alluvial fan, there is a reminder of the attraction of pockets of such fertile soil to early man in the form of a well-preserved chambered cairn. Several large upright stones of the façade remain, as well as the chamber, which was divided into three compartments by two transverse slabs. It is a characteristic example of the Clyde class of tomb. It was excavated in 1955–7 and the remains of both inhumation and cremated burials were found, together with some neolithic pottery.

Eileach an Naoimh Monastery, Garvellachs

NM 640097. There is a boat service from Toberonochy on the island of Luing, weather permitting.

The island group known as the Garvellachs is situated off the NW tip of Jura and the boat trip from Luing passes through some of the most beautiful scenery of the west coast. It also passes the small island of Belnahua, the centre of a flourishing slate-quarrying industry in the late C19 and earlier C20. But it was for reasons of tranquillity, perhaps coupled with accessibility to important seaways, that a small monastery was founded in Early Christian times. A well-preserved beehive cell as well as an underground chamber, which may well originally have been associated with another, are of this early date, along with a small enclosure known as Eithne's grave, and traditionally said to be the burial-place of St Columba's mother. One of the upright slabs that edge this setting is decorated with an incised cross. Ecclesiastical use of the island continued into the medieval period and a small chapel, the foundations of a medieval church, as well as other buildings can still be seen.

A visit to Eileach an Naoimh is remarkable in allowing the traveller of today the chance to experience the solitude of the eremitic life within the natural grandeur of the surrounding islands.

IONA   ★★

Of the abbey, only the Early Christian remains fall within the chronological span of this volume, but these are an important part of a visit to the island, and the crosses have become icons of Scottish heritage and culture. Occupation of the island in the Iron Age is shown by the presence of a small fort on **Dun Cul Bhuirg** (NM 264247), where excavations have revealed pottery dating to the early centuries AD. This fertile island was given to St Columba in AD 563 as a place for prayer and meditation within a monastic community. The importance of the monastery grew with St Columba's teaching and the key role of the Columban Church in the establishment of Christianity in Scotland. This phase was brought to an end about AD 800, when following Viking raids most of the community moved to Kells, Co. Meath. The medieval abbey and nunnery are the main focus of visitor attention today, and it would be difficult to imagine the layout and way of life of the early monastic community were it not for the *Life of Columba* written by Adomnan, ninth abbot of Iona, in the late C7. We can imagine the simple church, individual cells for the monks constructed of timber or perhaps of drystone beehive shape, communal buildings, all enclosed within a bank and ditch designed to delimit the

▲ St Martin's Cross (RCAHMS)

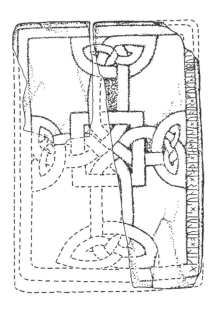

▲ Inscribed grave-markers (RCAHMS)

monastic area; a corner of this earthwork can still be seen to the NW of the abbey to the west of the road. To the west of the Abbey there is a rocky boss on which excavations have revealed the foundations of a small building interpreted as the site of St Columba's cell, which was said to be 'built in a higher place' than the rest of the community.

The high crosses are the principal surviving antiquities dating from the middle and later C8. **St John's Cross** is in the Abbey Museum (there is a cast in front of the Abbey) and the mortice and tenon construction can be clearly seen. It is decorated with panels of serpent and boss motifs and with panels of interlace. Standing in front of the Abbey is **St Martin's Cross**; there is serpent and boss ornament on the east face, but figural scenes on the other—the Virgin and Child at the centre, Daniel in the lions' den, Abraham's sacrifice of Isaac, David with musicians, and at the bottom a scene less firmly interpreted as Samuel about to anoint David.

The more fragmentary **St Oran's** and **St Matthew's Crosses** are in the Abbey Museum along with many other crosses and grave-markers, one with the worn carving of a boat and another with carvings in Norse runes of C10 or C11 date.

ISLAY

Two of the chambered cairns of Islay well illustrate the constructional techniques of the Clyde type of cairn. **Cragabus** (NR 329451) is close to the road, indeed parking is difficult, but one impressive stone of the upright façade as well as the overlapping stones of the chamber can be seen. Similar use of large upright slabs is present in the chamber of the denuded cairn at the edge of the playing-field SW of **Port Charlotte** (NR 248576); pottery recovered in the course of excavations between 1976 and 1979 is displayed in the attractive **Museum of Islay Life** in Port Charlotte, which has displays of the archaeology and history of the island. One of the few stone circles in Argyll is to be found at **Cultoon** (NR 195569) to the west of the road on the west of the Rhinns of Islay. There are three upright stones as well as twelve prone slabs. Careful excavation suggested that the intentions of the builders had never been completed and that the elliptical setting that had been envisaged was unfinished.

Ballinaby Standing stones, Islay

NR 219672.

There were formerly three standing stones to the north of Ballinaby, but only two now survive. The taller is, however, one of the most impressive uprights of western Scotland, measuring almost 5 m. in height, but only 1.1 m. × 30 cm. at its base. The preparation of the pillar and the engineering involved in setting it up are testimony to the organizational and technical skills of the early inhabitants of Islay. The second stone is situated some 220 m. to the NNE, but it is now only 2 m. in height, following damage in an attempt to break it up.

Look round and consider the setting, for not only is Ballinaby a name of Norse origin, but several burials with Viking artefacts have been discovered nearby. Norse settlements are difficult to identify, and it is important to remember this strand in the cultural history of the west.

Dun Nosebridge Fort, Islay   ★

NR 371601. From Bridgend take the minor road to Neriby, park about NR 363598, and walk up the track on the E. side of the road.

The fortified ridge of Dun Nosebridge is a spectacular, if puzzling, monument. Clearly a defensive establishment commanding the respect of a large area, given the scale of the earthworks, the period at which this was happening is difficult to gauge. The topmost defence is a stout wall enclosing an area about 25 × 15 m., but below the summit outer works on the west flank of the ridge there are outer works which give the site its distinctive profile. In the absence of excavation the date of the site is unknown.

Kildalton Cross Islay   ★

NR 458508.

This splendidly proportioned ringed cross, carved from single slab of

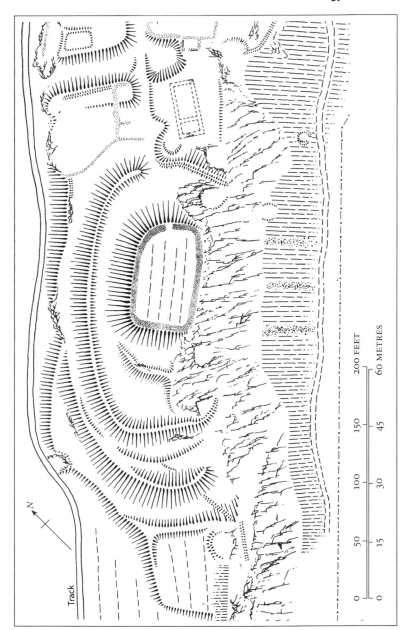

▲ Plan of Dun Nosebridge fort (RCAHMS)

epidiorite, stands in the churchyard of the medieval parish church of Kildalton. Dating to the second half of the C8, it joins the high crosses of Iona among the major achievements of the Early Christian art of

▲ Kildalton Cross (RCAHMS)

Dalriada. The west face has serpent and boss ornament with four lions around the central boss of the cross. There are four figural scenes on the west face of the cross. From the top, the upper scene may be David slaying the lion with two angels looking on; the arms of the cross may show Cain's murder of Abel, and Abraham's sacrifice of Isaac; at the top of the shaft the Virgin and Child are flanked by angels.

Look for the late medieval grave-slabs within both the church and the churchyard in distinctive West Highland styles.

Kilnave Cross Islay

NR 285715. To the W. of the medieval church of Kilnave on the E. side of the Ardnave peninsula 4.5 km. N. of Gruinart.

The cross is a worn example of a C8 cross, but one on which the fine decoration links it firmly with the IONA tradition and the manuscript art of the period. Two grooved slabs of the original cross-base can still be seen, and it is suggested that these were the top and bottom slabs of a box-like arrangement with four upright slabs forming the sides of the box which acted as the basal support for the cross.

KINTYRE

Blasthill Chambered cairn, Kintyre

NR 720092. The cairn is situated about 600 m. NE of Blasthill, off the road that follows the E. side of the southern tip of Kintyre.

This is an example of an unexcavated chambered cairn that nevertheless implies a long chronological evolution set within a landscape that has itself been part of the agricultural patterns of Argyll. The final period of the site is an impressive long mound with two megalithic chambers and an upright façade of stones at the east end. It is possible, however, by analogy with excavated sites elsewhere, that the chamber at the centre of the cairn is

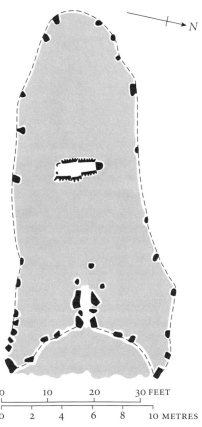

▲ Plan of Blasthill chambered cairn (after RCAHMS)

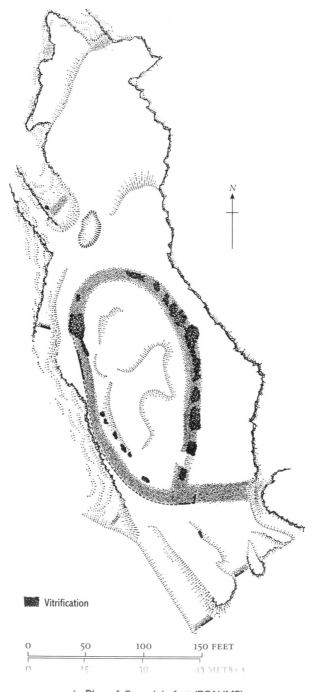

Vitrification

0   50   100   150 FEET

0   15   30   IN METRES

▲ Plan of Carradale fort (RCAHMS)

the earlier, perhaps surrounded by a small round cairn. That cairn was subsumed within a larger cairn with a chamber at the east end and a monumental façade on either side of the entrance. When the tomb went out of use, stones were piled in front of the entrance, sealing it for the last time.

Carradale Fort, Kintyre

NR 815364. To the S. of Carradale village off B879.

Situated on a rocky promontory of Carradale Point on the east side of Carradale Bay there are the remains of what has been an oval timber-laced fort measuring about 56 × 23 m.; it has been destroyed by a fire of such ferocity that the stones of the walls have fused together to form large vitrified masses, which are particularly impressive on the east side of the fort. The fire has raged with such force that some of the wall-core on the SW side has tumbled into the interior in fused lumps. A few stretches of outer facing-stones can still be seen. Additional defence was provided by a series of walls cutting off the gullies that might have allowed access to the summit, and one cross-wall (also vitrified) runs between the SE tip of the fort and the cliff edge.

Dun Skeig Fort, Kintyre

NR 757571. A series of minor and farm roads to the NNW of Clachan on A83 leads to a point where the summit of Dun Skeig may most readily be reached.

The fortifications on the summit of Dun Skeig offer a fascinating sequence of building. They occupy a formidable position overlooking the entrance to West Loch Tarbert with wide views in all directions. In the earliest phase the whole of the summit area appears to have been enclosed by a stone wall, but this is only clearly visible on the SE side; if such a wall did indeed surround the summit area the fort would have measured about 113 × 36 m. There is a smaller fortification at the SW end of the summit, now consisting of a circle of the fused or vitrified core material of what was once a substantial timber-laced wall, enclosing some 26 × 18 m. The burning was so intense that the position of the entrance cannot be identified. The best-preserved period of fortification is the dun at the NE end of the ridge; the drystone wall is up to 4 m. in thickness and encloses a central area about 13 × 14 m. in diameter. The entrance passage is particularly clear, and the door-jambs against which the stout door would rest are clearly visible, along with the bar-hole, in which the securing bar that kept the door in position in the north side of the passage. The dun was additionally protected by an outer wall, traces of which can be seen around the NE end of the ridge.

Dun Skeig evokes a sense of continuity of the imposition of authority through the fortification of high places, although many generations of people and several different political structures may be involved. The views alone should encourage the visitor to think about the interaction of the landscape of Scotland, its indented coastline, and the framework of Iron Age society.

Kildonan Dun, Kintyre

NR 780277. On the E. side of the road between Campbeltown and Carradale some 3.5 km. S. of Saddell.

This well-preserved dun is characteristic of a class of small stone-walled fortifications of the early centuries AD and there is easy access from the road. D-shaped on plan, the dun measures about 19 × 13 m. internally within a wall over 2 m. in thickness. The impressive entrance is in the SW, with the door-jambs, bar-hole, and bar-slot, into which the bar would be inserted to hold the door firm, all clearly visible. The double stairway to the wall-head on the west side and a mural cell on the NE remain intact.

What is particularly important about Kildonan dun is the fact that excavations have given some indication of the chronological range of use of such structures; objects of C1 or C2 date offer a likely date for the construction of the dun, while C9 and C12 or later finds show that such a stronghold was an important focus for powerful leaders in later times. The finds are in Campbeltown Museum.

Ranachan Hill Fort, Kintyre

NR 689250. This interesting fortification is situated 800 m. E. of Balnagleck farmhouse.

The once formidable stone-built fortification is now much reduced in height but the outline is clear and there are many sections of the outer face surviving to over 1 m. in height on the south side. The position is commanding, as with so many forts of this period, and the surviving remains have to be appreciated within their setting overlooking Machrihanish Bay. There are entrances to the west and north; an internal revetment within the thickness of the wall in order to increase its stability can be seen on the NE and south.

The fort has been provided with additional defence on its east flank by lines of walling. The scale of the fortifications shows that this was an important centre of power in the early part of the first millennium AD.

KILMARTIN, ARGYLL ★★

The monuments around Kilmartin are among the most evocative of the prehistory and early history of Scotland. Antiquarian interest in the C19 and the enlightened interest of the local landowner in the earlier part of the C20 have had vital parts to play in elucidating the monuments and in making them available for public inspection. William Daniell prepared a

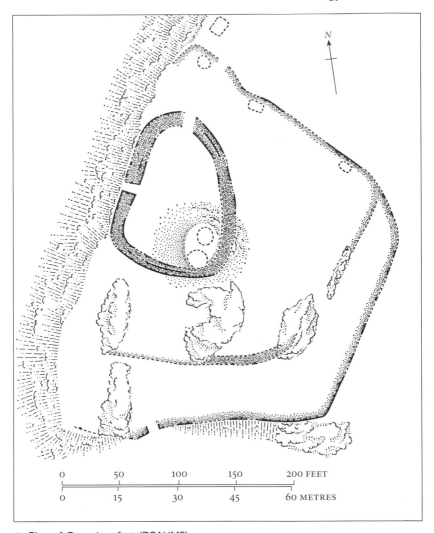

▲ Plan of Ranachan fort (RCAHMS)

view of the stone circle of Temple Wood in 1813 at a time when the character of the floor of the valley was changing. The land was not yet enclosed, indeed peat extraction was steadily removing the superincumbent peat from what is agricultural ground today, and the peat-diggers and the bank of stacked peat can just be seen. In the background the stones of Nether Largie and the massive cairn of Nether Largie South are clearly visible. By the time when Canon Greenwell examined the cairn in 1864 it had been severely robbed to provide material for field-walls and drains, and the ordered landscape that we see today, including the planting of trees to create the wood of Temple Wood, was in place. The

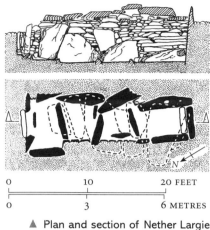

0   10   20 FEET

0   3   6 METRES

▲ Plan and section of Nether Largie
South chamber (RCAHMS)

beginning of the peat cover over the floor of the valley has been dated to around AD 900, and it is likely that the marginalization of the agricultural potential of the area for the next millennium or so has helped to preserve many archaeological monuments.

The chambered cairn of **Nether Largie South** (NR 828979) well illustrates the importance of such burial-places over many generations and with differing fashions of burial practice. The chamber is of Clyde type, with overlapping side-slabs and bracing cross-slabs allowing the equivalent of a horizontal house of cards of massive slabs to be erected, the bracing slabs and the supporting cairn providing the essential stability. A burial-chamber of four compartments was thus created. The excavations revealed deposits associated with neolithic pottery as well as later deposits in the chamber with Beaker ware. There were two later burial deposits in cists, one of which is still visible to the south of the main chamber.

Temple Wood has been examined on several occasions, and the central part was clearly already open by the beginning of the C19. Excavation between 1974 and 1979 laid bare the sequence of construction and reconstruction. The earliest phase is the ritual circle of timber and later stone uprights, some 10 × 10.5 m.; radiocarbon dates confirm that this setting was in being in the fourth millennium BC; it is now indicated by a series of concrete markers.

The circle of twenty-two stones that forms the SW circle formed the focus for a series of ritual and burial acts over many centuries and it was not possible to disentangle the precise sequence. Two of the stones are decorated, one with a double spiral, the other with a double oval. Burials within small cairns took place both within the circle and immediately outside it, and finally the whole site was covered with cairn material. Only the central cist, which originally was set within its own small kerbed cairn, remains visible. It is recorded that a great many coins were found in digging at the centre of the circle, presumably a coin hoard of medieval date, but none appears to have survived. Opposite the circle is a setting of stones that should be viewed only from the road as the site, like many others in the area, is in private ownership; a linear setting of standing stones, one decorated extensively with cup-marks, must certainly be an important part of an as yet little understood ritual landscape of the Kilmartin Valley.

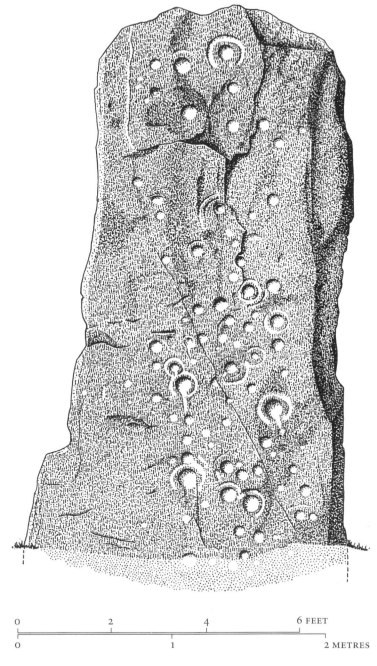

0   2   4   6 FEET

0   1   2 METRES

▲ Standing stone with cupmarks at Ballymeanoch (RCAHMS)

The linear settings at **Ballymeanoch** (NR 833964) can now be visited as part of an access agreement and the stones and the decoration on two of them can be appreciated at close quarters. The purpose of such linear settings cannot be guessed at, but their presence within a pattern of burial-cairns and such monuments as henges and stone circles suggests that the totality of the landscape was one in which ritual rather than agricultural activities were paramount. The little henge monument some 150 m. SW of the standing stones can still just be seen; there is a very slight outer bank and inner ditch with breaks to north and south. Two cists, excavated by Canon Greenwell in 1864, are still partially visible.

There are several cairns of Bronze Age date in the vicinity of Kilmartin which give good impressions of the scale or chronological complexity of such sites: **Dunchragaig** (NR 833968), where there were formerly three cists, although only one is now visible; Nether Largie Mid (NR 830983), North (NR 830984), and Ri Cruin (NR 825971), where cists, decorated slabs, and the sequence of deposits are outlined in display panels.

Achnabreck Cup-and-ring markings, Kilmartin ★

NR 855906. Take the road to the farm of Achnabreck and park in the signposted space; follow the signs across a field to the edge of the conifer forest, where a large fenced enclosure surrounds the rock-sheets.

The spectacular rock outcrops with multiple ring-markings should be seen in a low light, particularly late in the day. In some cases there are as many as seven rings surrounding a cup. In a number of instances gutters lead from the central cup to the edge of the outer ring or beyond. On the uppermost rock-sheet, that is the NE sheet, there is a greater variety of carving, although some are very worn, and there are two double spirals and one triple spiral.

A second rock-sheet should not be overlooked; the path leads through trees from a gate at the SE corner of the main enclosure. There are over fifteen ringed cups, with up to six surrounding rings.

Exploration of sites such as Achnabreck and CAIRNBAAN inevitably prompts the question of why people carved the profusion of symbols on the rock-sheets, and no satisfactory solution has yet been put forward. They are clearly part of the ritual landscape of Kilmartin Valley, with examples on standing stones at Ballymeanoch and elsewhere. The double spiral at Achnabreck finds its closest local parallel at TEMPLE WOOD. Thus the neolithic landscape involves a whole series of sites that must have been viewed in an integrated way. Bronze-Age artists used cup-marked slabs, perhaps reused the slabs, adding axes at Ri Cruin and Nether Largie North. Kilmartin presents a remarkable number of pieces of evidence that can be experienced to allow an extraordinary picture of a social framework in neolithic and Bronze Age times that made possible the construction of sophisticated monuments utilizing massive slabs, chambered cairns, stone alignments and stone circles, round cairns, and decorated rock surfaces. Archaeologists have not worked out what the markings may mean, but increasingly see the integration of the relationships of different categories of evidence—field monuments, a consideration of their topographical position, as well as the designs on pottery and other artefacts associated with them—as one way of informing the broader picture.

Cairnbaan Cup-and-ring markings, Kilmartin

NR 839910. There is a signposted path from the restaurant at Cairnbaan.

▼ Rock art at Cairnbaan (RCAHMS)

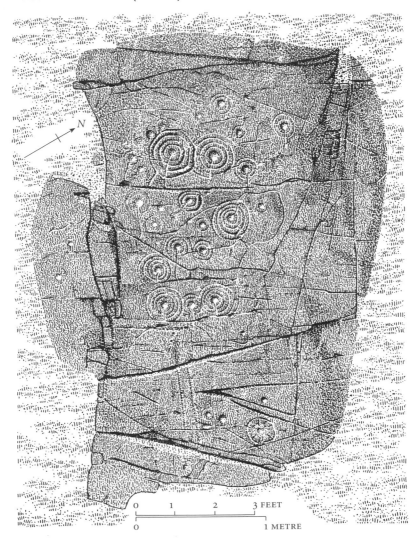

0   1   2   3 FEET

0   1 METRE

There are two rock outcrops with simple cupmarks, cup-and-ring mark-ings, some with gutters from the centre. The markings are of importance in themselves, but it is also important to appreciate the placing of the site within the wider landscape with extensive views to the south.

Dunadd Fort, Kilmartin ★

NR 873935. Follow the signposts from the A816, 1.5 m. N. of Kilmichael Glassary, park in the indicated area, and walk to the summit of the hill along the official path.

The rocky massif of Dunadd rises abruptly from a flat valley floor, an ideal site for a fort that was one of the strongholds of the kingdom of Dalriada. The plan should help to orientate the visitor and an evocation of Heroic society may help to explain the importance of such high-status sites. What we see now are the stout stone walls within which timber halls and roofed buildings would offer a robust residence and workshop area for a Dark Age magnate. The lowest terrace would have had a strong timber gateway half-way along the defile that leads to the interior. There was clearly indus-trial activity on the next terrace for metalworking finds include crucibles and moulds, implying activity in the C8 and C9 AD. The terrace immedi-

▼ Plan of Dunadd fort (RCAHMS)

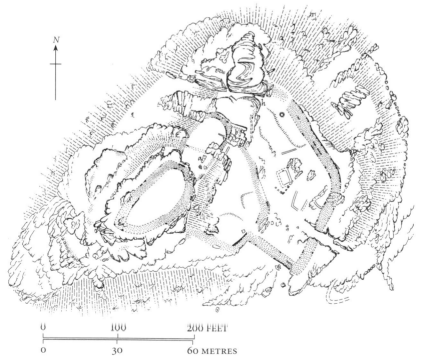

N

| 0 | 100 | 200 FEET |
| 0 | 30 | 60 METRES |

▲ View of the fort at Dunadd (RCAHMS)

ately below the summit has unusual carved rock surfaces. There is a large rock-cut basin and about 2 m. NE of the basin a shallow footprint and an incised boar. There is also the modern incised head and shoulders of a man smoking a pipe with the inscription King Fergus. Farther to the north there is another footprint and an ogham inscription, the reading of which remains obscure. While there is little doubt that the identification of Dunadd as the capital of Dalriada by W. F. Skene increased archaeological interest in the site in the first quarter of the C20, the scant resultant evidence should be linked with the tales of the Heroic Age in Ireland and the visitor should try to see the site as one of the centres of a complex of sites supported by considerable sea-power and inter-family authority and loyalty.

Kintraw Cairns and standing stone, Ardfern

NM 830049. The site is situated by a sharp bend on the A816 at a point 1 km. SE of the road junction to Ardfern. Park very carefully to view the cairns and associated standing stone in a field to the E. of the road.

The cairn is a dramatic monument set on a terrace with wide views down Loch Craignish, a position that emphasizes the sense of location that is so often a feature of Highland archaeology. It is some 15 m. in diameter and almost 3 m. in height. When excavated in 1959–60 a setting of stones on the SW side with two stones at right angles to the kerb with a massive slab in front formed an unusual feature, but unfortunately this can no longer be seen. The small and low cairn to the SW belongs to the same distinct category as that from STRONTOILLER (Lorn), in Glen Lonan, and BALLYMEANOCH (Kilmartin).

The standing stone is an impressive example about 4 m. in height above ground. It fell over in the winter of 1978–9, and subsequent excavation revealed that it had originally been set with about 1 m. of its total length into the ground, a proportion that can be confirmed at other sites.

The monuments at Kintraw attract visitors not only because of their intrinsic archaeological interest, but also because a platform on the hillside above was the subject of one of the first excavations designed to test the theories of Professor A. Thom about the possibilities of the use of megaliths in solsticial observations. This is not an area where certainty is ever likely to be proved. What is important for the visitor is to consider such a complex monument within the topographical setting all around and to remember the unknowable cosmologies of earlier times.

LORN

Caisteal Suidhe Cheannaidh Dun, Kilchrennan, Lorn

NN 029243. This well-preserved dun occupies a commanding position to the W. of the Taynuilt to Kilchrenan road (B845), 1.5 km. N. of Kilchrenan.

This circular dun measures between 12 m. and 13 m. in diameter within a wall some 5 m. thick. The entrance is on the NE and has the characteristic door-checks against which a stout door would be secured. Limited excavation in 1890 indicated the position of several hearths as well as settlement debris. The height of the surviving wall-face is impressive at over 2 m., but it is also the location of the dun and an appreciation of the surrounding terrain that makes this an interesting site to visit.

Leccamore Dun, Luing

NM 750107. The dun is approached from the road to Leccamore farm, where permission should be sought to visit; it is clearly visible from the road.

The well-preserved dun has many characteristic features of this class of monument; the thick stone wall encloses an area some 20 × 13 m. More unusually there are two entrances; that to the SW shows the door-jambs against which the door would be supported and the bar-slot in which the bar would be housed when out of use. The door-jamb on the SE side is a slate slab decorated with thirteen cup-marks. The NE entrance has no door-jambs, but there is an intramural cell and a flight of stairs leading to the wall-head on the NW.

The dun is additionally protected by an outer work and by two rockcut ditches, which may also have served as quarries for building stone. The

▲ Strontoiller cairn (RCAHMS)

views from the site over the inner seaways at the mouth of Loch Melfort are impressive.

Strontoiller Cairn and standing stone, Lorn

NM 907289. The cairn and standing stone are situated just to the N. of the secondary road between Oban and Taynuilt that passes through Glen Lonan, beside a cattle-grid, at a point 450 m. S. of Strontoiller farm.

The impressive standing stone is a tall block about 4 m. in height, and it has the traditional name of Diarmid's Pillar, after the mythical figure of the Irish tales who is said to have hunted boar in these parts. The cairn, Diarmid's Grave, is a small Bronze Age cairn about 4.5 m. in diameter with large granite erratic kerbstones. It contained small deposits of cremated bone. At the base of the kerbstones were deliberate scatters of white quartz pebbles, which were clearly part of the ritual activities involved in the construction of the burial monument.

Tirefour Broch, Lismore

NM 867429. The Port Appin ferry lands the visitor to Lismore at the N. tip of the island where a walk of rather more than 4 m. will be rewarded by one of the best-preserved brochs in the area. Follow the road SW and after about 3 km. take the farm track to Balure. The broch will be visible near the coast after about 1 km.

The broch, situated atop a limestone ridge, is about 12 m. in diameter and still stands to a height of almost 5 m. on the SE. The entrance is on the SW, and several of the classic architectural features of brochs can be seen in the interior, such as a distinct scarcement, on which internal timber floors may have rested, as well as long sections of narrow galleries within the thickness of the wall, which were designed to increase the stability of the drystone construction. The broch is additionally defended by outerworks which cut across the ridge on the NE and SW sides.

As with so many of the later prehistoric monuments of Scotland, part of the interest lies in relating the site to its position within an island framework and also a wider landscape and in trying to evaluate the role of such a status-conscious construction in the society of the times.

TIREE

Dun Mor Broch, Vaul, Tiree

NM 042492. The broch is situated on a rocky knoll close to the shore some 300 m. NW of Vaul township on the N. coast of Tiree. Park at the N. end of the township and walk to the NW coast.

The broch is about 9 m. in diameter within a well-built drystone wall some 4.5 m. thick and over 2 m. high. There is an internal gallery at ground level with several doorways from the central court, but the main one seems to be that on the north side where there is also a stairway that allows access to the upper levels of the structure. The gallery is a constructional technique and it would originally have been spanned with lintels at about this level, rather like the cross-ties in cavity-wall construction today, and the upper levels of walling would continue in a similar way with an outer and an inner wall. The entrance arrangements are impressive, with door-checks against which the door would be jammed from the interior, and the pivot-stone on which the door turned. The door was kept in position by a wooden bar, which, when not in use, was pushed back into the appropriate slot on the north side of the passage; when the door was shut, it was drawn across the back of the door and wedged into the slot on

▼ Plan of Dun Mor broch (after RCAHMS)

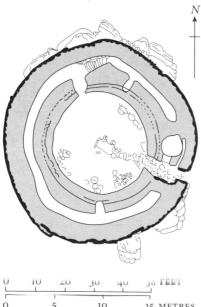

N

0   10   20   30   40   50 FEET

0   5   10   15 METRES

the opposite side. The guard-cell on the north side of the passage is also a characteristic feature of many brochs and duns; in this case it is a corbelled cell about 2 m. in diameter.

The internal arrangements of the broch are to some degree a matter of conjecture and debate; certainly roofing of all or part of the interior is only sensible, but at what height and in what style cannot be known. The central hearth implies a central opening to the roof structure, and an internal range of concentric timber rooms and stores is the most likely; there was doubtless much internal rearrangement while the broch was in use. Excavation produced evidence to suggest that the construction may be placed in the middle of the C1 BC, but that reconstruction and reuse continued until Viking times.

▲ Soroby cross-slab (RCAHMS)

The broch is further protected by an outer wall which was built close to the edge of the knoll; it is possible that this represents an earlier fortification, but it is less regular than many independent structures and would surely have been robbed to provide material for building the broch if it had not been a part of the defensive strategy.

Soroby Cross-slab, Tiree

NL 984416. Just at the N. of the junction of B8066 and B8067 at the SW of Tiree to the N. of Balemartine.

The burial-ground at Soroby contains several Early Christian and medieval carved stones, the most remarkable of which is the cross-slab carved in deep relief and standing in its original socket-stone. On one face is a Latin cross with a dominant central boss and accompanying tendril motifs; on the other face is a ring-headed cross infilled with key-pattern. The cross-slab is powerful testimony to Early Christian activity on Tiree.

Aberdeenshire and Moray
(Map, p. xviii)

A particularly wide range of fortifications can be seen in this area, from Iron Age hillforts to Dark Age promontory forts, as well as C12 mottes and later stone castles. A speciality of Aberdeenshire is the recumbent stone circle with its implications of moon-worship. Some of the finest examples of Pictish stone-carving are to be found in the countryside here, including the great obelisk known as Sueno's Stone.

Burghead Fort and Pictish carved stones, Moray

NJ 109691. 11km. NW of Elgin on A96, B9013 and B9089 (well: Historic Scotland).

Beneath the early C19 fishing village lies one of the power-centres of the kingdom of the Picts. Burghead is easily the largest of known Pictish forts, and it possesses two other unusual features which underline its importance: a huge well and a series of bull carvings. This is likely to have been a royal fortress, strategically located on a promontory jutting out into the Moray Firth.

▼ Plan of Burghead fort (The Stationery Office)

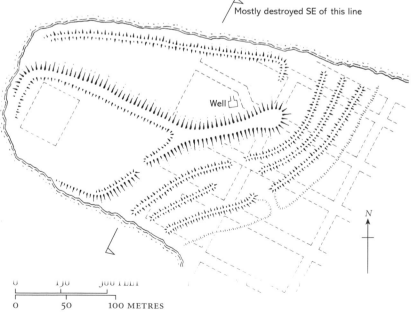

Mostly destroyed SE of this line

Well

N

0   150   300 FEET

0   50   100 METRES

Before the grid of streets and houses spread over them, the promontory was cut off from the mainland by three great ramparts and ditches. The area within them was divided into an upper citadel and a lower ward, each surrounded by a rampart, and these still survive. The grassy rampart round the citadel was originally a massive timber-laced stone wall, apparently decorated with a frieze of carved bulls as an appropriate symbol of power and prowess. Only six of these bulls survive, but some thirty were found when the ruined citadel wall was quarried for stone to build the harbour in the early C19; the six that survive have been rediscovered during subsequent repair works to the quayside. Two are displayed in Burghead Library, two are in Elgin Museum, one in the National Museums of Scotland in Edinburgh, and one in the British Museum in London.

More recently, samples of the burnt wood from the rampart on the seaward side of the citadel have yielded radiocarbon dates indicating that the inner part at least of this great fort was built sometime between the C4 and C6 AD and that it was destroyed by fire in the C9 or C10. It is tempting to attribute this destruction to Viking attack, but it could also have been the result of local resistance to the Scottish takeover of Pictland. It has been suggested that the outer defences across the promontory may belong to a prehistoric fort that was reused in Pictish times, but there is as yet no dating evidence to prove or disprove this idea.

Some excavation of the interior of the lower ward was carried out in the late C19, uncovering rows of buildings along either side. At the east end of the ward is the great well-chamber, cut out of solid rock, with a

The Moray Firth in Pictish times

The importance of this area with its fine harbours and rich hinterland is reflected by the number of symbol stones and cross-slabs that survive, as well as by the great fort at Burghead. Another Pictish fort may be seen at Portknockie on a precipitous rocky promontory known as **Green Castle** (NJ 488687), this time a tiny fort belonging to some minor chieftain. It was defended by a strong timber-laced wall, and excavation of the eroded interior revealed traces of a rectangular hall.

About half-way along the coast between Burghead and Lossiemouth is the **Sculptor's Cave** at Covesea (NJ 175707), so called from the carvings on its walls, some of which are Pictish symbols. Excavations have taken place here on two occasions, and it is clear that this large and dramatic cave has seen at least two major phases of activity, one early in the first millennium BC and another in Pictish times, contemporary with BURGHEAD fort. Symbols carved around the entrance to the cave include the triple-oval and the crescent and V-rod.

On the north side of the Firth was a major ecclesiastical centre at **Rosemarkie**, where some very fine Pictish sculpture may be seen in Groam House Museum.

water-filled cistern surrounded by a platform. Despite later modifications, this well is thought to have belonged originally to the Pictish fort.

In Burghead Library there are also two carved fragments from an early Christian stone shrine, suggesting that there was an important ecclesiastical foundation here, in keeping with the high status of the fort.

Capo Long barrow, Laurencekirk

NO 633664. 8 km. SW of Laurencekirk; from A94 take minor road (signposted RAF Edzell) for about 1 km. and park at forestry gate. Signposted path.

This type of burial mound is rare in Scotland but common in England. It is a well-preserved long mound of earth and turf, wider at the east end than at the west, which has not been excavated. Fully 80 m. long, up to 28 m. wide, and 2.5 m. high, this is a major earthwork that is likely to have involved stripping turf from a very large area. Information from excavated examples elsewhere, including one at Dalladies about 1 km. away, suggest that, under the wider end of the mound, there are likely to be traces of timber and stone structures and burials, dating perhaps as early as the fourth millennium BC.

Cullerlie Stone circle and cairns, Westhill ★

NJ 785042. 15 km. W. of Aberdeen on the A944, B9119, and B9125; signposted off a minor road to Peterculter (Historic Scotland).

This must surely rank as one of Scotland's most delightful prehistoric monuments. Eight tiny cairns nestle tightly inside a small stone circle, built on a tongue of gravel in the middle of nowhere. At the time of building in the second millennium BC, this low ridge was almost surrounded by wet bog, and the stones had to be transported here from higher ground.

The circle consists of eight irregular boulders arranged with the tallest to the north. Excavation has shown that these were set up first, along with the eight rings of kerbstones for the cairns. The largest cairn was built at the centre of the circle, with a double kerb, and the other seven were built in a ring around it. All but one of the cairns has a kerb of eleven stones— the odd man out has only nine. Before these rings were filled with smaller stones to form cairns, branches of willow were burnt amongst them and handfuls of cremated bone were placed inside them (although it is not known whether this ritual took place at the same time in all the rings).

Cullykhan Fort, Pennan

NJ 838661. From the B9031 W. of Pennan, a carpark is signposted for Cullykhan Bay.

The rocky promontory known as Castle Point has a long history of defensive use from soon after 1000 BC to the C18, encouraged by the fine natural harbour alongside. Excavation has shown that initially the promontory

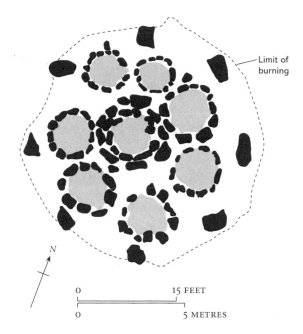

Limit of
burning

N

0   15 FEET

0   5 METRES

▲ Plan of Cullerlie stone circle (after H. E. Kilbride-Jones)

was defended by a stout wooden stockade across the landward neck. Some 400 or 500 years later, a new fortification was built, consisting of a timber-laced stone wall with an impressive gateway. This was replaced sometime after 100 BC by another such wall built a little farther to the east, which was destroyed by fire. Two ditches were subsequently dug across the promontory, as a final phase of prehistoric defence.

The strategic potential of the headland was also recognized by the builders of first a medieval castle and later, in the C18, of Fort Fiddes.

Culsh   Souterrain, Tarland

NJ 504054. Beside the B9119, 7 km. N. of Aboyne (Historic Scotland; torch at Culsh farm).

This is one of the best-preserved and most impressive of Scotland's many souterrains or underground storehouses. It was built by digging a long curving pit and lining the sides with drystone walling, large boulders at the base and smaller above. It was then roofed with large flat slabs and covered over with earth. Inside, the souterrain is 14.3 m. long and up to 1.8 m. in width and height. The entrance at ground level is likely originally to have been within a large timber roundhouse, but there has been no excavation to reveal either the remains of the house or the date of the site.

Doune of Invernochty Motte, Strathdon

NJ 351129. 25 km. W. of Alford; from the A97, take the B973 westwards.

Built in the C12, this huge Norman motte was situated to dominate the confluence of the Water of Nochty with the River Don, making good use of a natural glacial mound. The motte is still more than 18 m. high, oval in shape, and surrounded by a ditch and bank. The remains of a thick stone wall enclose the summit, but the foundations of a large rectangular building are thought to belong to a medieval church. An unusual survival is the system of sluices by which the great ditch could be flooded with water from a nearby lake.

Castles of Strathdon

This stretch of Strathdon offers a wonderful variety of castles, from the C12 motte at Doune of Invernochty to the fortification built at Corgarff in response to the Jacobite rebellion of the mid-C18. A castle with a polygonal curtain wall and massive corner-towers was built in the C13 at Kildrummy (NJ 454163), as a bastion of royal power against the troublesome province of Moray. Farther west, overlooking the confluence of the Water of Buchat with the River Don, is the fine Z-plan castle built in the C16 at Glenbuchat (NJ 397148). Another C16 tower-house at Corgarff was converted into a soldiers' barracks in 1748, and a star-shaped curtain wall was built round the tower. From this base, the Hanoverian army could control the clansmen of Strathdon.

Duffus Castle Moray

NJ 189672. 6 km. NW of Elgin, signposted off the B9012 (Historic Scotland).

After rebelling against the Scottish king, David I, in 1130, several landowners in Moray were dispossessed and their estates given to newcomers. A Fleming named Freskin was given the lands of Duffus, and he built, amidst what was then the boggy Laich of Moray, a classic motte and bailey castle. It was in existence by 1151, when the king paid a visit, but the buildings were then of timber, including the tower set on the great mound or motte. Within a century or so, the castle was rebuilt in stone.

Here, both the motte and the bailey must be largely artificial. The surviving stone castle consists of a large stone tower, the weight of which caused some subsidence of the gravel mound, with the result that the NW corner of the tower has slipped downwards. The motte is still separated from the bailey by a deep ditch, but the ditch is spanned by a curtain wall which replaced the earlier timber stockade round the bailey. The bailey would have held domestic buildings such as the bakehouse and stables. Both motte and bailey are surrounded by an outer ditch, creating a large drained enclosure.

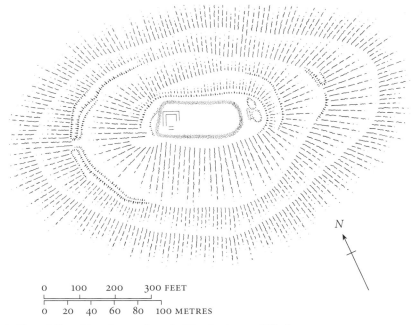

```
0       100     200     300 FEET
├───────┼───────┼───────┤
┌───┬───┬───┬───┬───────┐
0   20  40  60  80  100 METRES
```

▲ Plan of Dunnideer fort and castle (The Stationery Office)

Dunnideer Fort and castle, Insch ★

NJ 612281. 2 km. W. of Insch; track to the site from the minor road leading from the centre of Insch westwards, on the N. side of the hill.

The defensive potential of this hill has attracted at least three phases of fortification. The earliest is a sub-rectangular vitrified fort enclosing the summit, about 65 m. by 25 m. There seems later to have been a plan to build a multivallate fort taking in more ground, but this was apparently never finished, for the lines of ditch and bank are flimsy and incomplete.

Around AD 1260, one of Scotland's earliest stone castles was built within the old vitrified fort, using some of the stone from its predecessor. All that survives are the remains of a simple rectangular tower, but the best-preserved west wall includes a window that lit the great hall on the first floor.

Easter Aquhorthies Stone circle, Inverurie

NJ 732207. 3 km. W. of Inverurie on a minor road off the A96 (Historic Scotland).

A fine example of a recumbent stone circle, here the choice of stone underlines the use of colour and texture in prehistory. The circle is 19.5 m. in diameter, with eight stones of pink porphyry and a ninth of red jasper, whereas the two tall stones flanking the recumbent are of grey granite and the great recumbent itself is of red granite. There may once have been a

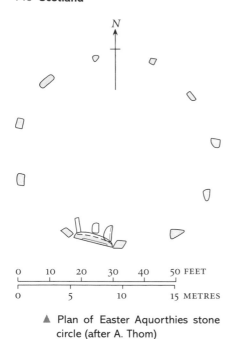

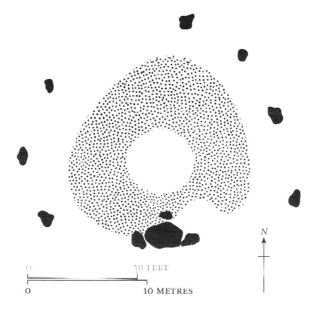

central cairn, for a cist was found here many years ago and there is still a slight bump in the ground.

Garrol Wood Stone circle, Mulloch

NO 723912. 4 km. SE of Banchory, signposted on a minor road between the B974 and the A957 (Forestry Commission).

Known also as Nine Stanes, this recumbent stone circle consisted originally of ten upright stones of red granite and a 16-ton recumbent grey boulder. The circle is somewhat flattened in shape, and it may be later in date than most true circles. A ring cairn was added within it some time after the circle itself was built; excavation in 1904 revealed a pit full of charcoal and burnt bone in the central space.

This is one of more than twenty stone circles on either side

0   10   20   30   40   50 FEET

0   5   10   15 METRES

▲ Plan of Easter Aquorthies stone circle (after A. Thom)

▼ Plan of Garrol Wood stone circle (after I. A. G. Shepherd)

10 FEET

0   10 METRES

of the River Dee, including another well-preserved example some 500 m. NW of the Garrol Wood circle (NO 717915). This is known as Eslie the Greater and it also has a secondary ring-cairn within the circle (yet another circle, Eslie the Lesser, lies to the NE at NO 722921).

INVERURIE Prehistoric ceremonial centre, Pictish symbol stones, and motte

NJ 7721.

The location of Inverurie at the confluence of the Rivers Don and Urie reflects the attraction of the area for settlement from early times onwards. As well as the monuments described here, there is a vitrified fort known as Bruce's Camp (NJ 768190) on a hill to the south and another Pictish symbol stone at Keith Hall to the east (NJ 788213). The museum in the Market Place displays many important artefacts from the area.

Broomend of Crichie Henge and stone avenue

NJ 779196. On the S. outskirts of Inverurie, minor road off the B993.

Set on a gravel terrace above the River Don are the remains of a major ceremonial centre of the later third millennium BC. Still visible is a henge, about 35 m. across, with two entrances across its ditch and bank and three standing stones within it. Two of the stones once belonged to a circle of six, which was an integral part of the monument, but the central stone is a Pictish symbol stone, which was moved here out of the way of ploughing in the C19. Carved on it are a crescent and a Pictish beast. Reused in this way in early historic times, it may originally have been part of the avenue of standing stones that once ran north and south from the henge, of which one survivor can be seen to the south. Old records of this avenue suggest that it consisted of two rows of thirty-six stones and that it ran southwards towards the river and northwards to a great stone circle, almost 50 m. in diameter, with three concentric circles of standing stones.

    Excavation inside the henge in the C19 revealed deposits of cremated bone at the base of the two original standing stones, a finely decorated stone battle-axe at the foot of the NW stone, and, buried deep at the centre of the henge, a stone cist containing both an inhumation and a cremation.

Brandsbutt Pictish symbol stone

NJ 759224. On the N. outskirts of Inverurie, signposted (Historic Scotland).

Sadly this slab was broken up as material for a field-wall, but the surviving fragments have been reassembled and they show that this is an outstanding example of the stonecarver's craft. The grooves outlining a crescent and V-rod and a serpent and Z-rod are particularly wide and well finished, and the ogham inscription alongside the symbols is similarly well executed. It reads 'Irataddoarens', a personal name. Nearby the site of a stone circle is marked out in the grass, and it may be that, like Broomend of Crichie, the symbol stone was a reused prehistoric standing stone.

Inverurie Cemetery Pictish symbol stones and motte

NJ 780206. On the SE outskirts of Inverurie, beside the B993.

The four symbol stones here have a long history, for they were formerly built first into the walls of the old church and later, after the church was demolished, into the churchyard wall, and now they stand in a neat line in the cemetery. They were presumably set up originally somewhere in the close vicinity, and there are likely to have been more such stones which have not survived. One is carved with two pairs of symbols: a crescent and V-rod above a circular disc and rectangle symbol, and a serpent and Z-rod above a double-disc and Z-rod. The second bears the circular disc and rectangle above an arch symbol, the third a disc above a double-disc and Z-rod and the fourth is carved with a horse.

The Bass of Inverurie is an artificial earthen motte which in the C12 was crowned with a timber castle and stockade.

Kintore Pictish symbol stone

NJ 793162. In the churchyard in the centre of Kintore, at the junction of the A96 and B977.

Unusually, this granite boulder bears a pair of symbols on either side, and the contrast in the quality of their execution suggests that they were carved at different times by different hands. On one side, professionally carved, are a fish and a triple-disc or cauldron symbol (note how the 'handles' of the cauldron hang from the horizontal spit, and how the fish-tail wraps round the edge of the stone). On the other side are the crescent and V-rod and Pictish beast symbols, clearly carved by a less experienced or less gifted hand.

Three other symbol stones have been found in Kintore (one is now in Inverurie Museum and two are in the National Museums of Scotland in Edinburgh). The latter two were found in the C19 in a prominent mound removed in the course of building the railway; this sounds like a motte, and the juxtaposition of motte and symbol stones echoes that at Inverurie. Were they centres of power in both Pictish and Norman times, the intervening centuries having left no physical record?

Loanhead of Daviot Stone circle, Oldmeldrum ★★

NJ 747288. Signposted from the A920 6km. NW of Oldmeldrum (Historic Scotland).

Information derived from excavation has made this one of the best understood, visitable, prehistoric sites in Scotland. There was ceremonial activity here over some fifteen centuries from around 3000 BC when the stone circle was built to around 1500 BC when the subsequent cremation cemetery went out of use. It is also now a very peaceful and evocative place to visit, its archaeology framed by low trees and its vista, typical of those chosen for recumbent stone circles, open to the south in order to monitor the movements of the moon.

The circle consists of eight standing stones and two flankers on either side of a huge, 12-ton, recumbent stone. The upright stones are graded in height from the tallest close to the recumbent to those at the 'back' of the circle, and there are cup-marks on the stone

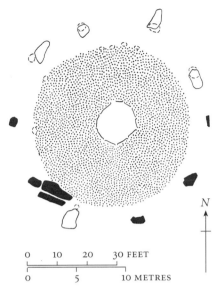

0   10   20   30 FEET

0   5   10 METRES

▲ Plan of Loanhead of Daviot stone circle and cemetery (The Stationery Office)

▼ Aerial view of Loanhead of Daviot (RCAHMS)

to the immediate east of the east flanker. Within the circle at some later date, perhaps towards the end of the third millennium, a ring-cairn was built, associated with sherds of Beaker pottery and token deposits of cremated bone. The cairn has a neat stone kerb, which curves round the back of the recumbent. Small stone cairns were added round the base of six of the standing stones.

Alongside the circle is a later cremation cemetery enclosed within a low stone bank with two opposing entrances. A central pit held the partially cremated remains of a man, apparently holding a stone pendant, and twenty deposits of cremated bone were buried around him, some in pottery urns and others in small pits. The deposits represented thirty-one people, including children, perhaps all members of one small community.

Maiden Stone Chapel of Garioch

NJ 703247. 7 km. NW of Inverurie, on minor road off the A96 (Historic Scotland).

This is a very powerful cross-slab, carved in the late C8 or C9 from a 3 m.-tall slab of pink granite. The cross faces west and has suffered from weathering, but the design is still clear: a ring-headed cross flanked by panels of decoration, with a human figure between two fish-monsters above, which is thought to represent the biblical story of Jonah and the whale. Below the cross is a panel of superb and elaborate decoration, based on a circle of spiral motifs, surrounded by a ring of key-pattern. Both narrow sides are decorated, one with geometric interlace and the other with continuous pairs of knots. The back of the slab is divided into starkly simple panels which create a pleasing contrast with the rest of the stone. At the top are at least three animals, and below are the notched rectangle and Z-rod symbol, the 'Pictish beast' (dolphin), and the mirror and comb symbols. The teeth on either side of this sturdy comb are carved individually.

This striking example of late Pictish art became part of later folk tradition, thus acquiring its name. The maiden in question was the daughter of the laird of Balquhain (the remains of the castle of Balquhain lie east of Chapel of Garioch). She is said to have been baking bannocks on her wedding day, when she rashly accepted a bet with a stranger that her baking would be finished before he could build a road to the top of Bennachie or she would be his. He was of course the Devil in disguise and he won the bet. She fled and was turned to stone as he caught her, the notch in the side of the stone showing where for a moment he held her.

High above and to the SW of the Maiden Stone, a great stone fort crowns the summit of the Mither Tap of Bennachie (NJ 682223). The design of this fort, with a citadel and annexe, is closer to that used in the Pictish period than in earlier times, but this intriguing possibility has yet to be proved.

Memsie Cairn, Fraserburgh

NJ 976620. Beside the B9032, between the A92 and A981 S. of Fraserburgh (Historic Scotland).

There is an astounding contrast between this huge primeval pile of stones and the cosy domestic landscape around it—like finding an elephant in a rose garden. It is fully 24 m. in diameter and 4.4 m. high and was doubtless once larger, a great cairn covering the grave of a revered leader of some 3,000 years ago. It consists of large water-worn pebbles and is as bare of vegetation today as when it was built. Two other such cairns are recorded nearby, but they no longer survive.

New and Old Kinord Settlements, cross-slab, and crannog, Aboyne ★

NJ 449001 and 444002. In Muir of Dinnet National Nature Reserve, 8 km. W. of Aboyne; access from B9119 N. of Dinnet on A93.

At New Kinord is a group of circular stone-built houses, one with a souterrain, set amongst stock-enclosures and droveways. Farther west, a similar settlement at Old Kinord is enclosed within stone banks and surrounded

▼ Plan of New Kinord settlement (after A. Ogston)

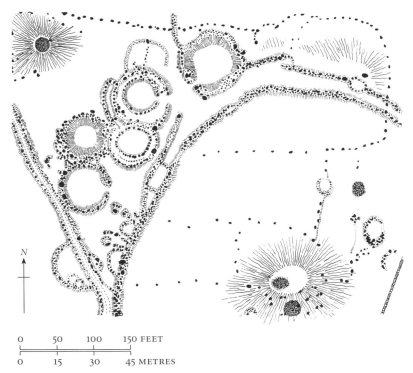

```
0        50       100      150 FEET

0        15       30       45 METRES
```

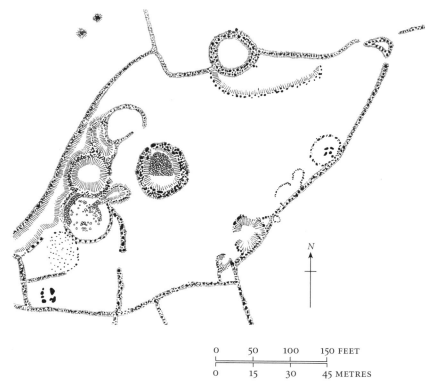

▲ Plan of Old Kinord settlement (after A. Ogston)

by fields and heaps of stones cleared from the fields to allow cultivation. Despite some excavation, neither farming settlement can be dated more closely than to the late first millennium BC.

From the track to the south of the two settlements, there is access to a well-preserved cross-slab dating to the C9 AD beside Loch Kinord at NO 440997 and a view from the lochside of a small crannog at NO 443995. Five logboats have been recovered from this loch.

Old Keig Stone circle, Alford

NJ 596193. From the A980 3.5 km. E. of Alford, take the B992 N. to Keig; from the crossroads, take a minor road NW past Old Keig, park at quarry, and follow belt of trees to S.

Although little remains of the rest of the circle, the recumbent stone is breathtaking in size, at 53 tons easily the largest surviving of any recumbent stone circle. The two flankers are still in position, and one other upright of a circle that was once 20 m. in diameter. The great recumbent is not a local stone. It is a boulder of gneiss and had to be hauled here from the Don Valley, some 10 km. away.

Peel of Lumphanan Motte, Lumphanan

NJ 576036. 15 km. NW of Banchory on the A980 and 1 km. SW of Lumphanan, signposted (Historic Scotland).

Passengers on the old railway between Banchory and Aboyne would have had a remarkable view of this C13 motte beside the line. The artificial mound survives 9 m. high above a wide surrounding ditch, and water may have been diverted into the ditch from the adjacent stream. Excavation has shown that the stone wall round the summit dates only from the C18, and the foundations of a late C15 manor house survive on the flat top of the motte. The original buildings were of timber, apart from a stone-cobbled trackway leading across the ditch and up to the summit.

The motte was built by the Durward earls of Atholl, possibly as a hunting lodge. Some 200 years earlier, Macbeth was killed at Lumphanan.

Rhynie Pictish symbol stones

NJ 499265. Rhynie lies at the junction of the A97 and A941 about 13 km. S. of Huntly.

The great stone fort on Tap o'Noth suggests that this area was a power-centre in Iron-Age times (see below), and the number of symbol stones found in Rhynie implies that it was also important in early Pictish times. Seven stones have been found in the vicinity, and another, known as the Craw Stane, still stands on a hillside above the Water of Bogie immediately south of the village. In the car park shelter near the church are two stones incised with symbols, one bearing a graceful beast's head (probably an otter), a double-disc and Z-rod, a mirror and a single-sided comb, and the other a double-disc and Z-rod, a crescent and V-rod, and a mirror. Two very weathered stones stand on the village green, and there is a cast of the slab known as Rhynie Man in the entrance to the school. It bears an incised male figure with an extraordinarily malevolent air about him; carrying an axe over one shoulder and dressed in a tunic, he has a great hooked nose, glaring eye, and bared teeth. He may represent some character from Pictish mythology.

▲ Rhynie Man
(I. A. G. and
A. N. Shepherd)

(The original stone is preserved in Woodhill House, the Council offices in Aberdeen.)

The Craw Stane is likely still to be in its original position, and aerial photographs show ploughed-out earthworks around it. This is an irregular slab of granite carved with a fish (salmon) and a 'Pictish beast' (dolphin) facing south.

Strichen Stone circle

NJ 936544. 1 km. SW of Strichen, access from the A981 along a track to Strichen Mains farm, turn right then left, park, and follow path up hill.

After destruction in the late C18, this recumbent stone circle was rebuilt to the south of its original position. This in turn was destroyed in the C20. But the original site was excavated, allowing the circle to be re-created to its first builders' design. About 15 m. across, the circle consists of a stony bank strewn with white quartz chippings, in which the upright stones are set. On the south side are the great recumbent and its attendant taller stones. Outside the circle on the east is a large pitted stone on which the quartz was apparently shattered. A stone with six cup-marks was found buried within the circle and a central small cist held cremated bone. The cremated remains of a woman were found buried in the bank.

Sueno's Stone Forres   ★

NJ 046595. On the NE outskirts of Forres, signposted off the B9011 to Kinloss (Historic Scotland).

Misleadingly named in the C18 after a C11 Danish king, this elegant obelisk is in fact the work of Pictish sculptors in the late C9 or C10. It has been described as 'a monument which invites superlatives', and it is indeed an outstanding and unique creation. The sandstone from which it was carved has weathered badly over the centuries, but most of the designs are still clear and it is now protected within a tall glass and steel pavilion. Excavation round the base of the stone yielded no evidence of burials but confirmed that it is likely to be in its original position.

The slab is more than 6.5 m. high and bears a cross on the west face and a complicated series of battle scenes on the other. The cross has a ring-head and interlace decoration, and the panel beneath its base shows two large figures bending over a central figure, with a smaller attendant on either side, which has been interpreted as illustrating the inauguration of a king. The battle scenes on the back show massed foot soldiers and cavalry and the beheading of the defeated. The history of the theories that have been put forward about the battle is a saga in itself, but most agree that the event commemorated is more likely to have been local than biblical. At present, the consensus of opinion favours a battle between the Picts and Scots in the C9, won by the Scots, whose ruler was inaugurated king over both peoples—either a provincial king in Moray or the high king of Scotland. If this was the case, the victorious Scots commissioned this piece of propaganda in stone from a Pictish master craftsman.

Both narrow sides of the stone bear interlaced decoration, including, on the upper part of the south face, spirals of foliage in which small human figures are perched, which is a motif borrowed by the Picts from Northumbrian art.

Sunhoney Stone circle, Echt ★

NJ 715056. About 22 km. W. of Aberdeen on the A944 and B9119; some 2 km. W. of Echt, take a track to the right to Sunhoney farm. The circle is in a clump of trees W. of the farm.

The circle here is more than 25 m. in diameter, with eleven standing stones of red granite or gneiss and a recumbent slab of grey granite over which the skyline of the southern hills may be seen. The slab seems to have toppled over, and its now upper surface is decorated with thirty-one cup-marks. A ring-cairn was added inside the circle, and excavation in 1865 revealed deposits of cremated bone in the central space.

Another fine recumbent stone circle may be seen about 2 km. to the west in Midmar kirkyard.

Tap o' Noth Fort, Rhynie

NJ 484293. A track leads up from the A941 W. of Rhynie to the top of the hill.

Perched on the apex of a hill at 563 m. OD, this fort is not only one of the highest in Scotland but also one of the oldest. There are two stone walls, an outer one enclosing about 21 ha. and a massive inner wall forming a rectangular citadel, 105 × 40 m., at the top of the hill. The inner wall was built with an internal timber framework and was set on fire, causing extensive vitrification; scientific dating of the melted stone suggests that the fire took place early in the second millennium BC. Excavation at the end of the C19 revealed the wall to be up to 8 m. wide and surviving to a height of 3.5 m. There was a large water-cistern at the south end of the citadel.

More than 100 house-platforms have been identified within the outer enclosure. Despite its elevation, this prestigious fort was clearly the home of a large tribal unit at a time when the climate was reasonably warm and dry.

Tullos Hill Cairn cemetery, Aberdeen

NJ 957036. Park in the car park at NJ 949029 (Altens Industrial Estate) and walk uphill to the NE.

Aberdeen must have been an important harbour for the NE coast of Scotland in prehistoric as in later times. The hills south of Nigg Bay still bear the remains of a group of burial cairns, which hint at the prehistoric archaeology which once underlay the city. The four surviving cairns are known as Crab's Cairn, Baron's Cairn, Cat's Cairn, and Tullos Cairn; up to 20 m. in diameter and 2.5 m. high, they represent an important burial-place of the early second millennium BC, which must have been visible and impressive from the sea. Nothing is known, unfortunately, of the burials that they covered.

Highland South (Map, p. xix)

For convenience, the southern part of the huge Highland area is taken to extend as far north as the Dornoch Firth on the east coast and Applecross and Skye on the west (Skye is accessible by bridge from the mainland). A special kind of chambered tomb is typified by the tranquil Balnuaran of Clava, and excellent brochs are to be found in Skye. The fertile lands around Inverness and the Moray Firth seem to have been at the heart of the early Pictish kingdom; it is here that the earliest forms of symbol are found, and here that St Columba came in AD 565 to seek audience of the Pictish king. The strength of Christianity in the Black Isle and Easter Ross in the C8 and C9 has tangible expression in the great cross-slabs such as Rosemarkie and Nigg.

Applecross Cross-slabs

NG 713458. From the A896 N. of Sanachan, a minor road runs NW to Applecross, and the church is at the N. end of the bay.

The monastery of Applecross was founded in AD 673 by an Irish monk, St Maelrubha, yet the old name Aporcrosan is Pictish and the sculpture here shows close links with ST VIGEANS, a Pictish monastery in Angus. The explanation is that, until the C9, the Applecross area was part of Pictland. The 3 m.-high cross-slab beside the modern gate is thought not to be in its original position; the ringed cross depicts a free-standing cross in Irish taste, but it is carved on a slab in Pictish tradition; lacking ornament, it is difficult to date but is probably C9.

Inside the church are three fragments of decorated cross-slabs, the larger of which displays a very high quality of carving. Only about a third survives of what must have been a magnificent work of art. It was a ringed cross with panels of interlace and key-pattern that show links with Rosemarkie, and the intact background panel is filled with superb triple-spiral work, including bird's head terminals such as those at St Vigeans, Arbroath (cross-slab No. 7).

Maintaining links across a Pictland without roads cannot have been easy, but the attraction of Applecross is clear, with its broad sheltered bay, fertile valley, and fresh water from the River Applecross.

Balnuaran of Clava Chambered cairns, Inverness   ★★

NH 757444. From the B9006 about 7 km. E. of Inverness, take the B851 and turn left at crossroads, signposted on the right after 1.5 km. (Historic Scotland).

One of the most beautiful legacies of Scotland's remote past, the three pale cairns lie in a serene woodland glade. Each of the cairns has a kerb of large boulders and is surrounded by a circle of standing stones, and both the kerbstones and the free-standing stones increase in height towards the SW. The cairns lie in line from NE to SW, and the importance of the SW orientation is underlined further by the fact that the entrance passages of the cairns at either end are also aligned to the SW. Clearly there is an interest here in the midwinter sunset. The central cairn has no passage, and three of its encircling standing stones are linked to the cairn itself by low banks of stone. Near the west side of this cairn is a ring of boulders only 3.7 m. in diameter, which is thought to be the remains of a kerb-cairn, perhaps later in date than the larger cairns.

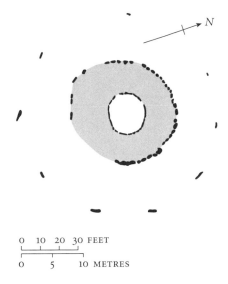

▲ Plan of central cairn at Balnuaran of Clava (after S. Piggott)

Four and a half thousand years ago or so, when the cairns were built, their centres would not have been open to the sky as they are today. The chambers of the two passage graves would have had corbelled domes beneath a covering cairn, and the space inside the central ring-cairn would have been filled with stones. A number of stones bearing cup-marks were built into the structure of these cairns, the most easily visible being those on a kerbstone on the north side of the most northerly cairn, and those in the passage of the same cairn (the last slab on the left before entering the chamber).

Caisteal Grugaig Broch, Totaig

NG 866250. From Shiel Bridge on the A87, a minor road runs NW along the shore of Loch Duich to Totaig; footpath W. through forest (Forestry Commission).

The broch itself is clear of trees and it is possible to appreciate a superb view across the loch—from here, the broch-dwellers would have been able to monitor traffic between three sea-lochs, Loch Alsh, Loch Duich, and Loch Long. The broch was cleared out at the end of the C19, and the surviving structure is impressive, solidly built with large blocks and displaying a triangular lintel over the entrance. The entrance passage shows checks and bar-hole for the door, and a spacious guard-cell opening off the left-hand side.

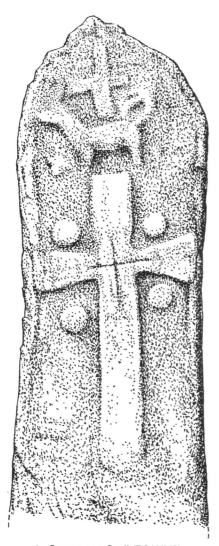

Internally, the floor is very rocky and irregular and suggests that this level was used for storage, while the living quarters were on a timber upper floor. Three doorways in the inner face of the wall lead to a finely corbelled cell, a stair and an intramural gallery. From the stair, another doorway led into the first-floor accommodation.

Camus nan Geall

Chambered cairn, Kilchoan

NM 560619. From the A861 at Salen, follow the B8007 W. along the Ardnamurchan peninsula to a car-park some 2.5 km. W. of Glenmore, and walk NW to the bay.

The Bay of Camus nan Geall neatly illustrates the importance of topographical location in our appreciation of archaeological sites. The tight confines of the arable land between the shore and the rising ground might well have been the principal farming area for the early agricultural community, whose burial-place lies at the head of the bay. Part of the chamber and forecourt survive, and the size of the portal stones, side-slabs, and displaced capstone illustrate powerfully the engineering skills available 5,000 years ago.

▲ Camus nan Geall (RCAHMS)

There is an impressive standing stone some 90 m. south of the chambered cairn, perhaps of neolithic or Bronze Age date. It was decorated in early Christian times with two crosses, one with pellets between the arms, and an animal, possibly a dog. The little burial-ground nearby is not itself ancient but was perhaps created for the Roman Catholic members of the family of the Campbells of Ardslignish in the C18.

Another fine chambered tomb can be seen by continuing west on the B8007 to Kilchoan; on the rising ground west of the village stands Greadal

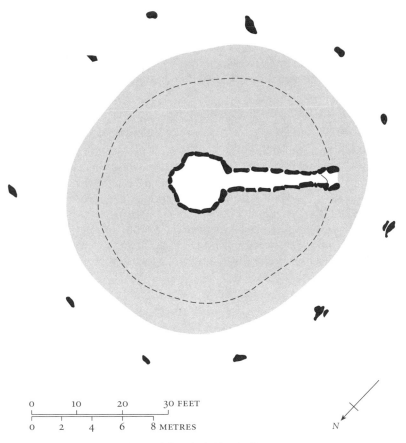

0   10   20   30 FEET

0   2   4   6   8 METRES   N

▲ Corrimony chambered cairn (after A. S. Henshall)

Fhinn (NM 476639), its orthostats almost bare of cairn, which has been robbed away to build field-walls. Two chambers are exposed, the main chamber of Hebridean type with a slipped capstone across its entrance and a smaller box-like chamber spanned by a single capstone. Both were originally enclosed within a round cairn.

Corrimony   Chambered cairn, Glen Urquhart

NH 383303. From Drumnadrochit on the A82 SW of Inverness, take the A831 W. along Glen Urquhart; signposted minor road on the left (Historic Scotland).

This is a Clava cairn, the type of tomb to which Balnuaran of Clava lent its name, and the similarities between the two sites are readily appreciated. Both lie on flat ground in river valleys, and Corrimony was built to the same plan as the two passage graves at Balnuaran of Clava. Here eleven stones surround the cairn, and both the chamber and the entrance-passage are still partially roofed. A large slab lies on top of the cairn, carved with more than 20 cup-marks, and this may have been the lintel at the apex of the corbelled dome over the chamber. Despite clearance in the C19 down to floor level, excavation in 1953 revealed, beneath the cobbled floor of the chamber, traces of a crouched burial.

Craig Phadrig Fort, Inverness

NH 640452. In Craigphadrig Forest 2.5 km. W. of Inverness from A862.

Although surrounded by forest, the fort on the summit of the hill is bare of trees, and the two ramparts are easily traced. Both were built of stone with a timber framework which subsequently caught fire, causing the stone to vitrify, and radiocarbon dating indicates that the fort was built in the C5 or C4 BC. Excavation in 1971 found evidence to suggest that the ramparts were later refurbished, and artefacts from the interior of the fort included imported pottery and a clay mould dating to the C6 or C7 AD. This may well have been the stronghold of a Pictish warlord.

Dun-da-Lamh Fort, Laggan

NN 582929. From the A86 Spean Bridge to Newtonmore road, about 3 km. SW of Laggan, park beside cottages on the W. side of the road and walk N. and then W. along a track into the forest.

This may be another Dark Age fort, now surrounded by trees but still commanding wide views over the two river valleys above whose confluence it was sited, Strathspey and Strath Mashie. The stone wall enclosing this craggy hill must have been immensely impressive in its day, for it was very thick and may have been quite high, and the shape of the hill resulted in pronounced 'corners'. It was also very well built, as can be seen where the fallen stone has been cleared away from the inner face.

Dun Telve and Dun Troddan Brochs, Glenelg ★★

NG 829172 (Dun Telve), 833172 (Dun Troddan). From Shiel Bridge on the A87, a minor road leads W. to Glenelg and thence SE along Gleann Beag (Historic Scotland).

The modern road from Shiel Bridge follows the line of the old military road to the Hanoverian Bernera Barracks built in the early 1720s against the Jacobite threat (NG 815197). Gleann Beag runs parallel to the south and contains two of the best-preserved and most informative brochs in Scotland—indeed, at 10 m. Dun Telve is the second tallest broch after Mousa in Shetland. This is despite its location on the valley-floor, which made it vulnerable to stone-robbing in the past. Such a non-defensive situation underlines the prestige element in broch-building. Dun Troddan is set on a terrace above the valley, but even there it was designed to impress rather than to be impregnable.

▲ Dun Telve, drawn by M. Griffith in 1772

There are outer structures built of huge blocks in front of the entrance into Dun Telve, but their relationship to the broch is obscure. A doorway in the entrance passage leads to a cell and to a stair, and, where the broch-wall has been robbed, it is possible to see five galleries within the wall still standing. On the internal face of the wall, the usual ledge to support a timber upper floor can be seen, and above it, at a height of almost 9 m. above the ground, another ledge to support either another floor or a roof over the first. The voids in the inner wall-face were a device to lighten the wall, especially over the entrance.

About 500 m. farther east along the glen stands Dun Troddan, but it is not known, unfortunately, whether the two brochs were contemporary. Part of the broch remains to a height of 7.6 m., and the corbelled guard-cell at the entrance survives intact. A doorway beneath a void in the inner wall-face leads to another cell and to a stair that rises nine steps up to an intramural gallery. Originally the stair continued above this level to upper galleries. Excavation in 1920 revealed a central hearth at ground level, encircled by a ring of post-holes which would have helped to support the timber upper floor. Such evidence of internal structures above ground level is rare, but elsewhere the posts may have stood on stone slabs. It is arguable whether the upper floor extended across the entire interior of the broch or took the form of a gallery around the inner face of the broch wall.

Edderton Pictish symbol stone and cross-slab

NH 708850 (symbol stone), 719842 (cross-slab). Edderton village is on the A9 about 8 km. W. of Tain.

The symbol stone stands in a field to the north of the A9. The shape and height (almost 3 m.) of the stone suggest that it was an early prehistoric standing stone to which symbols were added in Pictish times; the two symbols are worn but well carved, a fish above a double-disc and Z-rod. Edderton old church is about 1 km. east of the modern village, beside the A9 bridge over the Edderton Burn (there is a car-park). In the churchyard, a few metres from the gate, stands a cross-slab probably of C9 date, carved with a cross above two panels of horsemen. The rider in the upper panel in its arched frame perhaps represents the deceased warlord, while the lower panel (partly hidden in the ground) may indicate the warriors whom he commanded, each carrying spear, shield, and sword.

The carved stones at Rosemarkie, Nigg, and Shandwick make a splendid Pictish day out, particularly if it is leavened by exploring the many delights of Cromarty on the way. There was once another great cross-slab at Hilton of Cadboll, about 3 km. north along the coast from Shandwick; it is now in the National Museums of Scotland in Edinburgh, after an ignominious history in which it was converted to a grave-slab in the C17, moved to the grounds of Invergordon Castle in the C19, and in 1921 sent to London. Its stay in London was brief, however, for public pressure soon brought it back to Scotland and its final resting place in Edinburgh. This is an extreme example of the way in which even large carved stones can be treated as portable artefacts. The foundations of an early church in a rectangular enclosure may be seen at Hilton of Cadboll (Historic Scotland).

Farther north again, at Portmahomack, an ancient harbour, is **Tarbat** old church with a medieval burial-vault and a display of Pictish carved fragments. This was the site of an important Pictish monastery in the C8 and C9.

Nigg Pictish cross-slab ★

NH 804717. From the B9176 about 2 km. N. of Nigg Ferry, a minor road leads NE to Nigg; the stone is in the church.

The Nigg cross-slab used to stand in the churchyard, but it is not known whether that was its original location. Sadly it was blown down and broken, but it has been reassembled, some 2.2 m. high, and is still a magnificent example of sculpture carved in an effective blend of high and low relief. The decoration on the cross combines panels of geometric key-pattern and interlace with elongated animals intricately woven together. The background panels almost overwhelm the cross, with their great bosses encircled by snakes. There is strong Christian iconography here, for the eight bosses in one panel represent the eight days of Passion week from Palm Sunday to Easter Day, and the scene in the triangular pediment depicts the biblical story of Paul and Anthony in the desert, to whom a raven brought a loaf of bread.

The carving on the back of the slab gives the impression of looking through an ornate doorway into a landscape peopled with figures. In the foreground a hunt races across, the deer pursued by a hound and a horseman, and a man on foot at the rear. Beyond are biblical figures of David slaying a lion, a sheep and a harp representing David the shepherd and David the musician, and the armed figure of David the warrior. At the top of the scene, as it were hovering in the sky, are two symbols: the 'Pictish beast' and the eagle. The frame is divided up into panels of various ingenious interlace.

Rosemarkie Pictish carved stones ★

NH 737576. In Groam House Museum, High Street, Rosemarkie, on the A832, NE of Inverness.

Groam House Museum has become a centre for Pictophiles, with its excellent collection of carved stones and inspired bookshop. All the stones were found in the vicinity, in the church or its kirkyard or in the village, and it is clear both from the high quality of the sculpture and from historical sources that there was a major monastery here in the C8 and C9 AD. Like most of the modern village, the monastery would have been built on the raised beach above the shore. By tradition, Rosemarkie was founded by Curitan (also known as

▲ Rosemarkie cross-slab (RCAHMS)

Boniface) in the late C7 or early C8, and the great cross-slab carved around the end of the C8 testifies to the patronage enjoyed by the monastery.

This 2.6 m.-high cross-slab is an astounding work of art. Its designer lost no opportunity for decoration, with the result that every part of every surface has been carved with intricate ornament. It survives almost 3 m. high, but the very top is missing. There is a cross on both faces, but, instead of the normal full-length cross, these are equal-armed crosses within square panels, and it is likely that they echo contemporary fine metalwork such as jewelled fittings for illuminated gospel-books. The Rosemarkie cross-slab also bears Pictish symbols: two intact huge crescents and V-rods are separated by a double-disc and Z-rod, and above them are the remains of a fourth crescent and V-rod, while below are two mirror symbols beneath the lower crescent. The crescents are filled with interlace and the discs with ornamented bosses. The rest of the stone is covered with panels of exquisite animal interlace.

There are also fragments of other decorative cross-slabs. Even more importantly for information about the early church building, there are long slabs with panels of key-pattern and spirals, which are likely to have formed a low screen between nave and chancel.

Shandwick Pictish cross-slab, Balintore

NH 855747. From the B9176 between Nigg Ferry and the A9 S. of Tain, a minor road leads E. to Shandwick and Balintore, passing the stone in a field on the left just short of Shandwick.

This superb cross-slab is not only one of the few Pictish stones still in its original location, but also one of the few to have had excavation round its base. Despite old reports of graves in the vicinity, no trace of burials was found close to the stone. The reason for the excavation was that the stone was to be taken to Edinburgh for conservation prior to the erection over it of a protective glass box—all as a result of the concern and fund-raising efforts of the local community. Shandwick Bay has been an important harbour for many centuries, and the stone has been a useful sea-mark. The choice of this location may well reflect such a use in Pictish times, as well as its primary function as a prayer-cross.

Standing about 2.7 m. high, this great slab shows clear links with that at Nigg in its use of raised bosses, but they are less successful here. The cross is outlined with bosses, and there were once four gigantic bosses encircled with heavy snakes which simply meet head to head, unlike the fluid snakes of Nigg. But it is with the back of the stone that Shandwick comes into its own with wonderful panels of decoration. At the top are two huge symbols, the double-disc and 'Pictish beast', above a panel crowded with figures moving from left to right. In the distance are two horsemen and a hound pursuing a deer, in the middle distance on the left a horseman carrying a spear and a curious walking figure in a large headdress and carrying a drinking horn, surrounded by animals and birds (a god of the forest?). On the right beneath the deer is a small figure on what appears to be a goat. The foreground contains two men fighting with swords and shields, two cattle apparently watching the scene beyond, and an archer crouched with a crossbow aimed at a deer. The archer appears to have a falcon on his back.

The panel below is truly a *tour de force* of whirling spirals. There are fifty-two spirals arranged symmetrically in concentric circles, conveying almost a sense of gazing into a galaxy of spinning stars. There are panels of interlace decoration below, but they are partially hidden within the plinth in which the stone is bedded.

Strathpeffer Fort and Pictish symbol stone

NH 4858. On the A835 W. of Dingwall.

High on the ridge above the C19 spa at Strathpeffer is a fine prehistoric fort, **Knock Farril** (NH 504585). Its strategic location is best appreciated from the A835 approaching Strathpeffer, but the easiest route up to the fort is from Maryburgh to the south of the ridge. This was the scene of the earliest excavation in Scotland in 1774, which has left three distinct troughs across the interior and the defences. Sub-rectangular in shape, the fort was defended by a timber-laced stone wall, which was set on fire at some stage, resulting in vitrified masses of stone, particularly along the south side. Scientific dating of samples of the melted rock indicates that this is a very early fort, which was destroyed around 1100 BC. It is in such a defensive location, however, that it would be surprising if it had not also been used at later periods.

In Strathpeffer itself, signposted from the A835, is a Pictish symbol stone (NH 485585) carved with a decorative arch above a stylized eagle. The Gaelic name for this stone is Clach Tiompan, meaning sounding stone, and it is tempting to attribute the broken top right edge to repeated hammering to make the stone 'ring'.

SKYE

The romantic island of Skye has more than its fair share of well-preserved brochs and broch-like forts. There are also the remains of at least twelve chambered cairns, although most are very ruinous, and it would seem that the population of the island throughout prehistory was relatively high in number. The distribution of Viking Age finds and place-names suggests that Norse settlers took over the northern, more fertile, part of the island, leaving the southern part to the indigenous, dominantly Pictish, inhabitants.

Clach Ard Pictish symbol stone, Tote

NG 421490. About 7 km. NW of Portree on the A850, the B8036 leads N. and after 500 m. a minor road is signposted Tote and the stone is on the N. side of the road.

The original location of this stone is not known, for it was only recognized in 1880, at which time it was serving as a door-jamb at Tote. Not surprisingly, the stone is very worn, but it is still possible to make out a crescent and V-rod, a double-disc and Z-rod, and a mirror and comb.

This is one of three symbol stones found in Skye (another can be seen in Dunvegan Castle), and a symbol-bearing cross-slab survives in the garden of Raasay House, on the island of Raasay off the east coast of Skye.

Dun Ardtreck Broch, Carbost

NG 335358. From the A863 SE of Bracadale, take the B8009 through Carbost and the left turn for Fiscavaig; after about 1 km., a minor road leads N. towards Ardtreck Point.

This was a perfect spot for a fortified residence, a natural rocky knoll beneath which steep cliffs fall 20 m. into the sea. Effectively, this is half a broch, and excavation has shown that it was never a complete circle nor, with the natural defence of the cliff, did it need to be. A well-preserved wall survives to almost 2 m. and encloses an area some 13 × 10.5 m. The entrance passage has door-checks and a guard-cell, and there are openings on the inside of the wall to intramural galleries.

▼ Plan of Dun Ardtreck broch (after E. W. MacKie)

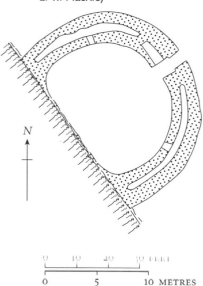

0   5   10 METRES

Dun Beag Broch, Bracadale ★

NG 339386. Signposted on the A863 just W. of Bracadale (Historic Scotland).

There is no obvious reason for this fine broch to be here. It stands on a knoll with little natural defence but with wide views over the surrounding landscape—as if staking a claim to territorial rights. The entrance is on the east, through a wall 4.3 m. thick and faced with good large blocks of stone. Notice the checks for a wooden door one-third of the way along the passage. The cells in the wall on either side are entered from inside the broch and appear not to have any control over the entrance passage, again suggesting that defence was notional. One cell gives access to a stair inside the wall, and opposite, on the other side of the broch-interior, is the entry to an intra-mural gallery.

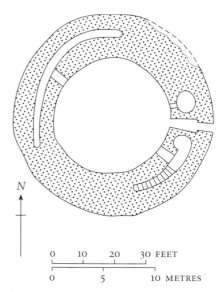

Dun Beag means 'small fort', and it has a partner, Dun Mor, 'large fort', a little to the north, although little trace can be seen of the Iron Age fort. There is also a round house and a souterrain in the vicinity. The area was clearly favoured for settlement from prehistoric through until later times, for there are foundations of rectangular buildings and bound-ary walls to the north and NE of the broch, and several small oval buildings which are probably shielings to the SE. When the

0   10   20   30 FEET

0   5   10 METRES

▲ Plan of Dun Beag broch (after E. W. MacKie)

broch was cleared in the early C20, medieval and later coins and artefacts were found, suggesting that it had continued to offer shelter.

Dun Fiadhairt Broch, Dunvegan

NG 231504. From Dunvegan, take the A850 N. past Dunvegan Castle and continue on the minor road over a causeway between two lochs; park and walk W. on to the Fiadhairt peninsula.

This broch on its rocky knoll was cleared out in 1914, and the internal wall-face rises to about 2 m. Most unusually, there are two entrances: the normal passage with its door-checks and flanking guard-cells, and, in the opposite wall, a low opening that not only allows access to an intramural gallery but also leads outside the broch. Another internal doorway serves a pair of cells within the broch-wall, and a fourth leads both to a short gallery and to stairs rising up inside the wall.

Another good broch is clearly visible to the left of the B884 about 2.5 km. SW of Dunvegan.

Dun Hallin Broch, Waternish

NG 256592. From the A850 about 5 km. NE of Dunvegan, take the B886 N. to Stein, thence a minor road NW along the peninsula to Hallin; turn right towards Geary and park after 500 m. The broch is in moorland to the S.

This is one of three brochs on the west side of the Waternish peninsula, all situated 500 m. to 1 km. inland, overlooking the habitable lower ground along the coast. Though ruinous, the outer wall-face of Dun Hallin is impressive with its neat courses of square blocks, and the locations of the entrance and intramural gallery are visible. Beyond the broch are traces of an outer wall enclosing the level plateau. There are also low mounds marking the sites of shielings. Farther north are Dun Borrafiach (NG 235637) and Dun Gearymore (NG 236649).

From the road junction, it is worth continuing another 1 km. towards Trumpan to see the remains of the C18 crofts of Halistra along the east side of the road. Halistra is a Scandinavian name and implies that settlement here goes back into the Viking Age. Late medieval graveslabs survive at the ruined church of Trumpan, the old parish church for Waternish.

Dun Ringill Fort, Kirkibost

NG 561170. The A881 from Broadford leads SW towards Elgol; park at Kilmarie and walk towards Kilmarie House, cross a bridge on the left just short of the house, and follow the path E. along the shore.

Somewhat irregular in shape as it fits snugly on its promontory, this is almost a broch and demonstrates the problems of terminology with many such small fortified sites. The entrance passage has door-checks and bar-holes, and there is a corbelled cell built within the wall. Its defensive potential was recognized in later medieval times, when it was refortified as a castle. A ditch was dug across the neck of the promontory, the original entrance-passage was elongated by adding masonry to the inner end, and two rectangular buildings were constructed inside the fort. Tradition relates that it was the residence of the chief of the clan MacKinnon.

▼ Plan of Rubh' an Dunain chambered cairn (after A. S. Henshall)

N

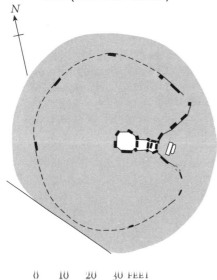

0   10   20   30 FEET

0   5   10 METRES

Rubh' an Dunain

Chambered cairn, Loch Brittle   ★

NG 393163. From the A863 SE of Bracadale, take the B8009 W. and, after about 2 km., a minor road S. to the head of Loch Brittle; a footpath leads SW to Rubh' an Dunain (a round trip of about 11 km.).

Choose a fine day for this long but satisfying walk below the famous Cuillin Hills. Almost at the end of the promontory is a loch, and the cairn is beside the wall running from the NW end of the loch to the sea. This is a round cairn with a concave forecourt in front of the entrance to the chamber. Despite robbing, the cairn is still 3.3 m. high, and the chamber and façade are impressive. On either side of the entrance, the façade is constructed with upright pillars connected with neat drystone walling, and this seems to have continued all round the cairn as a kerb. The same method was used to line the short entrance-passage and the chamber. Four lintels are still in place roofing the passage and the small antechamber, rising from about 80 cm. in height at the entrance to 1.6 m. at the innermost surviving lintel. The polygonal burial chamber is now roofless. Excavation in the 1930s recovered remains of five adults from the chamber, along with neolithic and Beaker pottery, flint and quartz chips, and pieces of pumice.

The south end of the loch is linked to the sea by a curious small water-way popularly known as the 'Viking Canal'; it is certainly artificial but far too small for boats, and some industrial purpose in medieval times is likely. On a promontory to the east is a small Iron Age fort (NG 395159).

Highland North (Map, p. xix)

Throughout time, settlement in the Highlands has been concentrated on the fertile land in river valleys and along the coast. The spectacular coastal landscape of Caithness and eastern Sutherland is thickly dotted with brochs, mostly surviving as prominent grassy mounds, but intrepid excavators of the C19 cleared out quite a number. Some have extensive domestic settlement outside the broch, and these have yielded vast assemblages of artefacts but not, alas, a matching record of the excavations. There are also excellent chambered cairns and, a Caithness and Sutherland speciality, fan-shaped settings of standing stones.

Achavanich Stone setting, Latheron

ND 187417. From the A895 Latheron to Thurso road, take a minor road SE at Achavanich, signposted Lybster. The stones are on the E. side of the road just over 1 km. from the junction.

Although the individual stones are little more than 1 m. tall, the overall effect of this U-shaped setting is impressive against the bare moorland. There are now about thirty-six stones visible, but the original number is thought to have been closer to fifty-four, and weathering of the surviving stones suggests that many may have been over 2 m. high. The axis of the setting lies SSE–NNW, perhaps aligned on the major setting of the northern moon. Such U-shaped settings are rare in Britain but much larger examples are found in Brittany.

An Dun Dun, Gairloch

NG 802753. From the car-park beside the A832 1.5 km. S. of Gairloch, walk down to the beach and S. to the headland.

Its vantage point on this steep and rocky promontory gave the occupants of the dun a wide view along the sandy bay. A stone wall encloses an area about 20 m. across, and an outer defence bars access from the landward side. This could have been the defended home of no more than a single family, living in the inner enclosure.

Cairn o' Get Chambered cairn, Ulbster

ND 313411. Signposted from the A9 at Ulbster (Historic Scotland).

There is a remarkable concentration of prehistoric monuments in the area between the Lochs of Yarrows and Watenan, ranging from chambered cairns and standing stones to forts, hut-circles, and brochs (*see also* under YARROWS). A good path has been laid out to the chambered cairn in state care known as Cairn o' Get, and from there it is possible to explore other features in this ancient landscape.

Cairn o' Get (or Garrywhin) was excavated in 1866. Now roofless, the passage and chamber may be entered and the carefully symmetric design of the tomb appreciated. The original shape of the cairn was square with concave sides within a double wall-face (known as a short-horned cairn), and the entrance passage opens between two low portal-stones in the centre of the south side. The passage leads first to a small antechamber between two pairs of portal-stones and then into the burial-chamber. The portals of the burial-chamber are particularly prominent. The chamber is polygonal in shape, defined by three large slabs set slanting outwards with neat drystone walling between them. The entire tomb had been filled with earth and stones at the end of its life, and the floor deposit contained large quantities of burnt and unburnt human and animal bone, flints, and pottery.

If you look at the skyline to the SW, the mound of another chambered cairn is visible (ND 310408), and there are several cairns probably of Bronze Age date in the vicinity. To the north of the cairn is the fort of Garrywhin, where a stone wall encloses a long oval hill (ND 312413), while to the east, beside Loch Watenan, are the remains of two brochs (ND 317411 and 318414). Less easy to make out in the rough peaty moorland are traces of three sets of stone rows (the best just SE of the fort).

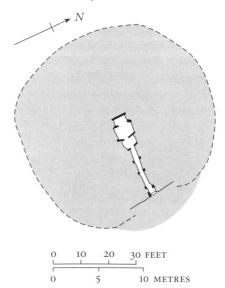

▼ Plan of Camster round cairn (after A. S. Henshall)

0   10   20   30 FEET

0   5   10 METRES

▼ Plan of Camster long cairn (after A. S. Henshall)

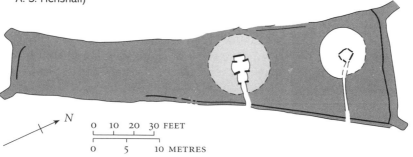

0   10   20   30 FEET

0   5   10 METRES

Camster Chambered cairns ★★

ND 260440 (round cairn), 260442 (long cairn). From the A9 about 1.5 km. E. of Lybster, take a minor road N. towards Watten and park after about 8 km., signposted (Historic Scotland).

Known as the Grey Cairns of Camster, these great piles of bare pale stones looked quite remarkable against the brown moorland surrounding them before the recent forest plantation was created. The round cairn is approximately 20 m. in diameter and almost 4 m. high over an intact chamber, the entrance to which opens from a straight façade on the east side. The passage runs for almost 6 m. before entering an antechamber through a pair of portal-slabs. A larger pair of orthostats mark the entrance into the main burial-chamber, itself divided unequally into two by a further pair of stones, and a single large slab acts as the end wall. The original roof is virtually intact apart from a modern skylight. Excavations in the mid-C19 revealed human bones, pottery, and flints on the floor of the chamber, and the entire tomb had been filled with earth and stones when it went out of use.

The profile of the long cairn has been restored to reflect the incorporation within it of two separate tombs, each with its own round cairn. Both lie within the broader and higher NE end of a cairn that is fully 60 m. long—an immense stately home for the ancestors. Excavation in the 1970s found evidence for a double-horned shape to both ends of the cairn, and thus it has been reconstructed. Both chambers are entered from the east long side and both are lit by modern skylights.

Carn Liath Broch, Brora

NC 870013. On the seaward side of the A9 between Golspie and Brora; signposted (Historic Scotland).

The location of this broch lacks natural defence and therefore the builders not only made the broch particularly solid but also added a strong outer wall. A passageway leads from the outer entrance to the broch entrance; when the site was cleared out in the C19, this passage was still partially roofed with flat slabs. There are checks for a door in the passage as well as in the broch, and there was presumably a stout gateway in the outer wall, making entry into the broch highly controllable. Houses were packed tightly into the space between the broch and the outer wall, some contemporary with the broch and others later (those to the west of the passage are particularly clear). Artefacts include a copy in silver of a C4 or C5 Roman brooch, suggesting that the site was still occupied at least until that time.

The entrance into the broch has a fine thick lintel, and the walls have been restored to a height of some 3.5 m. The inner face is partly hidden by a secondary stone lining, probably contemporary with the later domestic buildings outside and representing reuse of the old tower. Stone lined pits in the floor were probably for storage of food and water. A doorway opposite the entrance gives access to a stair within the wall.

Cnoc Freiceadain Long cairns, Shebster

ND 012653. About 1.5 km. E. of Reay, a minor road leads E. to Shebster cross-roads; turn N. towards Achreamie and park at the signposted path for Cnoc Freiceadain (Historic Scotland).

These two cairns can be seen from afar on the Caithness skyline. They are only 60 m. apart, but they lie at right angles to each other, one along the crest of the hill and the other across it. Including their projecting horns, they are 73 m. and 78 m. long respectively, but the north cairn appears to have had horns only at one end. Neither has been excavated and their burial-chambers are invisible, but their multi-humped outlines suggest that, as at Camster and elsewhere, tombs enclosed in round cairns were subsequently enlarged into long cairns.

Dunbeath Broch, Dunbeath

ND 155304. Follow the path along the N. side of the river from the car-park beside bridges in Dunbeath; leaflet from Dunbeath Heritage Centre.

Set on a wooded hillside above the confluence of the Dunbeath Water and two burns to the north, this broch has been cleared out and survives well despite stone-robbing in the past. The wall rises as high as 4 m., and the entrance has two sets of door-checks and a guard-cell. A doorway opposite leads into a double cell within the broch wall.

Dun Dornaigil Broch

NC 457450. From the A838 between Tongue and Cape Wrath, take the sign-posted minor road from the foot of Loch Hope S. into Strath More (Historic Scotland).

This is an extraordinary sight, for the wall rises almost 7 m. high over the entrance, but elsewhere has collapsed to about 2.4 m. The reason for the collapse is that the broch was built too close to the edge of a terrace above the river, although the course of the river may well have changed over the centuries. Over the entrance is a splendid triangular lintel (the entrance appears to be very low, but this is because the level of the modern road is higher than the original ground surface). The inner face of the high section of wall has also collapsed, and a modern buttress supports the surviving outer face. The interior is 14.5 m. in diameter but is full of rubble. The broch is also known by the charming name of Dun Dornadilla.

Dun Lagaidh Fort and dun, Loch Broom

NH 142913. From the A835 some 12.5 km. SE of Ullapool, take the minor road NW along the W. side of Loch Broom to Loggie, park, and follow the footpath.

The rocky ridge of Dun Lagaidh overlooks the narrowest point along Loch Broom, and it was fortified at least three times between about 700 BC and AD 1200. Excavations in the 1960s revealed a sequence beginning with a fort enclosing the whole of the summit of the ridge within a very thick stone wall. The wall had a timber framework which was later set on fire, causing the stonework to vitrify. The entrance was at the east end, where there is an outer vitrified wall barring the approach to the fort.

Centuries later, a fortified roundhouse was built over the east end of the fort. It looks much like a broch with its entrance guard-cell and intra-mural stair, and it is arguable whether it should be termed a broch or a dun, but for its occupants it was simply a defensive residence. Sometime in the C12, its walls were rebuilt and heightened with mortared masonry, and its entrance was blocked (the new entrance would have been above ground level). Two outer walls were added on the west, turning the old fort into a bailey for the new castle.

Some 1.5 km. SE of Dun Lagaidh, on the hillside above the road, is another fortified residence dating from Iron Age times. This is Dun an Ruigh Ruaidh, anglicized as Rhiroy, which was excavated at the same time (NH 149900). Much of the stonework has been robbed or has collapsed on the downhill side, but elsewhere the broch wall stands 3.5 m. high. The entrance was on the SE but is now blocked, and an internal doorway gave access to a cell and a stair within the wall. A ring of post-holes was found in the broch floor; the original timber posts would have supported an upper floor resting on the ledge still visible in the inner wall-face. There was also a central hearth and evidence of a long period of occupation.

Embo Chambered cairn, Dornoch

NH 817926. In car-park near the shore in Embo, 4 km. N. of Dornoch on minor roads.

In its present surroundings it is difficult to imagine the cairn in neolithic times. It was built on a gravel ridge above the shore, an oval mound of stones from which the coast could be seen stretching away to Tarbat Ness to the south and the Ord of Caithness to the north. Excavation in 1960 revealed a chamber at either end of the mound, and these are now visible, one better preserved than the other. At the south end, a short passage leads between two upright slabs into an antechamber, and another pair of slabs marks the entrance into the burial-chamber, built with upright slabs and panels of horizontal walling. The bones of at least six adults and nine children were found in the chamber. The north chamber was similar but had been disturbed before the excavation.

Long after the tombs had been sealed for the last time, two Bronze Age cists were inserted into the cairn, one into the south chamber and one, still visible, about 2 m. to the north. The first contained the body of a woman, wearing a necklace of jet beads and accompanied by a type of pot now known as a food vessel. The other cist contained the remains of a new-born baby and another baby of about 6 months, along with a food vessel and some beaker sherds. Later still, deposits of cremated human bone were buried in the cairn, one with a bronze razor.

Farr Cross-slab, Bettyhill

NC 714622. The stone is in the churchyard outside the Strathnaver Museum beside the A836 at Farr, just E. of Bettyhill.

Living somewhere in the vicinity in the C9 AD was a patron wealthy enough to commission a decorated cross-slab but not, perhaps, wealthy enough to afford to have both sides carved. It stands 2.3 m. high and bears a ringed cross with a rounded base against a background of interlace pattern. The cross-head has a central boss carved in high relief with a triple spiral, and the base is occupied by a pair of intertwined birds. Above and below the cross are panels of key pattern. The museum displays are mostly concerned with life in the area in the C18 and C19.

Hill o' Many Stanes Stone rows, Lybster ★

ND 295384. Signposted from the A9 5.5 km. E. of Lybster (Historic Scotland).

▼ Plan of stone rows at Hill o' Many Stanes (The Stationery Office)

• Upright stones

◌ Fallen stones

This is an oddly moving remnant of an ancient way of life. Set on a gentle slope are some 200 low standing stones arranged in a fan-shape of at least twenty-two rows running southwards downhill. The individual stones are less than 1 m. high, each with its broad face along the axis of its row as if lining parallel footpaths. More stones have been recorded in the past than survive today, and, if the rows were complete, an estimate of more than 600 stones may give a better impression of the original monument. There is no obvious focus either at the higher and narrower end of the rows or at the other, although in the case of other comparable settings there is often a burial cairn as a 'target'. An argument has been put forward to explain this particular setting (also known as Mid Clyth) as a complex lunar observatory, but it depends upon the entire fan-shape having been constructed at once as the original design, which, in the absence of ex-cavation, is not at all certain.

Nybster Broch

ND 370361. Signposted 'Harbour Broch' on the A9 at Nybster, N. of Wick; from the car-park, follow the footpath S. along the cliffs.

Much of the charm of this monument lies in an extraordinary memorial to its excavator. Sir Francis Tress Barry of Keiss Castle excavated the broch (together with eight others along this stretch of the Caithness coast) at the end of the C19, and the adjacent memorial was built at that time by John Nicolson, a local farmer and sculptor who helped in the excavations. Known as Mervyn's Tower, it resembles a child's sandcastle but built in stone and embellished with sculptured figures.

If you can tear yourself away from this creation, the broch is worth a visit. It was very strongly defended, both by precipitous cliffs and by a thick stone wall across the neck of the promontory. The base of the broch is apparently solid masonry, with no intramural cells or galleries, and its entrance faces the sea. There are no traces even of door-checks or a bar-hole, although it is inconceivable that the broch lacked a door, and there may have been over-zealous restoration. As well as a large mound of rubble cleared out of the broch, the whole of the promontory is covered with remains of domestic buildings.

Ord Archaeological landscape, Lairg

NC 579062 (car park). Signposted from the A839 immediately W. of the bridge at the S. end of Lairg; leaflets from Ferrycroft Countryside Centre.

A large promontory at the south end of Loch Shin rises to 158 m. OD at the top of the hill known as The Ord. There are two chambered tombs on the hill, several later cairns, and a number of hut-circles and clearance cairns on the flanks to north and south. The Archaeological Trail takes in many of these monuments. On the summit of The Ord is a large round cairn of bare stones, covering a passage, antechamber, and burial chamber, and to the north is a larger cairn with vestiges of a horn but n⟶ remains of a chamber.

St Mary's Chapel Crosskirk, Thurso

ND 024700. Some 8 km. W. of Thurso, take a minor road N. to Crosskirk, park and follow signposted footpath (Historic Scotland).

A rare survival on the ground in Caithness of the late Norse earldom of Orkney, Shetland, and Caithness, this is a plain C12 church, which was probably built as part of a family estate. Like those of comparable date in the Northern Isles, it consists of nave and square-ended chancel, although the existing chancel seems to have been built on earlier foundations. The original doorways at the west and east ends of the nave display slightly converging sides and flat lintels.

Strath of Kildonan Archaeological landscape

The River Helmsdale runs from Loch Badanloch deep in the upland moors of Sutherland eastwards to the sea at Helmsdale, mostly along the dramatic Strath of Kildonan.

Between Kinbrace and Helmsdale, there are chambered cairns, long cairns, and stone rows, indicating quite dense neolithic settlement, although contemporary domestic sites have yet to be found. Numerous burnt mounds and hut-circles, some with souterrains, demonstrate a similarly high population in the later second and first millennia BC, with the wealth and sense of social competition to induce a period of broch-building towards the end of the millennium. It is difficult to identify sites of the middle and later first millennium AD, or, indeed, much before the deserted townships of the C18 and C19. The displays in Timespan at Helmsdale explore the latter turbulent period, including the Kildonan gold-rush of 1868–9.

Kilphedir broch is well worth the climb uphill from Kilphedir on the A897 (NC 994189). Although the broch itself has collapsed into a pile of rubble, there are formidable outer defences. There are also good examples of hut-circles to the NW near Kilphedir Burn (NC 991190). Part of a souterrain can be seen at Suisgill (NC 897250), and close to the river about 1 km. farther west are the remains of a broch, again with outer defences (NC 888253). A fine group of early cairns may be visited on the forested hillside near Kinbrace, to the east of the A897 (NC 871291, 868293, 872282).

STRATHNAVER Archaeological landscape

A long history of settlement can be traced in Strathnaver, from its estuary at Bettyhill, where mesolithic flintwork has been found, to the C18 township of Rosal some 20 km. to the south (NC 689416; Forestry

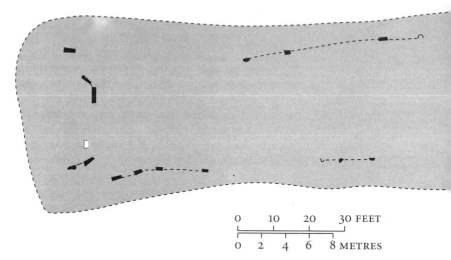

0	10	20	30 FEET

0	2	4	6	8 METRES

▲ Plan of Coille na Borgie southern chambered cairn (after A. S. Henshall)

Commission). There are chambered cairns, hut-circles, and brochs along both sides of the valley.

Coille na Borgie Chambered cairns

NC 715590. About 2 km. S. of Bettyhill, the A836 crosses the River Naver and a minor road continues along the E. side of the river towards Skelpick; take the minor road and park after about 1 km.

Set in line along the contours of the hillside to the east of the road are two impressive long cairns. The best preserved is the southern cairn, fully 72 m. long, with projecting horns at either end, and a burial-chamber visible at the broader northern end. The façade must originally have been very striking, lined with tall upright slabs; one still survives to a height of 2.4 m. The entrance passage and chamber are distinctly skew to the façade, suggesting that they may first have been enclosed in a round cairn, which was subsequently enlarged into a long cairn (at which point the tomb was effectively sealed for ever). Four roofing lintels remain in place.

Another fine long cairn may be seen at Skelpick, about 2.5 km. farther south along the same side of the valley (NC 722567; there is a burn to cross). The cairn is about 58 m. long with projecting horns and a well-preserved chamber entered from the façade at the north end. This is one of several chambered cairns in the vicinity of Skelpick, and there is another group on the other side of the River Naver about 1.3 km. to the south, all of which imply quite intensive neolithic settlement.

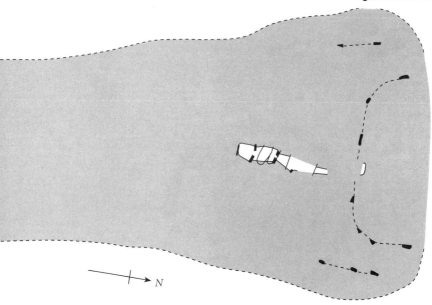

N

Wag of Forse Archaeological landscape, Latheron

ND 205352. From Latheron, take the A895 N. for 2 km., park in layby on left, and walk along track to E. to gate in stone wall and thence downhill to S.

A clear sunlit day makes you understand why people through the ages have chosen to live in the somewhat bleak landscape of Caithness—there is wonderful light and colours and an affinity of land and sea. Choose such a day to visit the Wag of Forse, when you can best appreciate the rich archaeology surrounding the Wag itself.

The Wag appears from a distance to be simply a great pile of stones. The pile was bravely excavated in 1939 and 1946–8, establishing a broad building sequence. Within a turf-walled enclosure, small round houses built of stone were replaced in time by a very large circular fortification, and this in turn was succeeded by a settlement of rectangular houses. At every stage of its history, this was the home of a small, self-contained, farming community. The circular fortification is thought to be a form of broch, and the striking triangular lintel over its doorway echoes, or perhaps anticipates, similar lintels at brochs such as CAISTEAL GRUGAIG and DUN DORNAIGIL. The later rectangular buildings with their internal stone pillars are common in Caithness and Sutherland and are known as wags (from the Gaelic *uamhag* meaning 'little cave'). They can also be seen outside brochs such as Yarrows, and they are likely to date to the middle centuries of the first millennium AD.

The landscape around the Wag of Forse contains ancient field-walls, cairns, and hut-circles to the NW, burnt mounds (cooking-places) beside

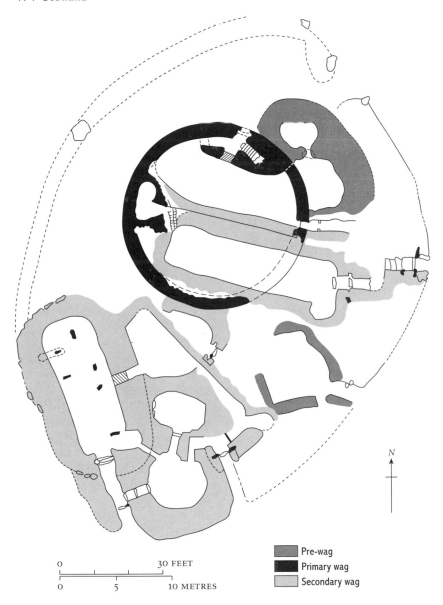

Pre-wag
Primary wag
Secondary wag

▲ Plan of Wag of Forse (after A. O. Curle)

an old stream-bed to the SW, and a great mound which probably covers a
broch to the north. C18 crofts survive to the south in the form of rectangular house-foundations, enclosures, field-walls, and the parallel ridges
left after cultivation of the fields.

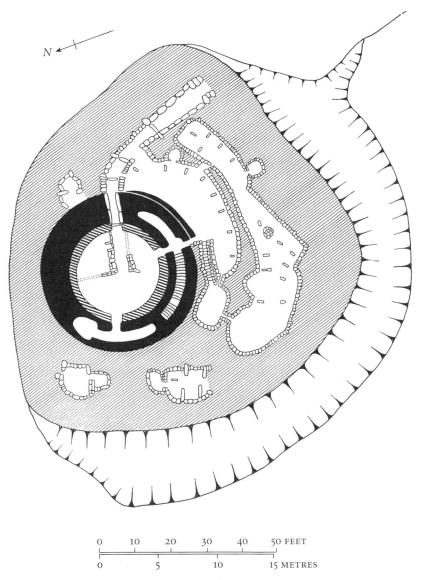

N

▲ Plan of Yarrows broch (Historic Scotland)

0   10   20   30   40   50 FEET

0   5   10   15 METRES

Yarrows   Chambered cairns and broch, Thrumster

ND 305435 (start of trail). Signposted from A9 at Thrumster, about 6.5 km. S. of Wick (trail leaflets are available from the Tourist Information Office in Wick).

Exploring this varied archaeological landscape has been made easier by a marked path and a leaflet with a detailed map. From the car park, it is only a short walk NE to the broch in boggy ground beside the Loch of Yarrows. The level of the loch is higher now than 2,000 years ago when the broch was built, but even so it seems likely that the ditch across the small promontory was designed to be waterlogged. The broch has a guard-cell on one side of the entrance passage and an internal stair on the other, and there is access from the ground floor to a double cell within the broch wall. Between the broch and the ditch are domestic buildings lined with upright stone pillars to help support their roofs. Despite excavations in the mid-C19, the chronological span of the settlement is not known, but it is likely to cover much of the first half of the first millennium AD.

Uphill to the west of the car park are two impressive long cairns, also excavated in the mid-C19. The south cairn is the better preserved, 73 m. long with horns at either end and a burial chamber visible at the broader east end (somewhat confused by the addition of modern walling both in the antechamber and outside the entrance). The north cairn is similar, with a burial chamber at the east end.

The trail continues southwards passing a small fort, a standing stone, cairns, and hut-circles (a round trip of at least two hours).

Northern Isles

Orkney (Map, p. xx)

The Old Red Sandstone bedrock of most of Orkney provides an easy source of superb building stone, with the result that a very high standard of drystone building was achieved from earliest times onwards. Where else can you find 5,000-year-old houses surviving to roof level as at Skara Brae and Knap of Howar? Monuments in mainland Orkney are described first, followed by those in the smaller islands (the Tourist Information Office in Kirkwall will be pleased to advise about inter-island travel, and there are leaflets about most islands). The terms 'brough' and 'broch' are pronounced in the same way and derive from the same Old Norse root, *burg* meaning stronghold, but, confusingly, a brough is a defensible island or promontory, whereas a broch is a stone-built tower.

Borwick Broch, Yesnaby

HY 224167. About 7 km. N. of Stromness on the A967, fork left on the B9056 and take the first minor road W. to Yesnaby. Walk over the Hill of Borwick and round the bay to the broch on the headland.

The grandeur of the cliffs at Yesnaby and the beautiful situation of the broch makes this a memorable walk. The seaward side of the broch is badly eroded but the landward side and the entrance are well preserved, displaying a high standard of drystone masonry to a height of almost 3 m. A guard-cell is visible on the right of the entrance passage. The site was excavated in the C19, revealing traces of buildings between the broch and a defensive wall across the headland, and the artefacts, including a Pictish comb, demonstrate that the use of the site continued into the mid-first millennium AD. The small bay to the immediate south of the broch is one of the few landing-places for boats along this inhospitable west coast.

Brough of Birsay Pictish and Norse settlements, Birsay ★

HY 239285. Signposted from Birsay village at the NW tip of mainland; a tidal island with a causeway accessible at low tide. High Water here is one hour earlier than at Kirkwall (timetable posted at Kirkwall Harbourmaster's Office), and it is impossible to cross during the three hours on either side of High Water (Historic Scotland).

The lands of Birsay are particularly fertile and the bay provides shelter, scarce along the west coast of Orkney, for boats and fishing. The area appears to have been important in both Pictish and Viking times, with the

▲ The Birsay Warriors (Historic Scotland)

Brough acting as the power-centre. Coastal erosion has been fierce and much has been lost into the sea even since Viking times, but it is nevertheless likely that the Brough was a tidal island then as it is now. With an area of some 21 ha., its economic resources were limited, and its inhabitants must have relied heavily on grain and meat from the mainland. Farmsteads of Pictish and Viking date have been excavated at several places round the bay: on the Point of Buckquoy, at Beachview in the village, and at Saevar Howe in the sand-dunes to the south.

Excavation in the 1970s revealed traces of extensive Pictish settlement, but the only visible structures relating to this period are a small well and the cast of a symbol stone, respectively east and south of the church. Around the well was debris from a brief episode of bronze-working, in the form of small clay crucibles and moulds in which small penannular brooches, finger-rings, and dress-pins were cast, presumably at the behest of a wealthy Pictish patron. The symbol stone was found in fragments (now in the National Museums of Scotland) and is a most interesting stone. It was a thin flagstone, decorated on one side with a circular disc and rectangle symbol, a crescent and V-rod, a Pictish beast, an eagle, and a wonderful vignette of three warlords in ceremonial robes, armed with spears, shields, and swords.

The visible house-foundations span the Viking Age from the C9 to C12, but it is not possible, unfortunately, to trace the history of the settlement in detail. Upslope there are hall-houses typical of early Viking times, most of which have been modified at a later date, and part of a very large hall-house survives close to the cliff-edge. A small rectangular building nearby may have been a bath house or sauna, for it has a central large hearth, footings for benches round the walls, and a drain. At the north end of the settlement is a blacksmith's workshop, one end truncated by coastal erosion but identifiable from the remains of a smelting hearth and quantities of iron slag. Between the churchyard and the cliff is a mass of walling representing a sequence of houses built and rebuilt over some three hundred years, the latest having a plan of two or three conjoining small rooms.

Artefacts from the early Viking levels show a mixture of Pictish and Norse types, while later levels yielded a good range of Norse combs, pins, and domestic equipment.

The church consists of a rectangular nave with stone benches and wall niches on either side of the opening into the chancel; the altar is now in the chancel but originally it would have stood in the semicircular apse at the east end of the church. Wall-footings at the west end suggest that there may once have been a porch or tower. A side-door provided access for monks from the domestic buildings ranged round a simple cloister to the north of the church.

Pictish and Viking Birsay

Orkney was evidently part of the Pictish kingdom but had its own local ruler. Adomnan's *Life of Columba* records that, during his visit to the court of the Pictish king Bridei son of Maelchon near Inverness in AD 565, Columba met the contemporary ruler of Orkney and requested of him safe passage to the islands for his missionaries. The image on the Brough of Birsay symbol stone of the three warriors is so strong that it invites speculation as to whether the chief of the three represents an Orcadian king and whether Birsay was foremost among the royal estates. This would explain why the incoming Vikings were swift to take over Birsay, as a political statement of their colonization of Orkney.

According to *Orkneyinga Saga*, the Norse Earl Thorfinn's seat was at Birsay, and there was certainly occupation on the Brough at his time in the mid-C11. The Saga records that, after a pilgrimage to Rome around 1050, Thorfinn built 'a fine minster' at Birsay known as Christchurch. The architecture of the church on the Brough dates it to half a century or so later, and Thorfinn's church is believed to have stood in Birsay village, perhaps on the site of the existing C18 church. It is possible that the Earl had his primary residence in mainland Birsay and a retreat on the Brough.

Brough of Deerness Settlement and chapel, Skaill

HY 596087. About 30 km. SE of Kirkwall; take the A960 and B9050 to Skaill, and a minor road N. to a car-park, where a signposted path leads N. to the Brough (Orkney Islands Council; the cliffs are precipitous).

Thorkel, foster-father to Earl Thorfinn, had a farm at Skaill in the C11, beside the only landing-place along this dramatic coast. Remains of a

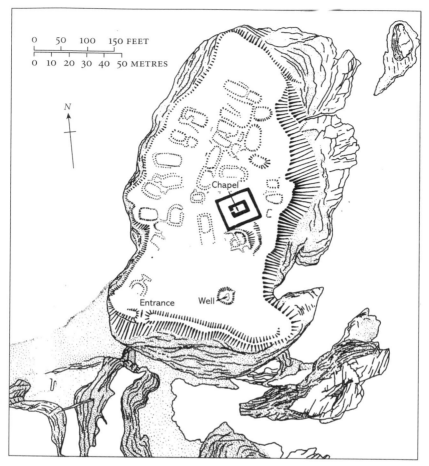

0 50 100 150 FEET

0 10 20 30 40 50 METRES

N

Chapel

Entrance Well

▲ Plan of the Brough of Deerness (C. D. Morris)

Norse farm and an earlier Pictish settlement have been excavated here but are no longer visible. In the nearby church there is a fine hogback gravestone dating to around AD 1100, which was found in the churchyard and which belonged originally to a Viking-Age church on the site.

The little stone chapel on the Brough of Deerness was contemporary with the Skaill church and may have been served by the same priest. The Brough is a detached promontory, accessible now at beach level; it is difficult to estimate the rate at which it has become detached and whether in Norse times access was easier. There is certainly a wall across the seaward side of the Brough, suggesting that some need for extra defence was felt by the inhabitants.

As well as the chapel in its walled enclosure, there are foundations of rectangular buildings on the Brough. The settlement could be either monastic or secular in character, but current opinion favours a secular status similar to that of the Brough of Birsay. None of the houses has been excavated, but an earlier stone and timber version of the chapel has been discovered by excavation, and both phases dated to the Norse period. (The many pits scattered over the site are the result of target practice during the Second World War.)

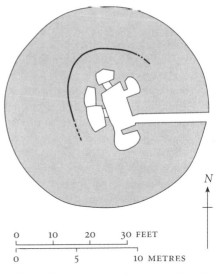

N

Cuween Hill Chambered

tomb, Finstown

HY 363127. Signposted from the A965 S. of Finstown (Historic Scotland; key at farm; torch needed).

0	10	20	30 FEET
0		5	10 METRES

▲ Plan of Cuween chambered tomb (after A. S. Henshall)

This cairn was well placed on the hillside to overlook the sheltered Bay of Firth. It is a Maes Howe type of tomb with a rectangular chamber and four side-cells, one of which is double. The masonry is particularly fine, using very long thin flagstones (the roof is modern), and it is worth the effort of crawling down 3 m. of very low passage—the experience also gives you some impression of how formidable entering the tomb would have been during its lifetime, when it contained rotting corpses. Remains of at least eight people were found during C19 excavations, and there were twenty-four dog skulls on the floor of the main chamber, which are likely to have had some totemic significance.

Traces of a contemporary settlement have been found nearby.

Gurness Broch and settlement, Evie ★★

HY 381268. Signposted on the A966 between Finstown and Birsay (Historic Scotland; visitor centre).

Gurness is the most complete and extensive visible example of a broch and its external settlement. It is one of a series of brochs lining either side of Eynhallow Sound, and it was built at the narrowest point of the Sound. Erosion by the sea has destroyed the northern part of the encircling defences and some buildings, but the major part of the site survives in excellent condition. The site was a huge grassy mound until its excavation in the 1930s, and it gives a graphic impression of what may lie beneath some of the other broch-mounds of Caithness and the Northern Isles.

Excavation failed, however, to clarify the building sequence, and it is not known whether the outer defences of three ramparts and ditches were contemporary with or earlier than the broch. The broch was built with a solid wall-base and guard-cells on either side of the entrance, to which an external porch was added later. The broch survives to a height of 3.6 m. but it was originally much higher. Inside it is crowded with hearths and stone partitions, most of which represent secondary modifications, but one original feature is the deep well reached by stone steps.

The space between the broch and the outer defences is filled with domestic buildings, some of which encroach upon the defences in such a way as to suggest that they outgrew any real need for defence. The maze of walls and upright slabs, hearths and cubicles, presents a mute but evocative image of teeming life round the chieftain's broch. These are semi-detached units consisting of houses within yards. Many artefacts were found, mostly pottery and bone and stone tools but also debris from bronze and iron manufacture. The broch and its settlement appear to have spanned some four centuries until about AD 400.

After about 200 years, the ruined buildings were levelled and Pictish houses were built. The best-preserved of these was rebuilt after the excavation and may be seen in front of the visitor centre. It consists of a stone-built inner wall-face (the outer part of the wall was evidently built of turf) outlining five cells round a central hearth. Part of a long rectangular building was also rebuilt, but it is uncertain whether this was of Pictish or Norse date. There was certainly Norse activity here, for Viking Age arte-

Kirkwall

The oldest upstanding part of Kirkwall is an archway tucked away in St Olaf's Wynd at the north end of the old town. This weathered but still ornately carved arch is all that is left of a C11 church of St Olaf, which stood somewhere in the vicinity (the arch has been reused). A hogback tombstone of the same date and from the site of the churchyard can be seen in Tankerness House Museum. St Olaf's was probably the church indicated by the place-name, Kirkwall or 'church bay', and at this time there were only a few houses according to *Orkneyinga Saga*.

Excavations have shown that formerly the bay stretched farther inland, and that, when the building of St Magnus Cathedral began in 1137, the shore was roughly along the line of the modern Albert Street, Broad Street, and Victoria Street. Thus boats carrying red sandstone from Eday for the cathedral could unload very close to the building site. Although 300 years were to pass before this splendid cathedral was finished, it began as the most ambitious project of Romanesque building in the Northern Isles and embodies the spirit of Orkney's C12 Golden Age.

facts were found, and a stone-lined grave contained a female skeleton with typical Scandinavian oval brooches and iron necklet, knife and sickle (these gravegoods can be seen in Tankerness House Museum in Kirkwall).

Orphir Norse farm and church

HY 334044. About 14.5 km. SW of Kirkwall and signposted from the A964 along a minor road (Historic Scotland and Orkney Islands Council; visitor centre).

Orphir is not only mentioned as a place of importance in the C12 in *Orkneyinga Saga* but two of its buildings are described: 'in front of the hall, just a few paces down from it, stood a fine church' (chapter 66). The church was round, one of a number of round churches built in Europe on the model of the round Church of the Holy Sepulchre in Jerusalem. Orphir was the seat of Earl Haakon Paulsson, who went on pilgrimage to Jerusalem 'where he visited the holy places' (chapter 52). The foundations of the nave survive, 6 m. in diameter, despite having been demolished in the C18, and the small east apse is intact.

The earl's hall is described as having side rooms as well as the main feasting-hall and an upper storey. Stone walls which may belong to this building have been excavated and are visible near the church. Closer to the road, remains of a small corn-mill have been discovered, the earliest example known in the Northern Isles of a mill with a horizontal water-wheel. Dating from the C10 or early C11, this must have been part of an earlier Norse farm than that belonging to Earl Haakon.

Quoybune Standing stone, Birsay

HY 253263. In a field to the W. of the A967 between Twatt and Birsay.

The Stane o'Quoybune is one of Orkney's tallest (almost 4 m.) and most striking monoliths, apparently standing guard over the Loch of Boardhouse. According to legend, this is a giant turned to stone, who comes alive at the turn of the year and goes down to the loch for a drink— but he must be back in his place before dawn breaks on New Year's Day. And anyone who watches will not live to celebrate another new year!

Rennibister Souterrain

HY 397125. Signposted from the A965 between Kirkwall and Finstown (Historic Scotland).

Although the chamber of this sturdily built souterrain is reasonably spacious, access was down a very low and narrow passage. The modern visitor enters by way of a hatch in the roof and a ladder, but the original passage can be seen from the interior. Lined with walling, the oval chamber has four stone pillars to support the roof and the weight of soil above. There are small recesses in the walls for storage of special items. When it

A

B

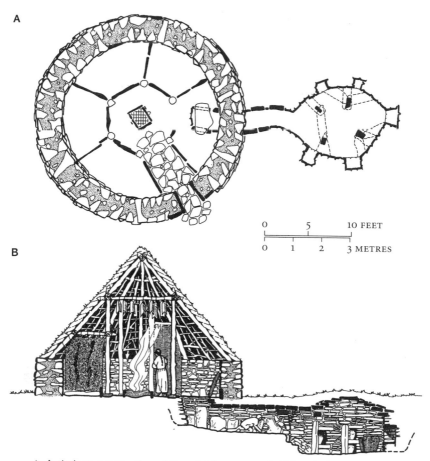

0   5   10 FEET

0   1   2   3 METRES

▲ Artist's reconstruction of Rennibister souterrain (Historic Scotland)

was discovered in 1926, the chamber contained the bones of six adults and twelve children, and their presence in this underground storehouse has never been explained. All trace of the original house from which the souterrain was entered has been destroyed by later farmyard activities.

Another well-preserved souterrain may be seen at **Grain** on the NW outskirts of Kirkwall (HY 441116; Historic Scotland).

Skara Brae Neolithic settlement   ★★

HY 231187. Beside Skaill Bay on the W. coast, some 10 km. N. of Stromness and signposted on the A967 and B9056 (Historic Scotland; visitor centre).

This extraordinarily well-preserved settlement lies at the present shore-line of Skaill Bay, but there is environmental evidence to show that originally it lay in open grassland some distance from the sea. Skaill Bay has

▲ Plan of Skara Brae settlement (after Historic Scotland)

0   10   20   30 FEET

0   5   10 METRES

N

▲ Neolithic house at Skara Brae (Historic Scotland)

always been one of the few sheltered landing-places on this bleak Atlantic coast, but it is subject to severe erosion which has scoured it out over the centuries. Erosion of the sand-dunes blanketing the settlement led to its discovery in the mid-C19 and still threatens it today.

The visible houses and passages were not all in use at the same time. After the major campaign of excavation in the late 1920s, the site was laid out for public view showing all the main structures regardless of date. The earlier buildings are obvious, however, from their lower level and less well-preserved appearance compared with the later buildings. All the houses were built to the same basic design, with a single entrance, a central hearth, a dresser opposite the entrance, and a bed on either side of the hearth. The only difference between the earlier and the later houses in design is that the beds were first recessed into the thick walls and later built against the walls and projecting into the room. But what is astounding about Skara Brae is that all this furniture was built in stone—and in the case of the later houses survives almost intact.

At any one time, there were probably some six to eight houses in occupation, a small but tightly knit farming settlement. Easiest to envisage is the latest phase, in which houses 1–8 were in use, most in two terraces on either side of the main passage. House 8 is the only detached building and its oval plan is distinct from the rest of the settlement. The presence here of large quantities of burnt stone and chert debris suggests that this was a workshop in which chert tools were manufactured, perhaps using heat to improve the flaking qualities of the stone.

House 7 is part of the main village but reached by a side-passage off the main passage, and it has unusual features that suggest a special purpose. Whereas the doors into the other houses could be barred from inside, here the door was barred from outside, as if it were a prison. These two buildings, 7 and 8, are also decorated, whereas all the other decorated stones are set into the walls of passages (mostly incised lines and hatched lozenges, these decorated stones are protected now with glass plates, which also makes them easy to locate).

The economy here was based primarily on mixed farming, including barley and wheat crops, and fishing. Excavations in the 1970s as well as those in the 1920s have produced a very large assemblage of artefacts, notably Grooved Ware, flint and chert tools, bone tools, beads and pins, and stone tools and ceremonial objects. Radiocarbon analysis indicates that the settlement flourished for about 500 years from around 3000 BC.

STENNESS Ceremonial complex

An extraordinary ceremonial landscape from 5,000 years ago can be seen in the heart of mainland Orkney. Centred between the lochs of Harray and Stenness is a complex of monuments spanning at least 2,000 years and representing many thousands of man-hours of labour. It is likely that in those days the two lochs were separated by a narrow neck of land (the modern causeway is artificial), Harray being a freshwater loch and Stenness partially if not wholly saltwater. Concepts of duality may well have played a part in the choice of this location for the spiritual centre of Orkney: earth and sky, land and water, freshwater and saltwater, Harray towards sunrise, Stenness towards sunset.

The earliest monuments are likely to be the chambered tombs of Bookan and Unstan, the earthen circle known as the Ring of Bookan and the Stones of Stenness, all probably built before 3000 BC. They would have been followed sometime before 2500 BC by the Ring of Brodgar and the great tomb of Maes Howe, and by the end of the third millennium the landscape was beginning to be dotted with smaller burial mounds.

Maes Howe Chambered tomb   ★★

HY 318127. Signposted on the A965 between Finstown and Stromness (Historic Scotland; visitor centre).

Maes Howe invites superlatives, for its architecture is a recognized pinnacle of European prehistoric achievement. The effort involved in its

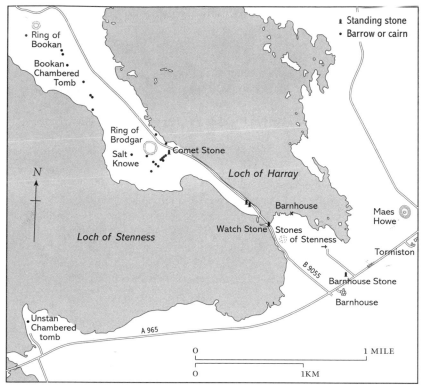

▲ Map of the Stenness ceremonial complex (after G. Ritchie)

building has been estimated at around 100,000 man-hours, tempting speculation about the dynasty of rulers who commissioned it. The huge mound rises from flat ground to the east of the Loch of Harray and has been a landmark through the centuries. Not surprisingly, the mound was opened certainly in the C12, if not before, as well as in the C19, with the unfortunate result that nothing is known of its original contents.

Modern excavations outside the mound have found evidence to indicate that the tomb was built on a natural knoll in open grassland, and that there was once a large standing stone in the space between the mound and the encircling ditch and bank. The orientation of the passage into the tomb suggests that the standing stone known as the Barnhouse Stone, visible in a field to the SW, was deliberately sited to mark the position as seen from the tomb of the midwinter setting sun, the rays of which shine down the passage and into the chamber.

Both the passage and the chamber are built on a grand scale, and the three side-cells open symmetrically from three walls of the square chamber, the fourth wall being occupied by the passage. The cells are above floor level, and the blocks used to seal their entrances lie on the chamber floor. Many of the stone slabs used in the walling of chamber and passage are monumental in scale, and the overall design is both ingenious and pleasing.

The Norsemen who broke into the mound on several occasions in the C12 carved not only a stately lion but also some thirty runic inscriptions on the walls of the chamber.

Ring of Brodgar Henge and
stone circle ★

HY 294133. Beside the B9055 just over 2 km. N. of its junction with the A965 Stromness to Kirkwall road (Historic Scotland).

This magnificent circle of standing stones is almost 104 m. in diameter. Thirty-six stones remain in position, some up to 4.5 m. high and some only broken stumps, yet still very impressive—the intact circle of sixty stones must have been an

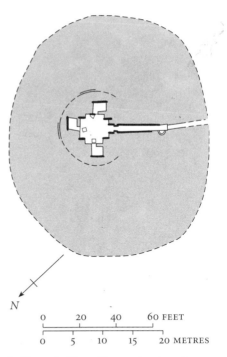

N

```
0        20       40       60 FEET
|--------|--------|--------|

0    5    10    15    20 METRES
|----|----|----|----|
```

▲ Plan of Maes Howe chambered cairn (after A. S. Henshall)

awesome sight. The circle is surrounded by a rock-cut ditch, some 3 m. deep and 9 m. wide, from which it is possible that some at least of the stones were cut. There are two opposing entrances across the ditch, one to the NW and one to the SE, each facing one of the lochs. One section has been excavated across the ditch, but there has been no recorded excavation in the interior. This is Scotland's largest stone circle, and the space enclosed contrasts with the constricted (and presumably· élitist) areas inside most circles. But Brodgar's interior may yet prove to have been littered with equally inhibiting structures!

Stones of Stenness Henge and stone circle ★

HY 306125. Beside the B9055 some 600 m. N. of its junction with the A965 Stromness to Kirkwall road (Historic Scotland).

Only four stones survive of the twelve that once stood here in a circle 30 m. across—one is a curiously crooked stone and the other three are graceful tapering slabs up to 5.7 m. high. The Watch Stone, another tall stone close to the causeway between the two lochs, may be an outlier of the Stenness circle. The circle is clasped within the ditch and bank of an

▲ The interior of Maes Howe in 1861 (J. Farrer)

earthen henge, with an entrance towards the Loch of Harray and the Barnhouse settlement described below. The 2.3 m.-deep ditch was dug into solid bedrock and represents considerable effort on the part of its builders. Excavations in the 1970s revealed a square stone setting of four flat slabs at the centre of the circle, and there were traces of stone and timber settings inside the henge entrance. Animal and human bones, together with Grooved Ware pottery, were found in the ditch.

A short distance away to the north, beside the Loch of Harray, there are the reconstructed remains of a contemporary settlement known as **Barnhouse** (HY 307127; Orkney Islands Council). The design of the houses is very similar to those at SKARA BRAE, and the artefacts associated with them show close links both with Skara Brae and with the STONES OF STENNESS. The settlement was occupied from about 3200 BC until about 2800 BC, and there must have been a close relationship between its inhabitants and the ceremonies taking place at the stone circle nearby.

Unstan Chambered tomb

HY 282117. Signposted on the A965 Stromness to Kirkwall road about 4 km. from Stromness (Historic Scotland).

This is the tomb after which the neolithic pottery known as Unstan Ware was named, because excavations in 1884 yielded the broken remains of at least thirty of these finely decorated bowls. The tomb stands on a promontory in the Loch of Stenness, overlooking the point at which the loch waters mingle with saltwater from the Bay of Ireland. The tip of the

▼ Plan of Stones of Stenness stone circle (after G. Ritchie)

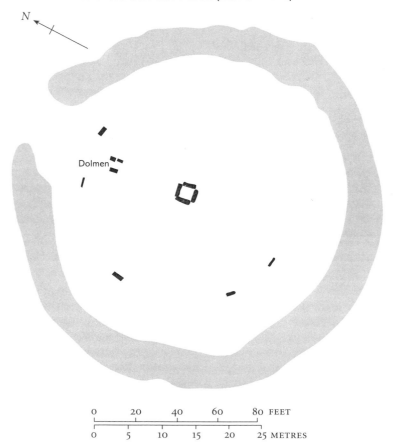

Dolmen

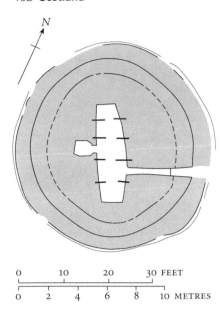

0   10   20   30 FEET
0   2   4   6   8   10 METRES

▲ Plan of Unstan chambered cairn (after A. S. Henshall)

▼ Plan of Wideford Hill chambered cairn (after A. S. Henshall)

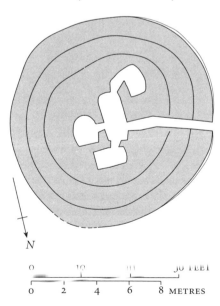

0   10   20   30 FEET
0   2   4   6   8 METRES

promontory is spanned by a low earthwork of unknown date.

The oval cairn encloses a stalled chamber with a passage entering through one of its long walls. The chamber is divided into three central compartments and a shelved compartment at either end (only the projecting slabs that supported the shelves survive). A large quantity of human and animal bones was found but was not, unfortunately, either recorded or preserved; it included intact and crouched skeletons, some in the main chamber and two in the side-cell.

Wideford Chambered tomb

HY 409121. Signposted between Kirkwall and Finstown both from the A965 and from the minor road to the S. of the main road; a walk of about 1.5 km. (Historic Scotland).

Wideford Hill is a notable landmark to the west of Kirkwall, and at least two chambered tombs and a contemporary settlement were located on its flanks, with wide views over both land and sea. The tombs are excellent examples of the Maes Howe type, one at Quanterness (HY 417129 but inaccessible) and one known as Wideford Hill. Here a rectangular chamber was originally reached by a long low passage (modern entry is by hatch and ladder through the roof), and there are three side-cells. Nothing is known of the burials from the C19 exploration, but excavation in 1935 revealed the way in which the cairn had been built, with a vertical outer face and two internal revetment walls, which are still visible.

EDAY

Before the major growth of peat some 3,000 years ago, this island appears to have enjoyed an agricultural economy which has never been regained. By contrast with Shapinsay, there was no wealthy and enlightened landowner to introduce improvements. But this has meant that there survives an extensive archaeological landscape, with visible burial-cairns and standing stones, and field-systems still largely submerged beneath the peat. As yet, early prehistoric settlements are elusive, apart from a house and field-bank excavated in the 1930s on the Calf of Eday and barely visible today.

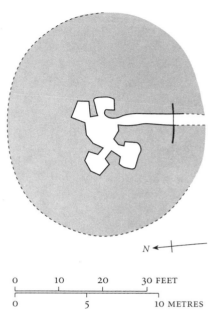

0   10   20   30 FEET

0   5   10 METRES

Vinquoy Chambered tomb

HY 560381. Signposted from the B9063 at the N. end of the island (Orkney Islands Council).

▲ Plan of Vinquoy chambered cairn (after A. S. Henshall)

The builders of this tomb chose a superb viewpoint—on a clear day it is possible to see almost the whole of Orkney from here. This is a Maes Howe type of tomb, although the local sandstone has inhibited the usual standard of neat masonry; four side-cells open in pairs off a central chamber, reached by a passage almost 4 m. long. It was explored in the C19 and nothing is known of its original contents.

Below and to the SE are the remains of two other tombs, Braeside (HY 563375) and two-storeyed Huntersquoy (HY 562377), and the 4.5 m.-tall Stone of Setter (HY 564371).

Calf of Eday Chambered tombs

HY 578386. Near the SW coast of the island (ask at Eday Co-operative about a boat from Calfsound).

Walking north-westwards along the coast from the landing-place, you will encounter two small tombs, 58 m. apart, in which the entrance passage merges almost imperceptibly into a chamber of the same width, with four compartments formed by upright slabs, enclosed within a round cairn. Another 40 m. farther on is a larger oblong cairn, about 20 m. long, which encloses two separate chambers. To the west is a small chamber similar to the tombs just described. A stalled chamber of four

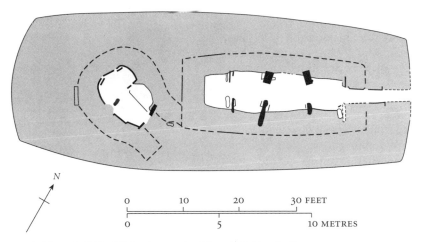

▲ Plan of Calf of Eday long cairn (after A. S. Henshall)

compartments was later built to the immediate east, and both were enclosed within the long cairn. Excavation in 1936 produced pottery and flint tools. A·little uphill from the cairn are the remains of an Iron Age house and field-walls.

HOY

The Norse name of this island means 'high isle', and the western part with Ward Hill and the Cuilags at 479 m. and 433 m. respectively is by far the highest area of Orkney. Apart from the prehistoric tomb known as the Dwarfie Stane and the beautiful Melsetter House, Hoy is chiefly famous for its military monuments, from the early C19 martello towers to defences of the two World Wars of the C20.

Dwarfie Stane Rock-cut tomb, Hoy

HY 243004. Signposted off the B9040 on a minor road to Rackwick (Historic Scotland).

The only chambered tomb in Hoy and the only rock-cut tomb in Britain, this must surely be the work of a neolithic eccentric. A vast block of sandstone on a hillside provided the inspiration for someone to hollow out a short passage with a small cell on either side, and the tool-marks of this painstaking process can still be seen. In addition, a suitable boulder had to be found to fit the entrance as a 'door'—this now lies outside the tomb but it was seen in place in the C16. Nothing is known of any burials, but the plan of the passage and cells appears to be related to those of simple chambered tombs in Orkney. This extraordinary monument has attracted much interest in recent centuries, and the carved graffiti go back to one H. Ross in 1735. In 1850 it was visited by Major W. Mounsey, formerly a British spy in Persia, who not only carved his name backwards in Latin but added a line of elegant Persian calligraphy which records: 'I have sat two nights and so learnt patience'—thought to be a reference to the perils of camping amongst the Hoy midges!

NORTH RONALDSAY

This island and neighbouring Sanday are very similar in their low-lying landscapes and in their archaeology, although the archaeological poten-tial of North Ronaldsay has yet to be realized. There are large settlement mounds and remains of two linear earthworks, which are likely to be of prehistoric date. Known as trebs, these earthworks survive up to 2 m. high and divide the island into three units of land.

Burrian Broch

HY 762513. At the S. end of the island, SE of the pier (access along the foreshore).

The coast is low but rocky, and the broch was built on a small promontory, defended on the landward side by four concentric ramparts. The broch entrance faces out to sea, but this side of the broch has suffered both from coastal erosion and from being incorporated into the sheep dyke (the wall that runs round the entire island to confine the seaweed-eating sheep to the foreshore). Oddly, there were no guard-chambers at the entrance, and only one cell within the broch wall on the NE. Traces of domestic build-ings can be seen between the broch and the outer defences. Excavations in the 1870s yielded a large assemblage of finds, including evidence of occu-pation in Pictish times.

PAPA WESTRAY

This fertile island slopes up from the low-lying south end to sheer cliffs at the north (a nature reserve). Its attraction for human settlement is attested from the middle of the fourth millennium BC onwards, although its historically recorded role as a Norse estate has yet to be supported by archaeological finds.

Knap of Howar Neolithic farmstead ★

HY 483518. On the W. coast of the island, reached on foot by a track from the road at Holland House (Historic Scotland).

Two buildings lie side by side, with their entrances facing out to sea. Today they are on the coast, but environmental evidence found during excava-

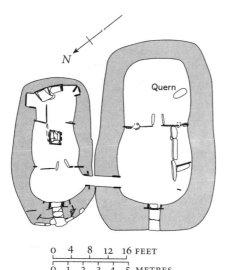

tions in the 1970s showed that, at the time that they were built some 5,500 years ago, the coastline was considerably farther west. The farm lay in open grassland behind sand-dunes—and it was windblown sand which finally engulfed it and preserved the walls of the houses to roof level.

The two houses are oblong in plan, with thick walls built with a stone face on either side of an earthen core. The larger building appears to have been a dwelling-house, divided into a living-room and an inner kitchen by low stone slabs. There was a simple hearth set in a shallow pit in the inner room, and traces of a wooden bench lining the walls. A massive quern-stone is still in position.

0 4 8 12 16 FEET

0 1 2 3 4 5 METRES

▲ Plan of Knap of Howar farm-stead (after A. Ritchie)

A low passage links this house with its neighbour. This smaller building is divided into three rooms, the central room containing a slab-built hearth and the inner room furnished with cupboards and shelves. Artefacts from both buildings and from the surrounding midden included Unstan Ware pottery, a small polished stone axe, flint and stone tools, and bone tools. Animal bones included domestic cattle, sheep, and pigs, together with deer, fish, birds, and shellfish, and there was limited evidence for barley and wheat crops.

Holm of Papa Westray Chambered tombs

HY 509518. At the S. end of the island (Historic Scotland; ask at the Papay Community Co-operative about a boat to the island; torch needed).

This small uninhabited island bears two very interesting tombs and traces of ancient field-walls. It seems likely that, 5,000 years ago when the tombs were in use, the island was a promontory attached to Papa Westray and thus more accessible than it is today. The tomb at the south end is an exaggerated example of a Maes Howe class of tomb, with a very long chamber divided unequally into three parts and no fewer than twelve side-cells, two of which are double. Entry into the chamber is by way of a hatch and a ladder through the modern concrete roof, but the original access was through a long and very low passage which is still visible. Although the main chamber is almost 3 m. high, all the entrances into the side-cells and end-cells are again very low, only 40 cm. to 60 cm. from

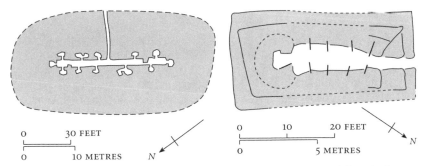

0   30 FEET

0   10 METRES   N

0   10   20 FEET

0   5 METRES

N

▲ *(left)* Plan of Holm of Papa Westray South chambered cairn (after A. S. Henshall)

(right) Plan of Holm of Papa Westray North chambered cairn (after A. S. Henshall)

floor to lintel. No artefacts or human bones were recorded when the tomb was opened in 1849. Several slabs in the walls are decorated, notably the lintel over the entrance into the SE-most cell, which bears pecked dots and 'eyebrow' motifs.

At the north end of the island is a small version of a stalled cairn, which was excavated briefly in 1854 and comprehensively in the 1980s. Although the rectangular cairn survived only to a height of about 60 cm., much of the interior of the tomb was intact and yielded much information about its use and ritual. The chamber is divided into four compartments by upright slabs and, unusually, there is an end-cell opening off the inner-most compartment. In fact, excavation showed that the stalled chamber had been added to a small oval cairn covering the cell, and the two were then encased in the visible rectangular cairn. The remains of more than eight adults and children were found in the tomb, along with pottery and flint tools, and the chamber and passage had been filled with earth and stones when the tomb was closed for the last time.

ROUSAY

Rousay is an island of scenic contrasts between rugged uplands and a fertile coastal fringe. The latter was very attractive to early farmers, and there are no fewer than fifteen chambered tombs. A famous archaeologist, Professor V. Gordon Childe, observed that the distribution of these tombs bore a remarkable similarity to that of C19 farms, prompting the idea that each tomb related to a particular community with its own unit of land. Childe and the Rousay landowner, Walter Grant, oversaw a number of excavations, including both tombs and the domestic settlement of Rinyo, which, though not so well preserved, consisted of the same sort of houses and artefacts as SKARA BRAE. Rousay has also yielded important Bronze-Age artefacts and burials, and at least five Iron Age brochs.

Blackhammer Chambered tomb, Rousay

HY 414276. Signposted on B9064 about 2 km. from the pier (Historic Scotland).

The tomb has a modern concrete roof, built after its excavation in the 1930s, and access is now by ladder from a hatch. The oblong cairn lies along the contours of the hillside, and the original entrance passage, visible from inside the chamber, faced south over Eynhallow Sound. It opened from the side rather than the end of the chamber, into the third (counting from the east) of seven burial compartments. The outer face of the cairn was built with a decorative effect of groups of alternately slanting slabs forming hatched triangles; these can still be seen on either side of the entrance.

Some of the slabs dividing the 13 m.-long chamber into compartments are missing, and there are blocks of masonry of unknown date in the chamber. This later activity had disturbed what remained of the original burial deposits, although there were traces of adult male skeletons, one in the west end-compartment and one in the passage.

Knowe of Yarso Chambered tomb, Rousay

HY 404279. Signposted from the B9064 about 3 km. from the pier (Historic Scotland).

This neat little tomb has yielded very interesting evidence of the way in which bones were sorted and rearranged during the use of the chamber. The cairn was built on a terrace above a steep slope, which drops down to a lower terrace on which lie the tombs of Blackhammer and Knowe of Ramsay (HY 400279). Yarso was excavated in 1934, revealing a sub-rectangular cairn with a decorative outer wall-face of slabs set slanting away from the entrance. The 4 m.-long passage leads into a three-compartment chamber (the roof is modern); the innermost compartment is twice the size of the others, but it is divided into two by a pair of low upright slabs. There were disarticulated human bones throughout the chamber and in the passage, but the skulls had been carefully arranged in the innermost compartment, lining the side-walls in such a way that they faced into the chamber. The remains of twenty-nine individuals were present. Many of the bones were scorched, and the walls of the chamber showed clear signs of fires having been lit

▼ Plan of Knowe of Yarso chambered cairn (after A. S. Henshall)

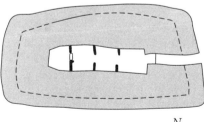

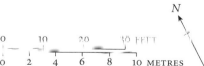

N

0   10   20   30 FEET

0   2   4   6   8   10 METRES

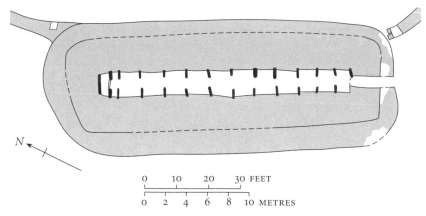

▲ Plan of Midhowe chambered cairn (after A. S. Henshall)

within it. Amongst the human bones and in the filling of the chamber were animal bones, including remains of at least thirty-six red deer. This is an unusually high number of deer. The artefacts included flint knives and no fewer than forty-three flint scrapers, and there may well be a connection between the deer and these tools, which could have been used in processing the deerskin for clothing and bedding. A single radiocarbon date suggests that the tomb was in use around 2900 BC.

Midhowe Broch and chambered tomb, Rousay ★

HY 371306 (broch), 372304 (tomb). Signposted from the B9064 about 8 km. from the pier (Historic Scotland).

The **broch of Midhowe** was excavated in the early 1930s and is in State care, with the result that its architecture and the design of its defences can be appreciated. Its builders chose a low promontory with a geo or inlet cutting into the rocky shore on either side, and gave the broch the additional protection and grandeur of a thick stone forework stretching in an arc between the two geos. There is a ditch on either side of the wall, and the stonework survives to a height of some 3 m. above the bottom of the ditches; it is difficult to estimate its original height, but, with a basal width of 8 m. or more, it could have risen at least another 3 m. without losing any stability. Its width is even greater at the entrance, creating an impressively long entrance-passage. It seems likely that this forework was designed more for visual effect than for real defence, for it stops short of the geo on the south side, leaving not only a rock ledge leading round the outside of the entrance but also providing access to a flight of steps through the south wall of the passage.

The periphery of the promontory has clearly been eroded by the sea, but the broch stands so close to the forework and its inner ditch—little more than 1 m. away—that it seems unlikely that the area available on the promontory was ever extensive. The broch survives to a height of about 4.3 m. and was originally a very tall and imposing tower. The entrance is in keeping with such a building, for it is unusually high and has a fine lintel. The wooden door would have been placed about half-way down the entrance-passage, where there are checks in the wall and a sill-stone and behind the door access on either side into small cells; the cell on your left as you enter leads into the gallery which originally ran round almost the entire circumference of the broch.

Inside the floor-area is divided into two rooms and seems crowded with slab-partitions, hearths, and tanks. These represent the final phase of use of the broch, and there is clear evidence that there had been modifications over the years—for example, a hearth overlaps an earlier underground cellar. Features of note are the post-holes on either side of the hearth, designed to take the uprights for a spit across the fire; an alcove with a corbelled roof supported on a single tall flagstone; the ledge projecting from the inside broch-wall at a height of about 3.4 m., on which a timber gallery is likely to have rested; a doorway in the wall-face, requiring a ladder to reach it, which leads to cells within the wall.

The excavations yielded many artefacts and animal bones, including Roman imports such as pottery and a bronze ladle. The buildings outside the broch appear not to be contemporary with the original design of the broch and its forework, for some were built over the inner ditch and into the inner face of the rampart.

Midhowe chambered tomb is encased in what looks like an enormous shed; you could be forgiven for thinking that you had come to the wrong place, for the site was excavated in the early 1930s, and the erection of the protective shed meant that the tomb could be preserved in the state in which it was found.

This is an extra long example of a stalled cairn, with twelve burial-compartments marked out by upright slabs along a chamber more than 23 m. long. It was found to be well preserved, with walls up to 2.5 m. high, and a decorative outer wall-face built in herringbone fashion. Its contents were particularly revealing, capturing the moment some 4,500 years ago when the vault was sealed off for the last time (the masonry blocking the entrance passage is still in position). Apart from a small heap of bones in the seventh compartment on the west side of the chamber, all the burials were on the east side, lying on low stone benches in the fifth to tenth compartments, and in the end compartment. Most consisted of heaps of bones, but there were eight almost complete and articulated skeletons lying with their backs to the wall, and these were presumably the last burials to be made here. In all there were the remains of twenty-five people. The first four compartments were empty, as if they played a different role in the use of the tomb.

Midhowe

There are two very different sites here with the same name, and both are extraordinary—the broch for its massive forework and the consummate skill of its builders, and the tomb for its long chamber and detailed information about its burials. Midhowe overlooks the NW end of Eynhallow Sound and the island of Eynhallow; Old Norse *Eyin-Helga* means 'holy isle', so named because there was a monastery there in the C12, of which the walls of the church still survive intact.

Midhowe also marks the point on Rousay where the low-lying and fertile coastal strip gives way to high cliffs and rough moorland, creating a wider range of natural resources which included the seabirds nesting on the cliffs and the deposits of copper and lead beneath the moorland. These natural advantages may explain why three brochs were built here in close proximity, for Midhowe (literally the middle mound) is flanked on either side at a distance of less than 300 m. by another broch; neither has been excavated and they both appear as low stony mounds.

Taversoe Tuick Chambered cairn

HY 425276. Signposted on the B9064 about 1 km. from the pier (Historic Scotland).

This unusual two-storey tomb was built on a knoll with wide views over the island of Wyre and beyond. It was discovered in 1898, when the owner of Trumland House attempted to create a garden-seat on the knoll, and excavated both then and again in the 1930s when a concrete dome was built to protect it.

▼ Plan of lower chamber in Taversoe Tuick chambered cairn (after A. S. Henshall)

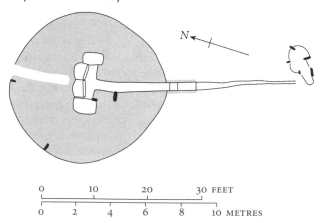

0	10	20	30 FEET

0	2	4	6	8	10 METRES

In effect, there are two tombs here, for although they are one above the other, and the slab-roof of the lower chamber acts as the floor of the upper, their entrances are entirely separate. The passage into the upper chamber opens from the north, while that into the lower chamber opens from the south. The lower chamber was built in a pit below ground level, and the chamber above is, as normal, at ground level. The surviving burials included both inhumations and cremations, but the total number of individuals is uncertain.

Another unusual feature is the miniature 'tomb', only 1.6 m. long, which was dug into the ground beyond the entrance into the lower chamber and which contained two pottery bowls and part of a third bowl.

SANDAY

The rich farmlands of this low-lying island have attracted settlement from earliest times to the industrialized 'model farm' of Stove in the C19. The Tofts Ness peninsula has a well-preserved prehistoric complex including many burial-mounds, and there are some very large settlement mounds—one excavated at Pool has yielded evidence of occupation in neolithic, Pictish, and Viking times. One of the few Viking boat burials to be excavated in Scotland in modern times was at Scar (the finds are in Tankerness House Museum in Kirkwall).

Quoyness Chambered tomb   ★

HY 676377. About 6 km. from Kettletoft on the B9069 and a signposted footpath (Historic Scotland; torch needed).

The low-lying peninsula of Els Ness appears to have been devoted to the dead of Sanday for about two millennia. There are certainly one and possibly two neolithic chambered cairns and at least twenty-six small mounds, some of which are likely to cover Bronze Age burials.

Quoyness is a spectacular example of the Maes Howe type of tomb. Its external appearance is somewhat misleading, because the front of the tomb has been reconstructed to show the stages by which the cairn was built rather than its likely final form. Three consecutive wall-faces are visible, representing an inner cairn enclosing the burial chamber, an outer skin of cairn material, and an outer casing round the cairn. The entrance passage is now roofed only for the inner 3.5 m., but originally it was roofed at a height of 60 cm. over a length of 9 m.—making entry to the chamber a truly daunting crawl.

The much shorter crawl for the modern visitor is well rewarded, for you emerge into a spacious chamber, the walls of which soar upwards into apparently never ending darkness. The chamber is intact, all but its roof (which has been reconstructed) at a height of 4 m. When it was first explored in 1867, the chamber was full of stones and the roof was missing;

with the hindsight of current knowledge, the roof is likely to have been removed when the tomb went out of use, and the chamber filled through the roof-space. The outer casing was probably added at the same time, because it covered the entrance-passage.

The burial chamber is 4 m. long and almost 2 m. wide, and there are low entrances in the side-walls which open into six small cells. All but two of the cells contained burials, and there were also bones in the main chamber, in the pit in the floor of the main chamber, and in the entrance passage. Artefacts included broken pottery, spiked stone objects, and a bone pin similar to examples from SKARA BRAE, but, oddly, no flintwork. Had this tomb been excavated with modern techniques, there is no doubt that it would have yielded an enormous amount of information.

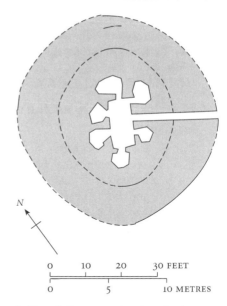

▲ Plan of Quoyness chambered cairn (after A. S. Henshall)

SHAPINSAY

Extensive agricultural improvements in the mid-C19 have left a fascinating array of industrial monuments but little visible prehistoric archaeology. The area of arable land jumped from 300 ha. in 1848 to some 2,500 ha. by 1874.

Burroughston Broch

HY 540210. At the NE end of the island, signposted from the B9058 (Orkney Islands Council).

Encouraged apparently by the recent spectacular discoveries at MAES HOWE, Col. David Balfour of Balfour Castle on Shapinsay hired workmen in 1862 to open the great mound known as Hillock of Burroughston. The result was the discovery of a well-preserved broch set within particularly strong outer defences, their strength compensating for the lack of natural defence on this low-lying coast. The broch entrance faces out to sea, and the defences, a deep ditch between two ramparts, probably once encircled it entirely. Traces of buildings were found between the broch and the defences.

The broch itself is solidly built with cells within the wall at ground level, a projecting ledge for an upper floor, and low radial partitions and a 3 m.-deep well in the interior.

SOUTH RONALDSAY

Burwick, St Mary's Church Foot-marked stone

HY 438843.

Known as the Ladykirk Stone, this intriguing fragment of Dark Age history lies now within the church of St Mary (hence Ladykirk). It is a flat and oval water-worn boulder, on which have been carved the impressions of two shod feet, and it is one of several such foot-marked stones in Scotland (*see* DUNADD in Argyll and CLICKHIMIN in Shetland for two others). They seem to be associated with the inauguration of kings, in which the new king literally follows the steps of his predecessors by placing his feet in their 'footprints'. Unfortunately the original provenance of this stone is not known, but there is a fort nearby known as the CASTLE OF BURWICK from which it could conceivably have come.

Castle of Burwick Fort

ND 434842. From Burwick at the S. end of the island, there is a walk of about 500 m. westwards to the coast (precipitous cliffs).

This fort should be excavated before coastal erosion cuts through the neck of the peninsula and isolates it! The narrow neck was clearly wider when the fort was built, for the outer defences of two ditches and three ramparts on the landward side are truncated at either end. The fort itself is a long oval within a stone wall, now grassed over, and there are outlines of house foundations within it. There has been no excavation but the surface traces suggest an Iron Age fort.

Isbister Chambered tomb ★

ND 470845. Near the S. end of the island; from the A961 just E. of Burwick, the B9041 leads E., signposted (Orkney Islands Council).

A fine example of a stalled cairn, this tomb has several unusual features. The oval cairn is backed on the landward side by an outer stone casing, while on the seaward side the entrance-passage opens through one of the long walls of the chamber rather than at one end, and there are three side-cells. The main chamber is divided into three compartments by upright slabs, and at either end there is a separate compartment, both of which originally were floored and shelved with large slabs. Excavation in the 1970s showed that, at the end of its long life, the roof had been removed from the main chamber and it had been filled with earth and stones. The side-cells had not been filled, nor had the entrance-passage, which had filled naturally with windblown sand. Apart from the end-compartments and one cell, the tomb was intact and proved to hold the partial remains of about 340 people. The two intact side-cells contained mostly skulls. There were also animal, bird, and fish bones, including an unexpectedly high proportion of bones and talons of sea-eagles, interpreted as a possible tribal emblem. Radiocarbon analysis indicates that the tomb was built sometime before 3000 BC.

Liddle Burnt mound

ND 464841. Near the S. end of the island; from the A961 just E. of Burwick, the B9041 leads E., signposted.

A rare opportunity to see what constitutes a burnt mound! Beneath the covering of dark soil and burnt stones, a communal cooking-place has been revealed. Sheltered by encircling stone revetments that kept the debris at bay, the dominant feature is the great stone trough, sunk into the ground and originally sealed with clay to make it watertight. Using peat as fuel for the hearth set in an alcove, stones were heated and dropped into the water-filled trough until the water came to the boil and joints of meat and fish could be cooked.

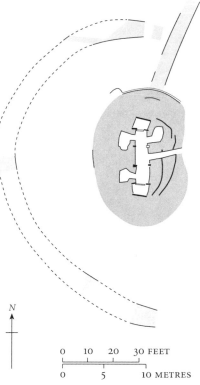

N

| 0 | 10 | 20 | 30 FEET |

| 0 | 5 | 10 METRES |

▲ Plan of Isbister chambered cairn (after A. S. Henshall)

WYRE

Cubbie Roo's Castle and St Mary's Church

HY 441263 and 443262. About 1.2 km. S. of the pier.

The earliest stone castle still standing in Scotland was built in Wyre in the mid-C12 by a Norseman named Kolbein Hruga (his nickname would have been Kubbie and his surname has been shortened to Roo, hence the modern name of the castle). Both he and his castle are recorded in *Orkneyinga Saga* (chapter 84), the castle described as 'a fine stone fort . . . a really solid stronghold', and the strength of the walls can still be appreciated today.

▲ Artist's reconstruction of Cubbie Roo's Castle (Historic Scotland)

What survives is the ground floor of a small tower, almost 8 m. square with thick stone walls, set within strong outer defences formed by a stone wall and deep ditch. The entrance into the tower would have been at first-floor level, reached by ladder, and the ground floor probably acted as a storeroom, with an access hatch through the wooden floor above. A tank cut into the bedrock floor of the storeroom may have held water. The original height of the tower is unknown, but at least three upper floors would be needed to accommodate the lord's family and retainers and to give a good view over both the island and Gairsay Sound. Subsequently, domestic buildings were added round the tower, some built over the original outer defences.

Dating to the late C12 and presumably part of the Norse estate is the nearby St Mary's Church. It consists of nave and chancel and was partially restored in the late C19 or early C20.

Shetland (Map, p. xxi)

'The air in these Isles is most wholesome, being well purged by great winds' (Robert Monteith, 1633). Wind-speeds have changed little over the centuries, but slightly warmer temperatures made farming easier in early prehistoric times. Remarkably complete archaeological landscapes of 5,000 years ago can be explored in Shetland, in areas such as Walls where subsequent farming activities have barely changed the surface of the land. The island of Mousa boasts the closest to an intact broch to be found anywhere in Scotland, while at Jarlshof you can wander amongst the remains of houses spanning prehistory, the Viking Age, and medieval times. Sites in mainland Shetland are described first, followed by island sites (the Tourist Information Office in Lerwick will be pleased to advise about inter-island travel; there are leaflets about several islands and areas of mainland).

Beorgs of Housetter Chambered tombs

HU 361854. To the immediate W. of the A970 Lerwick N. to Isbister road, about 7 km. S. of Isbister.

Despite the intrusion of the modern road, it is still possible to appreciate the natural drama of this place in which three tombs were built some four to five thousand years ago. To the east lies the Loch of Housetter, which was probably much smaller then, allowing space for cultivation in the valley. To the west the rocky face of the Beorgs of Housetter rises steeply above the terrace on which two tombs stand, known as the Trowie Knowe and the Giant's Grave, while on a shelf on the Beorgs itself there is a small and well-preserved heel-shaped cairn.

The Trowie Knowe is a ruinous round cairn of pink granite boulders surviving some 1.5 m. high, with a pair of upright stones which may have acted as portal-stones to the chamber. The Giant's Grave is easy to identify from the two standing stones, 2 m. and 2.7 m. high, that stand guard over the tomb. One of the attractions of the Beorgs to prehistoric builders must have been the fact that the granite outcrops display two colours, pink and white (the latter weathers to grey), and the Giant's Grave was designed using both. The standing stones are pink, while the cairn between them is grey.

Burland Broch

HU 445360. From the A970 some 10 km. S. of Lerwick, park on the lay-by and walk E. to the coast for about 1.5 km.

This is a spectacular and perilous site, to be approached with care. A small and precipitous promontory plays host to a well-preserved broch, but the effects of coastal erosion mean that there is little space now between the broch and the cliff. The neck of the promontory was defended by three ramparts and ditches, which are still very impressive in size.

Busta Standing stone

HU 348673. SW of Brae on the A970, a minor road leads S. to Busta, passing the standing stone about 300 m. S. of the junction.

A more commanding location could hardly have been found for this stout granite boulder. From here there is a wide view over Busta Voe and the hills of mainland south of Brae. Local tradition would have the stone thrown here in anger by the Devil, but the human effort involved in transporting the stone and wedging it into position must have been formidable too, for it is thought to weigh some 20 tons. A smaller triangular block to the NE may imply that this was designed as a pair of standing stones.

Clickhimin Broch and settlement ★

HU 464408. Signposted on the A970 on the outskirts of Lerwick (Historic Scotland).

This was once an island-broch set in the Loch of Clickhimin and connected to the shore by an artificial causeway, but C19 improvements to the loch caused its water-level to fall and the broch now stands on a low promontory. The site has a long history revealed by excavation, beginning in the mid-first millennium BC with a small domestic settlement, of which one oval house may still be seen to the NW of the broch. Late in the

▼ Plan of Clickhimin fort and broch (after Historic Scotland)

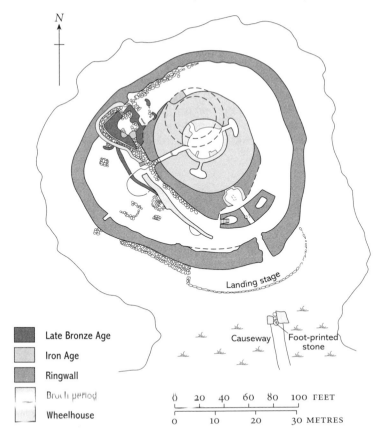

N

Late Bronze Age

Iron Age

Ringwall

Broch period

Wheelhouse

Landing stage

Causeway

Foot-printed stone

0   20   40   60   80   100 FEET

0   10   20   30 METRES

millennium, the island was fortified with a stone wall and a free-standing blockhouse, still an impressive structure today. There is a cell on either side of the entrance-passage through the blockhouse, but, unlike other Shetland blockhouses, the cells could only be entered from the first floor (the stair to which survives at one end) and may have been pit-prisons or cellars. There were traces of domestic buildings within the fort.

The next major development was the construction of a broch within the fort. Unusually, this broch has subsidiary entrances, which seem to underline the prestigious aspect of the building by reducing its defensive potential. Eventually the broch went out of use and a house was built within it, along with several houses outside. Unfortunately it is not possible to attach any precise dates to this sequence of building. It seems likely that the site remained in occupation, or at least in significance to the community, into Early Historic times, for a slab carved with two shod footprints lies at the island end of the causeway. Such carved footprints are associated elsewhere with the ceremonies surrounding the inauguration of kings.

Culswick Broch, Walls   ★

HU 253448. At 2 km. W. of Bixter on the A971, the B9071 runs S. to Culswick; a walk of some 2 km. over rough moorland W. to the coast.

Only for the energetic walker but well worth the effort, for the broch stands to a height of about 4 m. and commands a superb view over the approach to Gruting Voe and the island of Vaila. The broch-tower was originally surrounded by a strong outer wall, and the entrance into the broch itself is surmounted by a massive and striking triangular block of red granite.

Cunningsburgh Steatite quarries

HU 423270. Some 19 km. S. of Lerwick on the A970, the Catpund burn runs E. into the sea about 1 km. S. of Mail; a track gives access to the quarries at HU 426272.

The Catpund Burn cuts down through exposed steatite deposits on a steep slope, and there are traces of quarrying over a stretch of about 1 km. beside the burn. Steatite or soapstone is a relatively soft stone which, when fresh, can be cut with harder stone tools or with metal tools. It was used to carve vessels and weights from around 2000 BC until medieval times. Larger items such as round and square bowls were carved upside down as blanks on the rock-face, detached, and then hollowed out, and the most obvious surviving traces of quarrying are in the form of abandoned blanks or outlined platforms where such blanks have been removed.

In the Viking Age, the Norwegian colonists who had been accustomed to using steatite in their homeland continued to do so in Shetland, export-

ing artefacts to Iceland, Orkney, and the Hebrides. Aith Voe to the NE of the quarries is a fine natural harbour, and there is evidence here of occupation from Iron Age times onwards, including ogham and runic inscriptions and a fine Pictish carving of a wolf-headed figure, perhaps a god or a priest in a wolf-mask (in the Shetland Museum in Lerwick). The Scandinavian place-name, Cunningsburgh, means 'king's fort' and may well reflect the importance of the steatite industry in both Pictish and Norse times.

Dalsetter Broch and early settlement

HU 407156. From the A970 about 4 km. N. of Sumburgh Airport, a minor road is signposted to the excellent South Voe Croft Museum; remain on the minor road N. along the coast, park after

▲ The wolf-man from Mail (V. Turner)

about 2 km. just S. of Dalsetter farm, and walk SE along a track.

The track leads past a small field in which the remains of six oval houses and their field-walls can be seen; these are likely to date to the third or second millennium BC. About 500 m. from the road, the extensive remains of the broch-defences are encountered. Like CULSWICK, the broch was built well back from precipitous cliffs and was encircled by outer defences. Here, however, the stonework of the broch itself has been robbed to build the adjacent, now ruined, croft, but the encircling defences are still impressive, consisting of two ramparts and ditches. The mound covering the remains of the broch is sufficiently substantial to suggest that excavation might reveal a long sequence, and there are traces of contemporary and later domestic settlement outside the broch.

Gruting School Neolithic settlement

HU 281498. From the A971 less than 1 km. E. of Bridge of Walls, take a minor road SE for 1.5 km. until the school is on the right.

This example of a neolithic house has been chosen because it is both well preserved and close to the road. It lies on the gentle slope above the road and it takes a moment for the eye to pick it out against the rock-strewn landscape—look for the second telegraph pole NE from the school and the house lies just below it. A broad wall encloses an oval room with a stone bench against one wall and a small cell at the upslope end opposite the entrance. A little farther east, another oval house has been cut through by the road, and a third lies beneath a garage near the school.

Two groups of well-preserved houses set amongst walled enclosures may be seen on the southern slopes of the Ness of Gruting to the south (HU 276483–283482), and the STANYDALE houses lie just the other side of the ridge from Gruting School.

Jarlshof Multi-period settlement, Sumburgh ★★

HU 398095. Signposted from the A970 at the S. tip of mainland Shetland (Historic Scotland).

Despite erosion by the sea, Jarlshof has survived as a remarkable palimpsest of life over almost 4,000 years. Occupation is unlikely to have been continuous, but advantageous factors led people to choose the same spot time and time again: fertile well-drained land with freshwater springs, easy access to a sheltered bay, and plenty of building stone lying on the beach.

The **earliest houses** lie in front of the museum on the north side of the complex. A neolithic farm seems to have been established here by about 2400 BC, with an oval house sunk into the sand, the base of its walls little more than a revetment. Two pits in the floor hint of ritual activities, for one contained fragments of human skull, three stone clubs, and a stone knife, while the other contained the four feet of a cow. Sometime later **four better-preserved houses** were built, oval in plan from the outside and arranged inside as a series of small cells round a central space. The cells were probably used as sleeping areas and for storage. The ruins of one house were used as shelter for a bronzesmith's workshop around 800 BC—rare evidence in the Northern Isles for a community wealthy enough to commission the tools, weapons, and jewellery available in this prestigious metal.

Remains of three substantial stone roundhouses represent an **Iron Age farm**, complete with small underground cellars. The success of this farm may be gauged from the fact that, sometime in the last couple of centuries BC, the decision was taken to build a **broch**. The walls of the broch, its courtyard, and the wheelhouses within the courtyard, are better preserved than any other part of the pre-medieval sequence here, conveying a vivid impression of these monumental buildings. Coastal erosion has carried away part of the broch-settlement, which in its own time must have been very impressive. Originally there was the broch and a single roundhouse in the landward corner of the walled courtyard (although there may have been more buildings on the seaward side). The roundhouse was later replaced by a large wheelhouse, and later still by two

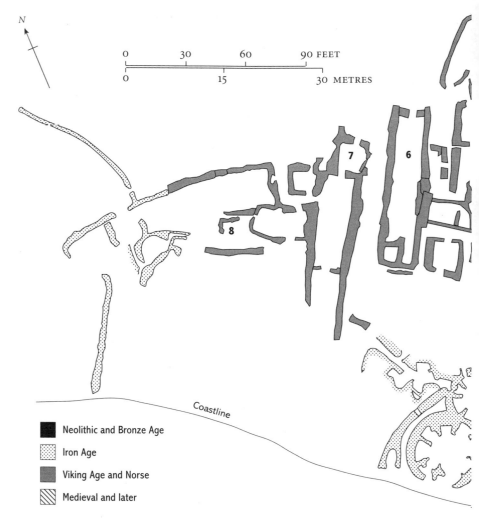

N

| 0 | 30 | 60 | 90 FEET |

| 0 | 15 | | 30 METRES |

Coastline

■ Neolithic and Bronze Age

▨ Iron Age

■ Viking Age and Norse

▨ Medieval and later

▲ Plan of the multi-period settlement at Jarlshof (after Historic Scotland): Buildings numbered 1–8 are the houses of the Viking Age and Norse period in chronological sequence.

smaller wheelhouses, one in the courtyard and one inside the old broch. Notice the hearths of these houses, carefully constructed with stone kerbs and paving.

In contrast to these magnificent wheelhouses, the only surviving buildings of the Pictish period are small and unimpressive, but the form of settlement may have been to the seaward side of the broch-complex. It is not clear whether the site was still occupied at the time of Viking colonization.

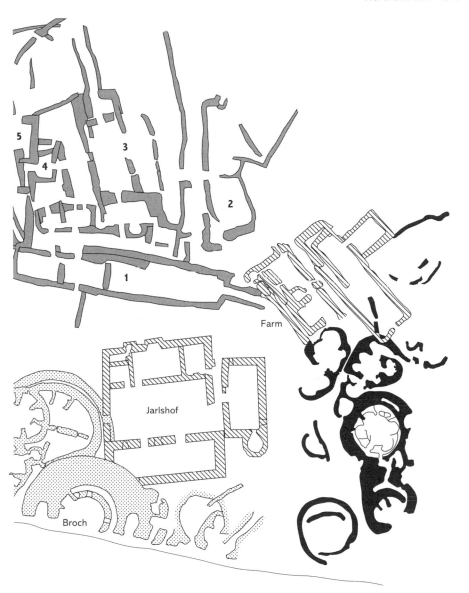

The **Norse settlement** appears as a confusing mass of interlocking walls, and its exploration is best begun with the primary dwelling, whose floor has been given a modern covering of white gravel and is thus easily distinguishable. In the C9 a farm was established here, with a dwelling house and separate outbuildings, and over the next three centuries this farm was modified and enlarged. It is possible to see here the earliest examples in Scotland of the true longhouse, in which people and cattle lived under the same roof. This seems to have developed in the C11. By the C12, additional rooms were being built on to the long walls of the core houses.

In the early C14, perhaps after a brief abandonment, a **new farm** was established at the north end of the site. A dwelling house and a barn were built alongside one another, with a small corn-drying kiln set into one corner of the barn, and the artefacts suggest that the farm survived for almost two centuries. Finally, the **laird's house** was built in the early C17, and its ruins have dominated the site ever since.

Jarlshof and Viking Shetland

The name 'Jarlshof' was invented by Sir Walter Scott, who visited the site in 1814 and subsequently incorporated it into his novel *The Pirate*. All that was visible then were the ruins of the C17 laird's house, which Sir Walter attributed to 'an ancient Earl of the Orkneys' and renamed 'Jarlshof' (Earl's Mansion). It was not until excavations in the early C20 that the existence of genuinely Norse buildings came to light. The original Norse name of the settlement is unknown, for it is not mentioned in the sagas, but the name of the whole promontory is Sumburgh, from Old Norse *Svinaborg*, meaning either 'Svein's fort' or 'fort of the pigs'. The fort could refer to the old broch or to the promontory fort on Sumburgh Head, traces of whose defences still survive.

Given its proximity to Norway, there should be many Norse remains in Shetland, but few have been identified—more excavation and field-work is needed before a clear picture will emerge of the Viking Age in these islands. Somewhere in the vicinity of Jarlshof, for instance, there should be a pagan cemetery. An excavated Viking farmstead may be seen at Underhoull in Unst (HP 573043), while in the Loch of Tingwall in central mainland there is an island known as Law Ting Holm, reached by a causeway and used, traditionally, as the Norse place of assembly or *lawthing*.

Loch of Houlland Broch, Eshaness

HU 213791. From the A970, just over 1 km. NE of Hillswick, take the B9078 W. and the minor road for Eshaness lighthouse. Park at the viewpoint and walk NE to the Loch of Houlland.

This is an impressive example of an island broch, although the 'island' is really a promontory with a narrow neck of land connecting with the mainland. Access is thus easy for today's visitor, although the remains of a stout stone wall across the approach show that the original access was well guarded. The broch has not been excavated and is half-submerged in the rubble fallen from its walls, but some 2 m. in height of the outer wall-face can be seen, along with the entrance. There are clear traces of buildings between the broch and its outer defences, some of which were built using the rubble from the broch and may represent Pictish activity.

An unusual feature of this site is that it is linked by a causeway to an adjacent island, and the island is also linked by another causeway to the shore. Could this have been a safe haven for livestock in times of trouble?

Mousa Broch ★★

HU 457206. Signposted from the A970 between Lerwick and Sumburgh, a minor road to Sand Lodge and the ferry (Historic Scotland; book the boat in advance).

The small island of Mousa is renowned for the best-preserved broch in the whole of Scotland. Used as a refuge in Viking times, this has become the ideal broch, a stout tower that was prehistory's version of a medieval keep. It stands sentinel over Mousa Sound, matched on the mainland opposite by another broch at Burraland, icons of Iron Age warrior society.

▼ Plan and section of Mousa broch (G. Ritchie)

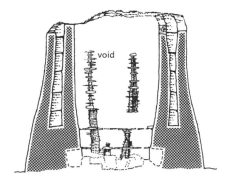

There are traces of a rampart on the landward side of the rocky promontory on which the broch stands, but nothing to match the outer defences of mainland brochs such as BURLAND. The broch entrance faces out across the Sound, and above the wall rises over 13 m. in classic tapering profile almost to the original wall-head. The base is solid masonry with three cells built within it—but no guard-cells at the entrance, as if its designer knew that this was one broch which no one would dare to attack. Even in Norse times, a thousand years after it was built, it was acknowledged to be impregnable to all but long-term siege.

Two ledges project from the internal face of the tower as supports for timber galleries. It is still possible to climb the stair within the wall, admiring its hollow construction on the way up to the

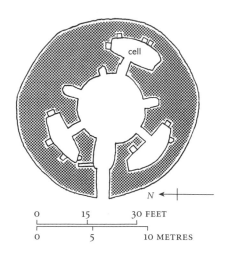

0	15	30 FEET
0	5	10 METRES

▲ Mousa broch (G. Ritchie)

top of the tower. The original floor of the broch is masked by the walls, hearth, and furniture of a wheelhouse built within the old tower after its heyday was over in the early centuries AD.

Ness of Burgi Fort

HU 388083. From the A970 shortly before Sumburgh airport, a minor road leads S. along Scat Ness. Park at the end and walk S. for about 1 km.; the approach to the promontory on which the fort lies is very dangerous (Historic Scotland).

The southern tip of Shetland forks into two rocky headlands, both of which were fortified in Iron Age times. The west headland boasts two examples of blockhouse forts along its east shore, one known as Scatness (HU 388087), where half the blockhouse has fallen into the sea, and the other known as Ness of Burgi. Both have been excavated but neither produced dating evidence for their construction (at Ness of Burgi, the stones from the excavation were built into a neat and rather misleading rectangular pile beyond the outer defences).

The approach to the blockhouse is guarded by a thick rampart, originally laced with stone, flanked on either side by a rock-cut ditch. A stone-lined passage leads through the rampart, and the blockhouse lies behind the inner ditch. Its sturdy masonry still rises well over a metre in height and is likely originally to have had an upper floor running over the entrance passage. Some of the slabs roofing the passage are still in place, showing that it was necessary to crouch low in order to enter, and door-checks and bar-holes indicate that there was once a stout door about one-third of the way down the passage. The bar was operated from a guard-cell opening off the east side of the passage. Another cell on the west side was entered from inside the fort, and a third from the west end of the block-house. Nothing is known of any other buildings in the fort.

Ness of Garth Fort, Sandness

HU 216582. From the A971 NW of Bridge of Walls, about 2 km. before it termi-nates at Melby, take a minor road E. to Crawton; walk N. along a track beside a small loch to the coast.

Although the Ness of Garth promontory is now cut off at high tide, in Iron Age times it would have been accessible across a narrow neck of land. There are traces of four ramparts across the promontory, the outer-most reduced to a string of boulders. Inside the fort, oval hollows in the grass along the west side are likely to be the remains of buildings, but there has been no excavation.

Punds Water Chambered

cairn, Brae

HU 324712. From the A970 about 6 km. NW of Brae, a minor road leads SW to Mangaster; parking place just before Mangaster, from which walk NW for about 750 m.

Today this area looks very inhos-pitable, just rough moorland and small lochs, but its appearance, and potential for farming, would have been very different before the major formation of peat. The tomb was built on a small knoll above what is now Punds Water, and a little farther to the NW are the remains of a substantial house and field-system (HU 323714). This is a good example of a heel-shaped cairn; although ruinous, the kerb, passage, and trefoil chamber can be seen, with well-built walls surviv-ing to a height of 1 m.

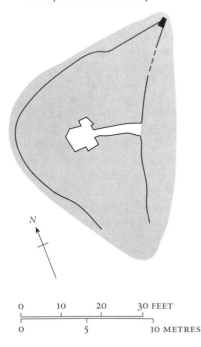

▼ Plan of Punds Water chambered tomb (after A. S. Henshall)

N

| 0 | 10 | 20 | 30 FEET |

| 0 | 5 | 10 METRES |

St Ninian's Isle Church, Bigton

HU 368208. Signposted from the B9122 through the village of Bigton; walk along the sand tombolo to the island.

Today this glorious sweep of sand has built up to the extent that the island is always accessible, but in early Christian times it is likely that the island was cut off at high tide. The visible remains are the walls of a small church built in the C12 to which a chancel was added in the C13. But excavation has revealed the traces beneath these walls of an earlier chapel and grave-yard, more famous now than ever it was in the C8. Beneath a slab of stone in the chapel floor was buried, around AD 800, a larch chest containing a fabulous treasure of Pictish silver.

Finely decorated bowls and implements for the table, intricate penan-nular brooches, and sword fittings of which a warlord could be proud, all made of gleaming silver—buried for safety and never recovered. This hoard, discovered in 1958, is a vivid demonstration of wealthy Pictish life in Shetland. (It is in the National Museums of Scotland in Edinburgh, but replicas may be seen in the Shetland Museum in Lerwick, along with carved stones from the site.)

Scord of Brouster Neolithic settlement, Bridge of Walls ★

HU 255516. The A971 forks at Bridge of Walls; take the Sandness branch and park after about 500 m.

The slopes above Gruting Voe and its subsidiary voes display some remarkable fragments of early prehistoric landscapes; some along the east side of the Voe are described under GRUTING SCHOOL. Perhaps the best way to gain a sense of this landscape is to explore the Scord of Brouster settlement and then to walk southwards, noting the meandering ancient field-walls, past the great chambered cairn on Gallow Hill with its encircling kerb of large boulders (HU 258508) to the settlement at Pinhoulland with its seven well-preserved houses amidst walled enclosures and clearance cairns (HU 259497).

The layout of Scord of Brouster can be appreciated even from the road, for the pale walls of the houses, cairns, and enclosures stand out clearly over an area of about 2.5 ha. Some of these features were excavated in the 1970s, and radiocarbon dates show that they span a long period from soon after 3000 BC to around 1500 BC, the whole complex representing a single farm on which the old farmhouse was replaced by a new one every now and again. The largest of the four houses (the one closest to the road) consists of an oval room, 7 × 5 m., with a hearth in the centre and massive boulders acting as piers between recesses along the walls. Close by is a ring-cairn of uncertain date and function. The economy of the farm was based on growing barley and keeping cattle and sheep; acid soil conditions led to poor preservation of bone, unfortunately, and there were no fishbones despite the likelihood that fishing was also important.

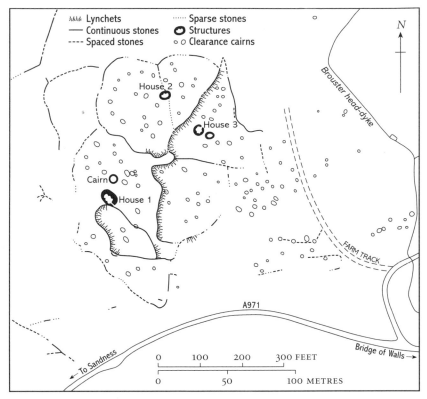

▲ Map of Scord of Brouster landscape (after A. Whittle)

Stanydale Neolithic landscape ★

HU 285502. Signposted from the A971 between Bixter and Bridge of Walls; foot-path marked by black-and-white poles (Historic Scotland).

Beside the third route-pole is a well-preserved house consisting of an oval living-room with a small cell at one end and a porch sheltering the entrance at the lower end. Excavation revealed a central hearth, alcoves in one side-wall and a stone bench along the other.

Farther west the path crosses an ancient field-wall, part of a system of enclosures visible to the SW. But the jewel in this particular landscape is the so-called Stanydale Temple. This is a very large and impressive building, the design of which combines the interior of a house with the exterior of a heel-shaped tomb. The use of huge boulders conveys a sense of megalithic grandeur. The entrance-passage leads through a concave façade, restored to a height of about 1.5 m., into an oval room more than twice the size of most houses. It appears to have had two massive wooden posts set in stone-lined holes to help support a timber-framed

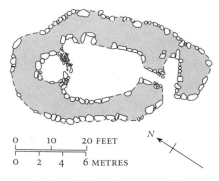

roof. Excavation retrieved fragments of spruce from one of the post-holes, indicating the use of tree-trunks borne across the Atlantic by the Gulf Stream from North America.

| 0 | 10 | 20 FEET |
| 0 | 2 | 4 | 6 METRES |

▲ Plan of Stanydale house (after C. S. T. Calder)

The inner part of the house has alcoves in the wall, separated by stone piers, and some of these alcoves had hearths. The great size and elaborate design of this building suggests that it may have been a meeting-place for the scattered farming communities of the time. A large burial-cairn with a boulder-kerb overlooks Stanydale from the top of the ridge to the south (HU 284500).

Vementry Chambered tomb

HU 295609. From the A971 Lerwick to Walls road at Bixter, the B9071 leads N. to Aith, where a minor road leads NE to Vementry farm and boat crossing to island (arrange boat in advance).

A superb tomb set in a stunning landscape—there is almost more water than land in this part of Shetland. The island of Vementry is separated from the mainland by a narrow but deep channel, and the tomb-builders chose the rugged summit of Muckle Ward, the highest point on the island. Its remoteness has ensured the good preservation of this heel-shaped cairn. The concave façade survives up to a height of more than 1 m., probably almost its original height, although the cairn over the chamber itself would have risen considerably higher. The chamber is set within a round cairn, and the cairn is encased by the heel-shaped platform, but the time-span of this sequence is unknown.

A passage opens from behind the façade into a chamber with three side-compartments. One of these compartments still has two

▼ Plan of Vementry chambered cairn (after RCAHMS)

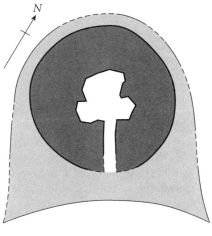

| 0 | | | FEET |
| 0 | 2 | 4 | 6 METRES |

roofing lintels in position, and it is likely that the whole chamber was originally roofed in this way with overlapping slabs.

FAIR ISLE

The population of Fair Isle has fluctuated over the centuries, but it can never have been an easy living. There is evidence of human presence from the second millennium BC onwards, although the island must have been known and at least visited over the preceding millennia. Burnt mounds, hut-circles, and field-systems suggest that there was a good-sized population during the first millennium BC, but there is just one fort and no broch. In 1588 there were just seventeen families on the island, but by the mid-C19 there were about 360 inhabitants (compared with 65 in the early 1990s).

South Haven Fort

HZ 222722. On the E. coast near the terminal of the Shetland ferry and the Bird Observatory.

A steep and narrow headland between South Haven and Mavers Geo offered the perfect location for a promontory fort. The neck of the promontory is guarded by a series of three ramparts with ditches between them, and beyond them a natural cleft reduces the width of the promontory to a narrow and easily defensible pathway. Another rampart spans the promontory above the cleft, the whole defensive complex looking somewhat paranoid given that this would seem to have been the only high-status Iron Age site on the island.

UNST

Unst has fared better than many parts of Shetland for archaeological studies in recent times. Norse farms have been excavated and are still visible, for example, at Underhoull on the west coast (HP 573044) and Sandwick on the east (HP 618023), and the steatite quarry at Clibberswick has been the subject of survey and excavation.

Bordastubble Standing stone

HP 578033. From the A968 about 4 km. NE of Belmont, a minor road runs NW to Westing; 1 km. from the junction, a track to Lund passes Bordastubble.

A huge chunk of gneiss in the middle of nowhere—the only rationale for its location may be that it marked the route down the valley to the sheltered bay of Lundawick. It is 3.7 m. high and up to 2.5 m. wide (a girth of 6.7 m.), and it now tilts markedly to the SW. A more slender cousin, 3 m. high, may be seen near Clivocast at the south end of the island (HP 604005).

WHALSAY

The island of Whalsay has attracted settlement since neolithic times, and it can boast Shetland's only example of rock-art. At Brough (HY 555651) on a rocky knoll, there are two groups of cup-marks, including three conjoined to make a trefoil. Aside from the prehistoric monuments described here, there is a well-preserved Hanseatic trading booth and an impressive Georgian mansion at Symbister. There are many well-preserved examples of planticrues, the small round enclosures with high stone walls in which in recent centuries vegetables were grown, protected from the wind.

Loch of Huxter Island fort

HU 558620. From the minor road leading E. from Symbister, a track leads to the shore of the loch, whence a boggy walk round the S. side of the loch to the cause-way linking the fort to the shore. Crossing to the islet is hazardous but it can be seen well from the shore.

Despite its tiny size, the islet was adapted for a blockhouse fort, nowhere more obviously a structure reflecting prestige rather than a real need for defence. The causeway is clearly artificial but the islet may be natural. The blockhouse is attached to a stone wall encircling the islet, but curiously its entrance is not aligned on the present causeway, prompting speculation as to whether access was originally by boat. In 1863 the blockhouse was still more than 2 m. high with traces of its upper storey, and it seems likely that since then stones have been robbed to build the planticrues on the adjacent shore.

On either side of its entrance-passage, the blockhouse contains a cell entered from within the fort. A bar-hole between the passage and the NW cell shows that the main door would have been barred by a long wooden beam operated from inside this cell.

Pettigarth's Field Neolithic settlement and cairns

HU 586652 (houses) and HU 584653 (cairns). Near Yoxie Geo on the NE coast of the island; walk either from Isbister NE or from Muckle Breck S.

This intriguing site consists of two truly megalithic houses on a slope above the sea and, overlooking them, a chambered tomb and a cist. Despite excavation, nothing is known of their sequence—was this a long-lived family farm where the old house was eventually replaced by a new one and the old burial vault replaced by a more fashionable cist? Both houses have acquired popular names in more recent centuries: the upper of the two is the Benie House and the lower is the Standing Stones of Yoxie (before excavation the taller slabs protruded from the turf like standing stones).

The two houses are similar in plan. Externally they are long and oval, while internally the Benie Hoose has one room and Yoxie two, both furnished with alcoves. A long passage leads out to an oval courtyard, which may have been open to the sky but could easily have been roofed as winter quarters for livestock. These were very substantial and snug dwellings. Their success and longevity may be gauged by the fact that more than 1,800 stone tools were recovered from the Benie Hoose alone (the huge rectangular pile of stones alongside the house is simply the debris from the excavation).

The tomb has an entrance-passage leading to a chamber with three alcoves, the whole encased within a square cairn. Alongside is a cist formed by four large slabs within a round cairn; the slab that once covered the cist is now slumped inside it. Both tomb and cist had been opened long ago and nothing is known of the burials that they must both have contained.

YELL

This is the second largest island in Shetland and has in the past supported grain crops as well as providing ample supplies of good peat. Its archaeological potential is remarkable but little studied, ranging from chambered cairns and standing stones to forts and brochs. The restored Old Haa of Burravoe (C17) has displays on local history.

Brough of Stoal Fort

HU 545873. From the B9081 about 7 km. N. of Burravoe, a minor road leads E. to Aywick, whence a walk of about 1.5 km. NE along the coast.

A place of immense natural defence, the promontory is flanked on either side by deep clefts or geos (its local name is Da Snooty, the Snout). Three impressive ramparts with deep ditches between them guard access on to the headland—there is now no trace of the entrance, which was presumably to one side rather than central and has been lost into the sea. There are traces of internal structures but it is impossible to tell whether they may once have included a broch. This site is very dangerous, and it is best viewed from the landward side of the fence.

Western Isles (Map, p. xxi)

A string of islands known as the Outer Hebrides trails from Lewis in the north down to Berneray in the south, roughly on the same latitude as Fort William. Their rugged landscape reflects the contorted gneiss bedrock, the oldest stratum of rock in the British Isles, but the shell-rich sands along their western seaboard was very attractive to early settlement. There are many well-preserved monuments, from chambered tombs and standing stones to brochs and medieval castles.

Visitors will find that road signs are in both Gaelic and English, and increasingly the Gaelic names for monuments are preferred—Calanais rather than Callanish, for example.

BARRA

Barra is the largest of the most southerly islands of the Outer Hebrides and is dominated by the hills of its interior, especially Heaval (383 m. OD) and Ben Tangaval (333 m. OD). The main road circuits the island, passing in the south the dramatic Kisimul Castle on its island before crossing the col between the two rocky hills.

Dun Cuier Dun, Allasdale

NF 664034. At the NW end of Barra just to the SE of the A888, on a rocky knoll behind the cemetery.

▼ Plan of dun at Dun Cuier (after A. Young)

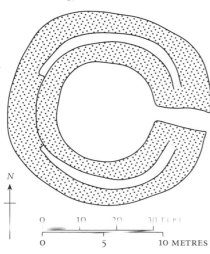

0   10   20   30 FEET

0   5   10 METRES

Dun Cuier is a well-preserved small but stoutly defended structure with a thick circular wall, with a median gallery to allow building to greater height than might otherwise have been possible. The entrance doorway is on the east, with the bar-hole, which housed the beam that held the door in position, on the south side of the passage.

Dun Cuier is one of the few excavated sites in Barra, and a wide range of finds was recorded, including both Iron Age material and objects of mid-first millennium AD date. Although opinion is divided as to the date of the original construction, and whether it is a broch or a dun, the excavation was undertaken at a time when radical reconstruction of the site would have been difficult to record. There is sufficient pottery to demonstrate Iron Age involvement in the construction, but the stratigraphy of the surviving central features, including a hearth, shows that it was still in full domestic use many centuries later.

LEWIS

For all that Lewis is graced by one of the great ceremonial centres of Scotland at Callanish, the island is remarkably free of evidence for intensive settlement before the Iron Age. Only six chambered tombs have been identified, and this total may be compared with that of about twenty tombs in the much smaller area of North Uist. But the natural resources of the two islands are also very different, and North Uist would have been far more attractive to early settlement. In addition, many sites may lie undetected beneath the peat in Lewis—in the C19, 1.5 m. of peat was stripped from around the standing stones of Callanish, revealing a small chambered tomb for the first time. Nevertheless, the question remains: why was Lewis chosen for what must have been the religious heart of the Western Isles? And where are the homes of the people who toiled to set up these standing stones?

Callanish Stone circles and alignments, Breasclete ★★

NB 213330. The village of Callanish, in Gaelic Calanais, is situated in a loop off the Stornoway to Butt of Lewis road (A858) a little NW of Garynahine; the visitor centre and car-park are signposted (Historic Scotland).

Like SKARA BRAE and the broch of MOUSA, the stone alignments of Callanish have become icons of the archaeology of Scotland. Callanish has inspired many artists, poets, and photographers, because the pale and sometimes ghostly stones have an extraordinary affinity with their landscape. The main setting lies along a low ridge, and consists of a small circle of thirteen tall stones which forms the focus of four rows of stones to north, south, west, and east, the north alignment being a double row or avenue. Within the circle is a particularly tall pillar, 4.75 m. high, beside a small chambered tomb with its entrance-passage facing east. Excavation has shown that the tomb was built a few generations after the circle, sometime after 3000 BC.

Although the stone rows are roughly aligned on the four cardinal points of the compass, this may reflect nothing more than the north–south situation of the ridge on which they stand. It is possible that the stones were sited here in order that people could observe the movements of the moon. Every 18.6 years, the moon seems to skim lightly along the tops of the hills to the south. Whatever the reason

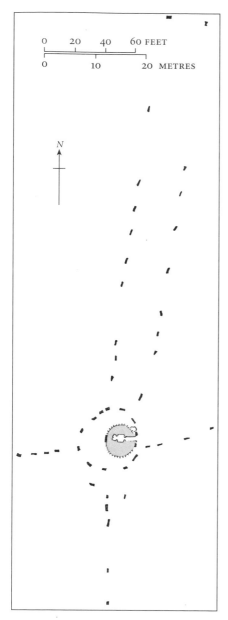

0   20   40   60 FEET

0   10   20 METRES

N

▲ The stone alignments of Callanish
(RCAHMS)

behind the choice of location, the stones must have acted as a powerful focus for communal life. And there are other smaller settings dotted about the landscape round Callanish. Two to the SE are signposted from the A858 (Historic Scotland): Cnoc Ceann a'Gharraidh is a circle with five upright stones and three fallen stones, and Cnoc Fillibhir Bheag is a double ring with eight stones encircling four inner stones.

Clach an Trushal
Balantrushal

NB 375537. Turn NW off the A857 Stornoway to Butt of Lewis road at Balantrushal, and turn left just before the last houses of the village.

This remarkable standing stone, some 6 m. in height, is one of the most impressive in the Western Isles. It tapers upwards from a massive base about 4.7 m. in girth, and would have been a landmark in prehistoric times; in more recent folklore, it is supposed to have marked the site of a great battle.

Dun Bharabhat Broch,
Bernera

NB 155355. At Garynahine on the A858, take the B8011 and B8059 to Bernera; after crossing to the island, park about 1.5 km. from the bridge and walk NW over moorland to the E. shore of Loch Bharabhat.

Great Bernera is an island of rocky knolls and myriad lochs, accessible by bridge from mainland Lewis. There are four standing stones at the island end of the bridge. Dun Bharabhat is a typical island dun in an inland loch, with a causeway some

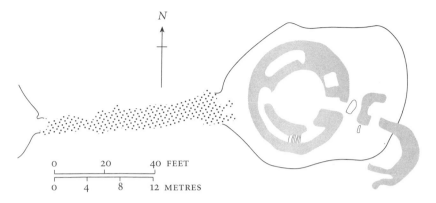

▲ Plan of Dun Bharabhat broch (after D. W. Harding and I. Armit)

30 m. long linking the island with the shore. This was a fortified family residence, so well built that the wall still survives up to 3 m. high. There is a gallery within the wall, and a projecting ledge on the inner face of the wall to support a timber upper floor. The entrance to such island duns is normally on the side opposite the causeway, thus making the approach even more difficult. Here the original structure is partially overlain by a later building, perhaps of medieval date.

There is another island dun, also known as Dun Bharabhat, on the Bhaltos peninsula of the mainland to the west of Bernera, which has been excavated and which is dated by radio-carbon analysis to the latter half of the first millennium BC. Perhaps the most surprising aspect of the excavation was to demonstrate the existence below the present water-level of external structures, making the settlement more extensive than it appeared from the visible remains. And the waterlogged conditions had preserved organic material such as wood and plant remains.

Dun Bragar Broch, Bragar

NB 285474. In Loch an Duna beside the A858 at the W. end of Bragar near the NW coast of Lewis.

Set on its island in the loch, this broch must have been a spectacular sight in its heyday. A stone-built causeway leads to the island from mainland, and there are the remains of three walls built across it to control access. The broch survives well enough to show traces of an upper gallery in the thickness of the wall and a ledge along the inner face to support an upper timber floor. There was also a good-sized annexe on the far side of the broch, enclosed by a substantial wall which is now partially submerged in the waters of the loch. This may have been designed to protect cattle or to provide working space.

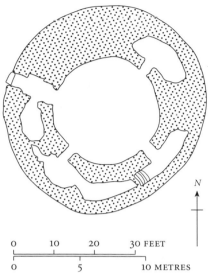

0   10   20   30 FEET

0   5   10 METRES

▲ Plan of Dun Carloway broch (after The Stationery Office)

Dun Carloway Broch, Carloway ★

NB 190413. Signposted from the A858, about 2 km. SW of Carloway in NW Lewis (Historic Scotland).

Perched on the steep end of a rocky ridge above a loch, Dun Carloway is a most impressive and well-preserved broch. The wall stands about 9 m. high above the steep drop, although on the other side, accessible from the top of the ridge, it has been robbed to build field-walls and blackhouses (of which there are good examples below the broch). There are likely to have been outworks beyond the vulnerable entrance to the broch, but no trace survives.

A guard-cell opens off the entrance-passage, and there are three low doorways inside the broch, leading to cells and a stair within the wall. A ledge protruding from the wall would have supported an upper floor, particularly necessary as living-space here because the ground floor, 7.4 m. across, is restricted by a large and inconvenient rock-outcrop. The interior was cleared out long ago (this was one of the earliest monuments to be taken into State care in 1887), but floor deposits survived in one of the cells, and excavation revealed a series of hearths and a surprising amount of pottery of a type that suggests that the broch continued in use into the early centuries AD.

Garrabost Chambered cairn, Eye

NB 523330. From the A866 1 km. NE of Garrabost, walk E. along a track for 500 m. and then uphill to the S.

Most of the stones of this square cairn have been robbed, but the outline is still marked by kerbstones except on the north where they have been removed. The entrance to the tomb opens from a shallow concave forecourt to the SE, and leads into an oval chamber.

Steinacleit Prehistoric structure, Shader

NB 396540. Signposted from the A857 in Shader on the W side of the A long (Historic Scotland).

It would take a brave archaeologist to be dogmatic about this site, hence the definition above, which gives nothing away! About 1 m. of peat was stripped off in the early C20, but there has been no excavation of the stone structures that emerged. Essentially, there is an oval enclosure defined by a stone wall, to one side of which is a substantial circular structure, about 16 m. in diameter, built with some very large stones. The amount of stone appears too large to be simply the remains of a massive domestic roundhouse, and it may be that this was originally a neolithic chambered cairn which was adapted as a round-house with a stock enclosure in Iron Age times. Only exca-vation will solve the problem, and meantime Steinacleit remains an impressive but enigmatic monument.

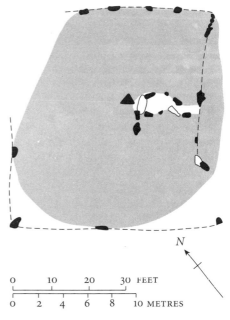

▲ Plan of Garrabost chambered cairn (after A. S. Henshall)

Downslope from Steinacleit, in Loch an Duin, there is a fine example of an island dun with a causeway connecting it to the shore.

NORTH UIST

North Uist is extraordinarily rich in prehistoric remains, particularly chambered cairns, which are more plentiful here than in any other part of the Western Isles, but also less obviously visible domestic sites dating from neolithic to post-medieval times. The reason for this richness is the fertil-ity of the island, which has attracted and sustained settlement over the centuries.

Barpa Langass Chambered cairn, Clachan

NF 837657. From Clachan on the W. coast take the A867 towards Lochmaddy for about 3 km.; the cairn is visible on the hillslope S. of the road.

This great bare cairn of stones gives a vivid impression of how the neolithic landscape must have appeared, dotted with numerous such cairns. This is a round cairn, 25 m. in diameter and 4 m. high, and

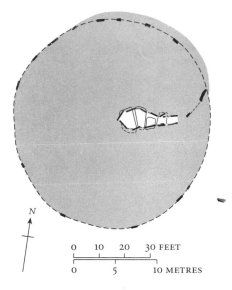

N

```
0    10    20    30 FEET
|----|----|----|
0         5         10 METRES
```

▲ Plan of Barpa Langass chambered cairn (after A. S. Henshall)

it has survived virtually intact, with a low kerb of pointed stones and traces of a deep V-shaped forecourt at the entrance to the tomb. The entrance-passage faces east and is about 4 m. long, roofed with flat lintels; it leads into an oval chamber, which is still intact and roofed by three large slabs, although it is not now accessible.

From here, looking north, it is possible to see the well-preserved chambered cairn of Tigh Cloiche, on the slopes of Mharrogh hill (NF 833695). To visit this cairn involves a long walk from the minor road between Ardheisker and Vallay Strand; within a round cairn, 24 m. across and more than 4 m. high, there is an intact entrance-passage along which you can see into the circular chamber.

Dun an Sticir Broch, Newtonferry

NF 897777. In Loch an Sticir, 500 m. S. of Newtonferry at the N. end of North Uist; visible from the B893. Walk across to the N. end of the loch and cross the causeway to the island via another island.

Dun an Sticir is one of the best preserved brochs in the Western Isles, with its wall remaining to a height of more than 3 m. It would have survived even better, had a rectangular house not been built within it, using stone from the broch, at some period in the Middle Ages. Tradition links this reuse of the island with one Hugh MacDonald, who failed to supplant his cousin as clan chief and sought refuge here around 1600; the wretched man was captured, taken to Duntulm Castle in Skye, and immured in the dungeon with a plate of salt beef and an empty jug.

It was probably at the time of this later occupation that a 3 m.-wide stone causeway was built to link the island with the adjacent island, Eilean na Mi-chomhairle, and thence to the mainland. Earlier access to the broch was probably along the narrower causeway from the south shore of the loch to Eilean na Mi-chomhairle and thence along an earlier version of the causeway to Dun an Sticir.

The entrance to the broch faces the causeway, and there are traces of a guard-cell and a gallery within the wall.

Unival Chambered cairn, Bayhead

NF 800668. From the A865 on the NW coast, take the minor road towards Vallay Strand for about 1.5 km., park, and walk SE across moorland.

There is no easy way to reach this monument without getting your feet wet, but it is worth the effort. It is a roughly square cairn, about 16 m. across, with a chamber and passage opening off the SE side, but the most striking feature is the presence of tall slabs marking the kerb of the cairn. These increase to a height of 2.5 m. at the entrance. There was excavation here in the 1930s, revealing rich deposits in the chamber and passage, which contained a lot of pottery and, in a cist in the chamber, the partial remains of a woman aged more than 25 years and the ribs of some-

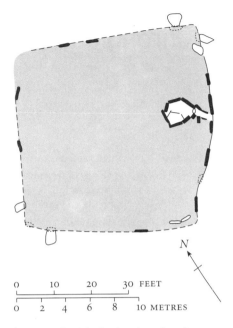

▲ Plan of Unival chambered cairn (after A. S. Henshall)

one less than 21 years old (the latter was thought to be the earlier burial). A stone ball was found on the floor of the chamber, and a pendant made of pumice in the upper levels of deposit in the chamber.

Some 7 m. from the SW corner of the cairn is a large standing stone, 3 m. high. During the Iron Age, a house was built into the north side of the cairn, the chamber roof was removed and the chamber is thought to have been used as a cooking pit.

Chronology

The rounded dates are approximate estimates, but the precise dates are derived from reliable historical records.

BC

10,000 hunters and gatherers move into Scotland as the ice retreats

4000 the first farmers arrive, bringing with them the knowledge of how to make pottery and polished stone tools, as well as growing crops and breeding cattle and sheep

2200 metalworking skills are introduced, using copper, tin, and gold

700 fortification becomes a major feature of settlements, and the knowledge of ironworking is gradually disseminated

200 evolution of the broch as a stone tower

AD

79 the Roman army, led by Agricola, marches into Scotland

83 Battle of Mons Graupius in which the Roman army defeated the Celtic tribes

142 the Antonine Wall is built as the northern frontier of Roman Britain

400 final withdrawal from Scotland of the Roman army

420 bishopric at Whithorn founded by Ninian

500 emergence of the kingdoms of the Picts and the Dál Riata

563 monastery on Iona founded by Columba

638 British fort at Din Eidyn falls to the Angles

673 monastery at Applecross founded by Maelrubha

685 Battle of Nechtansmere, in which the Picts defeated the Angles

795 first Viking attack on Iona

843 the Dál Riatan king Kenneth mac Alpin takes over Pictland

850 Viking settlement underway in Scotland

880 Norse earldom of Orkney established

995 official conversion of the Orkney earldom to Christianity

1100 Norman influence leads to the construction of earthen mottes with timber castles

Glossary

Barrow: an earthen mound covering a burial.

Broch: a circular drystone defensive structure of the Iron Age, with features of considerable architectural sophistication, such as intramural galleries and cells. The etymology is related to Old Norse: *borg*, castle.

Chert: a flint-like quartz used for making flake tools when good quality flint was lacking.

Chevaux de frise: in archaeology, a series of upright pointed stones set across possible line of attack and designed to impede access; Frise: French, Friesland, where metal arrangements were used to check cavalry charges in the C17.

Cist: a slab-built box or grave (Scots: *kist*, chest).

Crannog: built on an artificial offshore island, comprising a timber or timber and stone superstructure (Gaelic: *crann*, wood or beam).

Crop-mark: a difference in crop-growth owing to buried features, which is visible from the air and sometimes at ground-level.

Cup-mark, cup-and-ring markings: small pecked hollows in natural rock surfaces, in some cases surrounded by single or multiple rings.

Dun: drystone fortification of Iron Age or Early Historic date representing a single homestead (Gaelic: *dun*, fort or fortification).

Henge: a neolithic earthwork monument consisting of a ditch and external bank, with one or two entrances, sometimes enclosing circles of stone or timber uprights.

Hogback: a massive gravestone carved with an arched ridge and tegulae (roof-tiles) and sometimes animal ornament, dating to the C10 to C12 and reflecting Anglo-Scandinavian taste.

Midden: deposit of domestic rubbish.

Motte: earthen mound on which a timber castle was built in the C12.

Multivallate: having several concentric lines of defence, used of Iron Age forts.

Ogham: an alphabet consisting of straight strokes on either side of a central line, which was invented in Ireland by the C2 AD, for ease of cutting in wood and stone.

Orthostat: in archaeology, a stone set upright.

Picts: the descendants of the Celtic tribes whom the Romans encountered north of the Antonine Wall in the early centuries AD (Latin: *Picti*, the Painted Ones).

Planticrue: in Shetland, and to a lesser extent in Orkney, a small drystone enclosure within which young plants, particularly cabbage, can become established in an environment protected from the wind.

Runes: an angular alphabet used by Norsemen and other Germanic peoples, which was invented before the C2 AD but its place of origin is unknown.

Scots: settlers from County Antrim in Northern Ireland, who settled in Argyll in the C5 and C6 AD (Latin: *Scotti*, Irishmen).

Souterrain: an underground storage chamber, used in Scotland from about 800 BC to about AD 200, lined with stone and roofed either with stone lintels or with a timber-frame projecting above ground-level (French: *souterrain*, below ground).

Talus: a slope.

Vallum: a wall or rampart of earth, sods, or stone erected as a line of defence (Latin: *vallus*, stake, palisade).

Voe: in Shetland, a sea-loch.

Wheelhouse: a stone-built house with internal radial subdivisions, resembling a spoked wheel on plan.

Useful addresses

Many of the monuments featured in this book are in the care of:

Historic Scotland
Longmore House
Salisbury Place
Edinburgh EH9 1SH
tel. 0131 668 8600

Some monuments are on land owned by the:

National Trust for Scotland
5 Charlotte Square
Edinburgh EH2 4DU
tel. 0131 226 5922

Information about ferry timetables and accommodation can be obtained from local offices of the:

Scottish Tourist Board

More detailed information about individual monuments may be available from the:

Royal Commission on the Ancient and Historical Monuments of Scotland
National Monuments Record of Scotland
John Sinclair House
16 Bernard Terrace
Edinburgh EH8 9NX
tel. 0131 662 1456

Information about excavations and conferences may be obtained from the:

Council for Scottish Archaeology

and lectures, conferences, and an annual journal recording new research are available from the:

Society of Antiquaries of Scotland.

Both of these organizations are based in:

Royal Museum of Scotland
Chambers Street
Edinburgh EH1 1JF
tel. 0131 225 7534

Museums

Scotland's museums are constantly changing, new displays are being created and new institutions forged. The major archaeological collection, originally formed by the Society of Antiquaries of Scotland, will be at the heart of the **Museum of Scotland**, part of the **National Museums of Scotland**, which will open in the newly built museum in 1998, adjacent to the Royal Museum of Scotland, Chambers Street, EH1 1JF (0131 225 7534). The collections of the Society were the natural depository for many excavations in the last century, and in the absence of local museums in the first half of the present century continued to receive material from throughout the country. Exciting regional museums have been created in recent decades, and the story of Scotland's past is now presented in many more museums than before, and in many different ways. We have tried to include museums with primarily original material. Museums of country life have not been included, although these will include artefacts of perishable material missing from the earlier archaeological record and offer insights into life on the land and country pursuits that are relevant to much earlier times.

Aberdeen, Anthropological Museum, Marischal College, University of Aberdeen, Broad Street, AB9 1AS (01224 273131). The displays incorporate local antiquities in the exploration of general themes, including toolmaking, battle, ritual, magic, and medicine.

Dumfries, Dumfries Museum and Camera Obscura, The Observatory, DG2 7SW (01387 53374). A lively museum with a fine collection of Early Christian carved stones.

Dundee, McManus Galleries, Albert Square, DD1 1DA (01382 23141). An important collection of local artefacts, with a partial reconstruction of a prehistoric timber house from Douglasmuir and a vivid evocation of the discovery and excavation of a Bronze Age cist burial. Roman and Pictish carved stones.

Dunrobin Castle Museum, Golspie, KW10 6ZA (014083 3177). Here the Pictish carved stones form a fascinating group with several unusually well-preserved examples.

Elgin Museum, High Street, IV30 1EQ (01343 543675). Important collection of Early Christian stones from Burghead and Kinnedar.

Falkirk, Falkirk Museum, Orchard Street, FK1 1RF (01324 24911). Good local displays including material from the Antonine Wall.

Forfar, Meffan Institute, 20 West High Street, DD8 1BB (01307 468813). Small local archaeological display, interesting and well-lit collection of Pictish stones.

Glasgow Art Gallery and Museum, Kelvingrove, G3 8AG (0141 357 3929). This splendid Victorian museum has fine collections of artefacts from western Scotland and the decorated cist side-slab from Badden, Argyll.

Glasgow, Hunterian Museum, University of Glasgow, Hillhead, G12 8QQ (0141 330 4221). Important collection of Roman distance slabs from the Antonine Wall. Fine collection of coins. Archaeological material from the west of Scotland.

Inverness Museum and Art Gallery, Castle Wynd, IV2 3ED (01463 237114). The integration of natural history and archaeology makes for very informative displays of the early highlands. A small, but significant collection of Pictish stones.

Inverurie, Carnegie Museum, Town Hall, The Square (0779 7778). Local archaeological collection.

Kilmarnock, Dick Institute, Elmbank Avenue, KA1 3BU (01563 26401). Broad displays including local archaeology.

Kilmartin House, Kilmartin (01546 510278). New museum and visitor centre for this rich archaeological landscape.

Kirkcaldy, Museum and Art Gallery, KY1 1YG (01592 260732). Collections of Fife's archaeology and history.

Kirkwall, Tankerness House Museum, Broad Street, KW15 1DH (01856 3191). The archaeological story of Orkney is presented in a way that ideally complements visits to the monuments. The neolithic carved stone from Pierowall, Westray, is an important addition to the small number of pieces of early art.

Lerwick, Shetland Museum, Lower Hillhead, ZE1 0EK (01595 5057). Extensive displays of Shetland archaeology and ethnography on land and on sea. The slab from Papil, Burra, is particularly fine.

Meigle Museum (Historic Scotland; 0131 662 1250). See p. 101.

Montrose, Museum and Art Gallery, Panmure Place, DD10 8HE (01674 73232). Good displays of local archaeology, including the Pictish stone from Inchbrayock.

Perth, Museum and Art Gallery, George Street, PH1 5LB (01738 32488). The archaeological material is used in the display of general themes, sometimes with thought-provoking results; the ogham-incised slab from Inchyra is displayed beside a manual telephone exchange, both evoking communication.

Port Charlotte, Islay, Museum of Islay Life, PA48 7UA (0149685 358). Displays on the prehistoric archaeology of Islay.

Rosemarkie, Groam House Museum, High Street, IV10 8UF (01381 20924). See p. 157.

Rothesay, Bute Museum, Stuart Street, PA20 0EP (01700 2248). The displays clearly outline the natural and human history of the island. There is a fine display of the Early Christian sculpture of Bute.

St Andrews Cathedral Museum (Historic Scotland; 0131 662 1250). See p. 104.

St Vigeans Museum, Arbroath (Historic Scotland; 0131 662 1250). See p. 105.

Stirling, The Smith Art Gallery and Museum, Albert Place, FK8 2RQ (01786 71917). Wide-ranging displays with some local archaeology.

Stornoway, Museum nan Eilean, Francis Street (01851 703773). A new museum outlining the archaeology of the Western Isles.

Tarbat Discovery Centre, Portmahomack (01862 871443). Explores the Pictish and later history of Tarbat through excavations and artefacts.

Suggestions for Further Reading

Anderson, J. R., and Anderson, J. (1903), *The Early Christian Monuments of Scotland* (Society of Antiquaries of Scotland, Edinburgh; reprinted with an Introduction by Isabel Henderson, 1993, Pinkfoot Press, Balgavies, Angus).

Armit, I. (1996), *The Archaeology of Skye and the Western Isles* (Edinburgh University Press).

Ashmore, P. J. (1995), *Calanais: The Standing Stones* (Urras nan Tursachan Ltd, Stornoway).

—— (1996), *Ancient Scotland* (Batsford/Historic Scotland, London).

Baldwin, J. (1997), *Edinburgh, Lothians and the Borders: Exploring Scotland's Heritage* (The Stationery Office, Edinburgh).

Barclay, G. J. (1993), *Balfarg: The Prehistoric Ceremonial Centre* (Fife Regional Council, Glenrothes).

Bradley, R. (1993), *Altering the Earth* (Society of Antiquaries of Scotland, Edinburgh).

Breeze, D. J. (1982), *The Northern Frontiers of Roman Britain* (Batsford, London).

Burl, A. W. (1976), *The Stone Circles of the British Isles* (Yale University Press, New Haven and London).

—— (1995), *A Guide to the Stone Circles of Britain, Ireland and Brittany* (Yale University Press, New Haven and London).

Clarke, D. V., Cowie, T. G., and Foxon, A. (1985), *Symbols of Power at the Time of Stonehenge* (National Museums of Scotland, Edinburgh).

Close-Brooks, J. (1995), *The Highlands: Exploring Scotland's Heritage* (HMSO, Edinburgh).

Crawford, B. E. (1987), *Scandinavian Scotland* (Leicester University Press).

Davidson, J. L., and Henshall, A. S. (1989), *The Chambered Cairns of Orkney* (Edinburgh University Press).

—— —— (1991), *The Chambered Cairns of Caithness* (Edinburgh University Press).

Dunbar, J. G., and Fisher, I. (1995), *Iona: A Guide to the Monuments* (HMSO, Edinburgh).

Edwards, K. J., and Ralston, I. B. M. (1997), *Scotland: Environment and Archaeology, 8000 BC–AD 1000* (Wiley, Chichester and New York).

Feachem, R. W. (1977), *Guide to Prehistoric Scotland* (Batsford, London).

Fojut, N., and Pringle, D. (1993), *The Ancient Monuments of Shetland* (HMSO, Edinburgh).

—— —— **and Walker, B.** (1994), *The Ancient Monuments of the Western Isles* (HMSO, Edinburgh).

Foster, S. M. (1996), *Picts, Gaels and Scots* (Batsford/Historic Scotland, London).

Hanson, W. S., and Maxwell, G. S. (1983), *Rome's North-West Frontier: The Antonine Wall* (Edinburgh University Press).

Hedges, J. W. (1984), *Tomb of the Eagles* (John Murray, London).

Henderson, I. (1967), *The Picts* (Thames and Hudson, London).

Henshall, A. S. (1963) and (1972), *The Chambered Tombs of Scotland* (Edinburgh University Press).

—— **and Ritchie, J. N. G.** (1995), *The Chambered Cairns of Sutherland* (Edinburgh University Press).

Keppie, L. J. F. (1986), *Scotland's Roman Remains* (Mercat Press, Edinburgh).

Mack, A. (1997) *Field Guide to the Pictish Symbol Stones* (Pinkfoot Press, Balgavies, Angus).

MacKie, E. W. (1975), *Scotland: An Archaeological Guide* (Faber, London).

Renfrew, A. C. (1979), *Investigations in Orkney* (Society of Antiquaries of London/Thames and Hudson, London).

—— (1985) (ed.), *The Prehistory of Orkney* (Edinburgh University Press).

Ritchie, A. (1988), *Scotland BC* (HMSO, Edinburgh).

—— (1989), *Picts* (HMSO, Edinburgh).

—— (1993), *Viking Scotland* (Batsford/Historic Scotland, London).

—— (1995), *Prehistoric Orkney* (Batsford/Historic Scotland, London).

—— (1996), *Orkney: Exploring Scotland's Heritage* (The Stationery Office, Edinburgh).

—— (1997), *Shetland: Exploring Scotland's Heritage* (The Stationery Office, Edinburgh).

—— (1997), *Iona* (Batsford/Historic Scotland, London).

—— **and Breeze, D. J.** (1991), *Invaders of Scotland* (HMSO, Edinburgh).

—— **and Ritchie, G.** (1995), *The Ancient Monuments of Orkney* (HMSO, Edinburgh).

Ritchie, G. (1997) (ed.), *The Archaeology of Argyll* (Edinburgh University Press).

—— **and Harman, M.** (1996), *Argyll and the Western Isles: Exploring Scotland's Heritage* (HMSO, Edinburgh).

—— **and Ritchie, A.** (1991), *Scotland: Archaeology and Early History* (Edinburgh University Press).

Shepherd, I. A. G. (1995), *Aberdeen and North-East Scotland: Exploring Scotland's Heritage* (HMSO, Edinburgh).

Smith, B. (1985) (ed.), *Shetland Archaeology* (Shetland Times, Lerwick).

Stell, G. P. (1996), *Dumfries and Galloway: Exploring Scotland's Heritage* (The Stationery Office, Edinburgh).

Stevenson, J. B. (1995), *Glasgow, Clydesdale and Stirling: Exploring Scotland's Heritage* (HMSO, Edinburgh).

Walker, B., and Ritchie, G. (1996), *Fife, Perthshire and Angus: Exploring Scotland's Heritage* (HMSO, Edinburgh).

Whittle, A., Keith-Lucas, M., Milles, A., Noddle, B., Rees, S., and Romans, J. C. C. (1986), *Scord of Brouster: An Early Agricultural Settlement on Shetland* (Oxford University Committee for Archaeology, Oxford).

Wickham-Jones, C. R. (1995), *Scotland's First Settlers* (Batsford/Historic Scotland, London).

Index of Places

References in italic include illustrations.